CYCLING PLUS
TOTAL ROAD CYCLING

If you love to ride, then *Cycling Plus* is the magazine for you.

Cycling Plus is the manual for the modern road cyclist.
Whether you're cycling weekly, an occasional new rider
or a Tour de France fan you'll find everything you need.

Every issue is packed with unrivalled, expert reviews of the
latest road bikes and gear, inspirational routes and rides
from the UK and around the world, evocative features that
take you inside every aspect of cycling and unmatched
nutrition, fitness and training advice guaranteed to help
you get the best from yourself and your bike.

THIS IS A CARLTON BOOK
Published by Carlton Books Ltd
20 Mortimer Street
London W1T 3JW

Text © Immediate Media Company Bristol Limited 2016
Design © Carlton Books 2016

Hardback ISBN 978-1-78097-655-6
Paperback ISBN 978-1-78097-798-0

Project Editor: Matthew Lowing
Design Editor: Stephen Cary
Editorial: Adrian Besley & Lisa Hughes
Design: Ben Ruocco & Darren Jordan
Production: Rachel Burgess

A CIP catalogue for this book is available from the British Library

Printed in China

10 9 8 7 6 5 4 3 2 1

CYCLING PLUS
TOTAL ROAD CYCLING

CARLTON
BOOKS

CONTENTS

FOREWORD

I WAS RECENTLY ASKED WHY I LOVE RIDING MY ROAD BIKE SO MUCH. THE ANSWER IS SIMPLE.

I love it because it keeps me fit; because it gets me to work; because it allows me to push myself to my limits; because it takes me to parts of the world I've never seen before; because it helps me make new friends; because it lets me indulge my passion for machinery and gear; because it gives me incredible stories to tell. Like I said, the answer is simple!

I'm passionate about cycling and as you've picked up this book I'm guessing that you are too. Or maybe you're curious to find out exactly why your road riding friends are always going on about their bikes, their rides and their Strava segments!

Whatever your level as a cyclist, you'll find something in this book for you – from tips on starting out right through to advice on taking your performance to an even higher level. This book is packed with some of the very best articles gleaned from *Cycling Plus*, the only magazine that truly understands, and delivers, the passion that makes you a cyclist. Read on and you're guaranteed to become a better rider and that means you'll get even more from your bike and, most importantly, from yourself.

Rob Spedding
Editor-in-chief, *Cycling Plus*

INTRODUCTION

WELCOME TO A COMPREHENSIVE AND EASY-TO-FOLLOW GUIDE THAT WILL TAKE YOUR RIDING TO ANOTHER LEVEL.

Around the world, more and more cyclists are donning their lycra and tearing up their local roads as if they were fighting for victory in the Tour de France. Whether you are a novice cyclist or an established 'roadie', this book has the tips, tricks and training routines to get you escaping the peloton and riding to success.

If you like riding with friends, commuting to work, or have recently purchased a shiny new bike, you will already be aware of the joys of cycling. You could already be enjoying journeys unhindered by traffic jams or overcrowded buses; experiencing the thrill of speeding along country roads, or benefiting from the low-impact exercise of cycling. Many, however, will want more from their riding; dreaming of cycling faster, taking on long-distance rides or tackling those 'unassailable' climbs.

Cycling as a sport has its own demands in terms of fitness and techniques, and the advice on these pages will prove invaluable to those riders who are ready to develop their road riding. The major – and minor – gains suggested throughout the book could well be the difference in you out-pacing your mate up the local hill, winning the sprint at your club race or escaping the peloton on that long-distance étape.

Once upon a time you could turn up to an event on your old bike and rely on your fitness to put you among the leaders. Nowadays, those setting the pace will have featherlight frames, high-performance components and specialist handlebars. They could also have aerodynamic helmets, super-wicking jerseys, and, almost certainly, clipless shoes. Here you will find a guide to getting the best possible equipment, even if you are on a tight budget.

To get the best from your bike, you can follow the simple procedures to setting the saddle height, reach and cleat settings for the optimum riding position. Clear diagrams explain the maintenance basics required to keep your bike in roadworthy condition and how to deal with those unfortunate mechanical accidents that occur on the road.

The book also deals with the most important part of the bike: the rider. It suggests training rides and routines that can improve your endurance, climbing and sprinting performance, but also shows how much difference your off-bike workouts can make. Working on your stamina, cardiovascular fitness and muscular strength in the gym or at home will pay dividends on your next ride.

So if you want to be the Peter Sagan or the Vicenzo Nibali of your local roads, open the pages of *Total Road Cycling*. It has all the information you need to get you riding faster and further.

9

GETTING STARTED

From rolling along a country lane with friends to an adrenaline-fuelled sprint past your rivals on a finely tuned machine, cycling has an array of pleasures. If you feel daunted about where to start or just want to be perfectly prepared when you hit the road, the following pages give you the lowdown on getting on your bike...

THE BASICS

Puzzled by bike materials? Worried about getting wet? Daunted by traffic? Here are the answers to some of the most common questions asked by new cyclists

▼ Learning road riding techniques and trying out new skills help make cycling easier and more fun

ISN'T IT DANGEROUS?

Despite recent media campaigns to improve the safety of cycling on roads, it might surprise you to hear that cycling is not especially dangerous. Whether you prefer to stick to the tarmac or head for the trails, cyclist deaths are still very rare. Even when taking to the roads there are far more pedestrian and motor vehicle deaths.

Cyclist fatalities still attract disproportionate media coverage. Around 15 per cent of cyclist deaths are due to people falling off bikes with no other vehicle involved. Many more people die in falls while walking or falling down steps, but a cyclist killed in a fall makes the news – together with whether the cyclist was wearing a helmet or not.

Even when you throw motor vehicles into the mix, cycling remains stubbornly safe. It's a little more risky than driving, taken as an average, but not much. Especially if you consider that safe motorway or autobahn miles covered by drivers skew the stats in the car's favour.

It is the minority status of the cyclist that generates the fear. The perception of cycling risk really doesn't match the reality. As John Franklin, author of *Cyclecraft*, argues, "There's nothing in life that's risk free. It's about the management of risk, not simply the fear of risk. As a road cyclist, managing risk means being assertive, and behaving like traffic so that others will treat you as traffic."

WON'T I GET WET?

Probably not. If you keep an eye on the weather forecast there's no reason to get totally soaked, and if it does rain a local café will keep off what your waterproof doesn't. You'll find it rains less than you imagine. Even in wetter climates, it is surprising for a daily commuter to suffer heavy downpours more than three or four times a year.

If you regularly experience a particularly wet couple of months in the winter, you can always choose to forgo the bike for this period.

DON'T YOU GET PUNCTURES?

Just like getting soaked, a puncture is a rare event that's nevertheless annoying. For road riders one of the best preventions is to use puncture-resistant tyres. These have a protective layer under the tread that prevents bits of glass and similar small, sharp objects getting through to the inner tube. Quality puncture-proof tyres, such as the Continental GP 4 Season, practically eliminate punctures.

You can also protect yourself by simply looking where you're going. Ride around patches of broken glass, not through them, and avoid sharp-edged potholes that can cause a puncture by pinching the tube between tyre and rim. Fair-weather road riders will find they get hardly any punctures anyway. It takes water on the road to act like a cutting lubricant and help a shard of glass get through the tyre.

There are also various options for self-sealing inner tubes which utilize a liquid sealant. Tubeless systems are gaining popularity among mountain bikers. Rather like a car tyre, these use an air-tight tyre with a sealant that fills punctures instantly.

HOW DO ALL THESE GEARS WORK? AND WHY ARE THERE SO MANY?

Bikes have gears for the same reason cars do: to let the engine work at a comfortable and efficient speed. But a car's engine works well at a wide range of speeds, while your bike's human engine is best in a fairly narrow band of pedalling rates. Bikes therefore need a wide range of gears to cope with hills and those gears need to be fairly close to each other.

Most bikes use external gear mechanisms, known as derailleurs (or mechs), to move the chain up and down different-sized toothed cogs, called sprockets, on the rear wheel and chainrings at the pedal end. The smaller the chainring or the larger the rear sprocket, the lower and easier the gear.

Ideally you want to keep the chain in a straight line. The large ring at the front lines up with the small sprocket at the back. So if the chain is on the small inner ring it needs to be on the bigger sprockets at the back; likewise, when riding on the big outer ring stick to the smaller sprockets. Crossing the chain puts strain on it and it might not shift into extreme gears, as well as making a grating noise as it rubs against the gears. This noise gives you a clue to check your gear selection. A less common type of gear system hides the mechanism inside the rear hub. Hub gears are practical and tidy, but don't have quite the wide range of ratios provided by derailleurs.

Many new riders find the gears the most daunting feature of their bike. Get yourself to a flat, quiet place like a car park or bike path and shift up and down through the gears till you are completely confident with how they work and what they do. You'll soon find it becomes second nature, just like changing gear in a car.

WHY SO MANY BRAKE TYPES?

You've got to be able to stop quickly and remain in control of the bike. Quickly is no problem. The brakes on modern bikes are powerful enough that your ability to brake is limited by the laws of physics; brake too hard and you'll go over the bars. What you want is fine control over how hard you brake, and consistency in wet and dry conditions.

Disk brakes are now becoming more common on road bikes. Brakes either act on the rim of the wheel or – a more recent innovation – a special braking disc near the hub, like on a motorbike or car. Rim brakes are simple but affected by water and damage to the rim, while disc brakes are more complex, but more consistent and more powerful. Rim brakes include old-fashioned cantilevers, which were succeeded by V-brakes, and dual pivots. Road race bikes almost always have lightweight dual pivot brakes, because bikes for racing are designed to be as light as possible.

13

◤ Punctures are rare but it pays to learn how to fix a flat

▲ Lots of gears make riding easier by allowing you to pedal comfortably whatever the gradient

◀ Disc brakes are standard on mountain bikes from mid-range up

WHY DO SOME BIKES HAVE DROP BARS AND SOME FLAT?

Drop handlebars were developed for road racing, and work brilliantly if you want to get into a position that gives least wind resistance and maximum efficiency. In fact, they offer at least three hand positions, so you can move around if you get tired of one stance. But many riders like the more upright position of a flat handlebar, especially for more leisurely riding – where you can sit up and admire the view – or in traffic.

Wider flat bars give better control on rough surfaces, which is why they are the universal choice of mountain bikers, but for riding on the road it's worth trying both. In fact, mountain bike bars are rarely flat these days; most rise up at the ends so are called riser bars.

HOW HIGH SHOULD MY SADDLE BE?

Many beginners want to be able to put a foot flat on the ground while sitting in the saddle. The problem is that puts your saddle too low for comfortable, efficient pedalling. With your saddle too low, you'll get tired quicker, and put extra strain on your knees.

You should have your saddle high enough that your knee is at a 25–35-degree angle when your foot is at the bottom of the pedal's rotation – it will look like the knee is not quite fully straight. On most bikes you'll still be able to

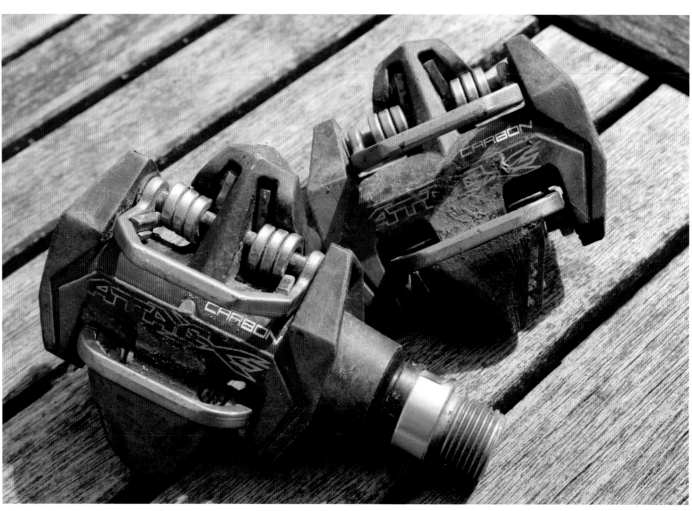

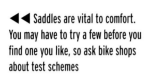

◀◀ Saddles are vital to comfort. You may have to try a few before you find one you like, so ask bike shops about test schemes

◣◣ Clipless pedals are popular with road cyclists and cross-country mountain bikers for the secure attachment to the pedals they provide. Getting out is a matter of a simple twist – once you've got used to them

▶ British Olympic track star Victoria Pendleton proves that you don't have to be muscular to be super-fast on a bike

reach the ground from the saddle in this position; you may have to shuffle sideways a little.

WHAT ARE CLIPLESS PEDALS?

Pedals come in two varieties: flat and clipless (confusingly named because you do actually clip into them). The simplest pedals are flat, and are found on most budget bikes and often on off-road bikes.

Clipless pedals have a spring mechanism, rather like a ski binding, that a dedicated cleat on your shoe fastens into. Clipless shoes for mountain biking have small cleats that sit in a recess in the sole so the rider can still walk in the shoes. Road clipless systems have larger, external cleats and are inconvenient to walk in, so many recreational and commuter cyclists use mountain bike shoes and pedals even though they never go off-road.

DO I NEED SUSPENSION?

Only if you plan to ride off-road. In short, the idea of suspension is to improve handling on rough surfaces such as dirt tracks. Good suspension is a boon for proper mountain biking, but if your ambitions don't involve crossing rugged landscapes or zooming down hillsides, you'll probably be fine with a rigid bike.

Even if you do fancy some suspension to take the sting out of those rocky trails, many of the low-end forks found on a lot of budget range bikes are quite poor quality and can be really heavy, so you need to do your research before you buy.

THAT SADDLE LOOKS UNCOMFORTABLE

Bike saddles need to be fairly narrow so you can pedal easily. As a result, they undeniably take some getting used to; it's a bit like breaking in a new pair of shoes. The trick to getting used to a saddle is to build up your miles gradually. Go for a ride one day, take a couple of days off, then go for another ride. Take another day off, then ride again. Build up both frequency and distance gradually and wear well-fitting padded bike shorts, ideally with no underwear (wash them after every ride).

Very wide and thickly padded saddles are counter-productive. While they might feel more comfortable at first, wide saddles get in the way of your thighs when pedalling and thick padding tends to bunch and pinch. They also add a big weight penalty that you'll notice on the climbs.

WILL I GET FIT?

In short, yes. Experts recommend at least 20 minutes of aerobic exercise (such as riding a bike hard enough that you get out of breath) at least three times per week to maintain basic fitness and health. How much fitter you get than that will depend on how much cycling you do. If you've been very sedentary or are a little overweight, it's sensible to check with your doctor before you start riding. Start with short, flat rides and build up gradually. Fitness is quite specific to activity. Being fit for riding a bike won't help you run a marathon (and vice versa), but it'll stop you getting out of breath running for a bus. And if you're looking to lose a few pounds cycling is a great way to do so.

REASONS TO RIDE

Road cycling has never been so popular, but if you're still unconvinced, here are 12 solid-gold reasons to get on your bike

◢◢ For those with a competitive edge, cycling offers countless opportunities to take part in events

The road bike scene is booming. There are hundreds of leisure rides, sportives and races for all abilities and many road cycling clubs are actively recruiting beginner members. So whether you're getting on a bike for the first time, dusting off your old bike after time off it, or you're looking to take your riding to the next level, there's never been a better time to pull on the lycra and get cycling. If you're still not convinced then here are 12 reasons why it's time to hit the road!

1 HEALTHY BODY

As hobbies go they don't come much healthier. Cycling is a great form of exercise without putting huge amounts of pressure on the knees like running. With obesity affecting around 25 per cent of adults and 10 per cent of children across Europe, finding fun ways to keep yourself and the family active makes a lot of sense.

2 CYCLING CITIES

As cycling becomes more popular, so the pressure increases for cities to provide facilities. The European Commission and most member states are committed to creating bike-friendly towns and cities throughout the continent. The introduction of more cycle paths, bicycle storage facilities and safer cycling environments will make cycling a more pleasant and convenient experience for all.

3 TECHNOLOGICAL ADVANCES

When the first Tour de France was held in 1903, riders pedalled 17kg steel bikes with wooden rims and no gears across stages averaging 400km. Nowadays, for less than a thousand pounds, you can get a quality lightweight bike. The aluminium frame, 20 gears and some top-class components would make your machine more than capable of tackling a Tour stage or two.

4 COMFORTABLE KIT

As well as the bikes the kit has also come a long way. Now there's no need to suffer over long distances when there's so much top-quality clothing on the market. Whatever the weather there's a material out there to keep you warm, cool, dry and, most importantly, comfy and happy. For everything you could possibly need head to page 32.

5 FOLLOW THE PATH OF THE STARS

Very few football fans ever get the chance to play at the Maracana stadium and only a handful of amateur tennis players get anywhere near Wimbledon's Centre Court, but cyclists can tackle the same famous climbs as their heroes; from the Tour de France's notorious Alpe d'Huez to the cobbled roads of the famous Spring Classics.

6 A BEAUTIFUL MIND

The physical benefits of cycling are understandably the ones that usually grab the headlines, but there are also huge mental gains to be had from riding your bike. Getting regular sunlight has been proven to increase levels of the feelgood hormone serotonin while researchers from Illinois University found that a five per cent increase in cardiorespiratory fitness from cycling led to an improvement of up to 15 per cent in mental tests.

7 CHARITY CHALLENGE

It's incredible how quickly your mileage threshold increases on a road bike. Before you know it you'll be clocking up 50 miles without thinking and be looking for bigger challenges. Raising money for charity is a great

way to harness this new desire for miles; there are plenty of organized rides out there or you could plan your own cross-country test for your favourite cause.

8 THE RIGHT TRACK

The number of signposted cycle routes worldwide continues to increase. EuroVelo's 14 routes criss-crossing Europe are intended for both cycle touring and for local people making short journeys. They currently cover 45,000 miles of road which should reach 70,000km by 2020. All of this will help to make travelling long distances by bike much easier – and make touring a great holiday option.

9 WINNING WAYS

For riders with a competitive edge there's plenty of opportunity to get out there and test yourself against fellow riders or the clock. New sportives and gran fondos are popping up all over the place with plenty of female-only events and beginner-friendly distances to choose from too.

10 TRAVEL AND TRAINING

For many cyclists the commute to work provides the perfect time for a training ride. Even if you only cycled one way you could still be getting your recommended daily dose of 30 minutes of light exercise. For quick-fire fitness results try some short interval sprints on your way home.

11 SAVE THE PLANET

Around a fifth of Europe's greenhouse gas emissions are produced by private motor vehicles. The more we can do to reduce this figure the better for us all. If just some of your journeys can be made by bike instead of car then your conscience can feel that bit clearer.

12 ROADS LESS TRAVELLED

Once you've got to grips with the road there are lots of new directions you can take your cycling. If you like the tarmac moving quickly beneath your wheels then why not try out a time trial, or if speed is your thing perhaps a velodrome could be the place for you. In winter months the cyclocross season takes over parks and trails, and provides cyclists with a great way to get off road and enjoy some mud. Beyond this there are plenty of mountain bike disciplines to choose from, each one more grin-inducing than the next.

" Getting regular sunlight has been proven to increase levels of the feelgood hormone serotonin "

BUYING A BIKE

Flat bar or drop bar, aluminium frame or carbon fibre, economy or high-end? There's such a variety of choice available. Here's how to select the right bike for you

►► Your local dealer is still the best place to begin your search for the right bike

▼ For those with a competitive edge, cycling offers countless opportunities to take part in events

Are you after a bike that you can do 100 miles on in a weekend, hammer the hills with, race or simply explore the open road on? Whatever bike takes your fancy, what follows is our guide to deciding how you can get aboard, explaining what you need to buy, how you go about buying it and where to find the best possible deal...

CUTTING THE COST
Many bigger shops and online retailers offer good – and often zero per cent – credit deals that have helped countless cyclists to access good equipment with relative ease by spreading the cost.

Your first step should be deciding on the budget you have available – and remember that you'll probably need some new kit to make riding your new bike a practical and enjoyable experience. If you've got less than a couple of hundred pounds to spend you should forget about buying a new bike, and buy second-hand instead. Machines below this price point are often made of poor-quality materials, low-grade component clones and will be very poorly assembled. A £150 bike can easily end up costing an extra £100 to £150 in order to get it adjusted correctly by a competent bike shop, so you should take that amount and put it towards a decent one instead.

You will also need to factor in a bare bones maintenance budget of about £75 a year. This breaks down to a couple of cheap tyres, a new chain, a couple of sets of brake blocks and some workshop labour. You could save yourself some of this by doing the work yourself, if you feel confident enough to give it a try.

WHERE TO BUY

Your local independent bicycle dealer (IBD) is still the best place to buy despite the many temptations of the internet, especially if you take a long-term view on warranty and after-sales service. Person-to-person contact should ensure that you don't get lost in the bike-purchasing woods.

Before you step over the threshold of your IBD, make sure you have a firm idea of your budget and what kind of bike you're in the market for. Keep in mind that most local shops will have deals on offer depending on the time of the year, and that they are always keen to move last year's stock.

There's no doubt that a lot of the best deals available on bikes new and old are to be found on the internet. Now that purchasing online is done with barely a flicker of concern, you should be able to find plenty of good deals that could save you money while helping to keep the parcel delivery industry afloat. But make sure to set aside at least £50–£100 to get things sorted mechanically during the first month because, unlike purchases made at your IBD, you won't be able to send a web-bought bike back for its required first service. Consequently, any problems or tweaks will most likely have to be dealt with at your local bike shop.

eBay and other auction sites are another obvious option. However, we only recommend purchasing here if you're an experienced bike mechanic. If you're looking at buying second-hand, it's best to do so in a situation where you can wheel the bike over to a shop for a professional assessment before you part with any cash.

In these days of pile-'em-high, sell-'em-cheap stock, large supermarkets and warehouse-sized toy stores are another increasingly high-profile option for bike buyers. Our advice? Stick with them for groceries and cheap inflatable paddling pools, and go elsewhere for bikes. The same goes for bikes advertised in newspapers or offered free with the purchase of a cruise or life insurance: stay away. These 'bike-alikes' will be nothing but trouble and feel hideous to ride.

BIKE CHOICE

For general riding such as commuting, a robust mount is obviously preferable, but if you want to add a bit more fun and speed to the equation, or start entering events, you can have your cake and eat it too – if you make the right choices.

For example, should you go for alloy, steel or carbon? The frame material will largely be dictated by the price, but expect either low-grade steel or aluminium to cost up to about £400. From this point onwards, oversized aluminium tubing is pretty much dominant. As you head towards the £1,000 mark you might start seeing the appearance of carbon in the fork and occasionally in the frame.

Whatever material it's made of, a road or racing bike will get you about faster than any other type of bike, whatever you ask of it. Fancy taking a sedate spin? Check. Fancy entering a sportive? Again, check. Fancy something competitive? Another check. Road bikes will take all of these activities in their stride. What's more, both main road bike variants – road race and endurance models – will happily handle anything you care to throw at them. The differences between them are subtle but can be important, especially if you find an endurance bike more comfortable for longer days in the saddle.

Road bikes can also be battle-hardened for commuting duties if you fit mudguards and slightly bigger and tougher tyres where possible. Also good for this are bikes fitted with disc brakes. Having long dominated mountain biking, disc braking is the latest technology making huge inroads into the world of road riding, the extra control really coming into its own in the wet. The increasing popularity of disc brakes has also given rise to a new type of 'adventure' road bike that's equally at home on gravel and tracks as it is on tarmac.

COMPONENT CHOICE

Such is the state of refinement and advanced technology in bikes today that virtually any widget or feature you could think of has been designed, tried, tested and put on the market, offering what amounts to an overflowing buffet of choice. Consequently, another way to fine-tune your bike is to think of some of the features you want and ask the helpful salesperson if that combination is already available off the peg.

SIZING

We strongly recommend you not to buy any bike until you've checked it for size. As with clothes and shoes, sizing tends to vary between manufacturers, so while you might need a road bike with a 54cm frame from one bike brand, you might require quite a different size from another.

A good bike shop will offer you advice on fitting, as it's about more than sitting comfortably at a standstill – it's about how it positions you when you're riding, which

▶ Do buy from a reputable or recommended bike shop

▶ Don't just add a bike to the ketchup and other groceries in your supermarket trolley

▶ Do spend as much on your bike as your budget will allow

▶ Don't be swayed by offers for 'free' bikes, such as those in newspapers and magazines

▶ Don't be intimidated by jargon or 'expert' staff. Make them explain!

▶ Don't buy with your heart – if a bike doesn't fit, walk away

◀◀ Road bikes are perfect for almost all paved terrain

◀ A good bike shop will always be happy to provide you with helpful cycle advice

has a huge effect on confidence, enjoyment, muscle health and joint pain (see page 30 for more about correct bike fitting).

Once you've worked out your budget, bike preference and purchasing method, you should stand over the bike with both feet flat on the ground, with your legs close together. Lift the bike up or look at the amount of clearance to your body: you should be able to lift the front and back wheels evenly off the ground by about 7–8cm, which should give the equivalent clearance between your crotch and the top tube (this is known as standover height).

Equally important is the reach, or distance from the saddle to the handlebar – there are several centimetres of adjustment possible here, but make sure your preferred set-up isn't at either extreme. You may find yourself tweaking it as you progress. A test ride will help hugely. If you're going for a race steed then expect a lower, more tucked position, while a bike designed for more leisurely use will have a higher bar so that you adopt a more upright stance when riding.

BASIC MAINTENANCE

Try to check over your bike once a week, because riding can be hard on kit. Get a floor pump for home – keeping your tyres at the right pressure means less rolling resistance and extends their life considerably. Pay extra attention to brakes and wipe grit off the rims and pads so they last longer. Be sure to keep your drivetrain clean, and use a suitable lube, plus check your tyres for broken glass or thorns. If your maintenance skills are lacking (see more on pages 102–113) consider a course. You can also find many bike maintenance walkthroughs at www.bikeradar.com.

ENJOY IT!

Hopefully, you're now armed with a bit of extra knowledge and have the confidence to know what to look for, what to ask for and how to buy it. Remember: riding a bike is both challenging and rewarding. But most of all it's fun. Yes, there are myriad health and wellbeing benefits, not to mention financial ones if you choose to commute by bike. But nothing can beat the genuine sense of happiness when all you focus on is the here and now of your ride and not the 'things to do' post-it note on the fridge door; nothing but movement, action and reaction. So go ride and enjoy the freedom!

"When choosing a bike, check it fits properly for maximum comfort, efficiency – and fun "

ROAD BIKE ANATOMY

Pure road bikes are designed to take you as far and as fast as your legs can manage. We take a closer look

At first glance the road bike hasn't changed a great deal over the years. Compared to complex full suspension mountain bikes, this is a traditional bicycle with a near identical silhouette to those raced 50 years ago, even if the technology has moved on.

It's important to know your way around a road bike in order to get the best from it. While the overall shape has altered little, the details have changed. The most important aspect is how the bike fits you. If you get that right at the start, everything else will be simple.

SADDLE AND SEATPOST
As you would expect, these parts have a big impact on the comfort of your ride. For road bikes especially, the comfort is more dependent on correct set-up than it is on having lots of padding. Road saddles are generally long, narrow, thin and sparsely padded. They look very uncomfortable, and do take some getting used to, but are actually better than wide and deep saddles for long rides of several hours.

CASSETTE
Road bikes use gears that are more tightly packed together to help you pedal at the ideal speed (cadence). Until recently the most common number of sprockets on road bikes was 10 but 11-speed is starting to take over, with the major manufacturers featuring it on their higher- and mid-range groupsets.

FRAME

The frame is the heart of any bike. Road bike frames are usually carbon or aluminium. Steel and titanium are used in niche models. Traditional road frames use a horizontal top-tube and a shorter seatpost. Compact geometry is now very popular, with a sloping top-tube to give more standover height. If you're a woman you may prefer a female-specific bike. These are often made with shorter top-tubes, more standover room and possibly an extended headtube. This combination is far more suitable for the average female's shorter torso and gives a slightly more upright riding position. Not every woman wants or needs to be riding a woman's frame though. The important thing is that you buy the right size and shape frame for your size and riding.

HANDLEBARS

Dropped handlebars mark out a road bike. They offer a number of positions. The tops, hands either side of the stem, are used for steep climbs or cruising. The hoods are the brake lever covers that provide a comfortable stretch and good leverage for climbing out of the saddle. The drops are the lower parts of the bar, used for a more aerodynamic position at speed. Bar width and shape varies to tailor your bike's fit to you. This set is an anatomical fit, with a straight section in the drops for a more natural grip.

BRAKES

Road bikes use dual-pivot brakes. They're compact, light and powerful, but only suited to road riding because they have no mudguard clearance at all.

CHAINSET

Road bikes traditionally feature two chainrings with tall 53/39-tooth combinations on race bikes. More usable 50/34 compact set-ups are now popular to aid climbing. Triple chainsets are optional on many bikes and give the widest range with a small inner ring.

WHEELS

Road bike wheels don't have to be as robust as their off-road brethren, so they use fewer spokes. The rims are deeper and narrower to improve aerodynamics. Tyres are also skinny, typically 23-25mm wide. Racing tyres go down to 18mm.

RACE BIKES

Speedy bikes that are bred for the rigours and drama of racing

You don't need to spend a fortune to enter the world of racing bikes. For less than £750 you can ride on the drops, spin through the gears and imagine that you're Marcel Kittel as you sprint against your mates to the next road sign, arms raised in victory... Spend over £1,000 and you're in the rarefied atmosphere of lightweight aluminium, carbon fibre or possibly titanium. Bikes get lighter, the number of gears gets higher, the ride gets faster. Two thousand Euros or more and you're looking at electronic shifting, super-light bling kit and aerodynamic wheels.

SADDLES
Race saddles can be pretty minimalist affairs that can be intimidating to new riders. It's important to remember, however, that a saddle's shape is often more important than its overall padding in terms of comfort but, as every bum is different, what one person may find comfy may be another's pain in the proverbial. So the key is to try as many as you can until you find the one that works for you.

PRICE & SPECIFICATION
At around £500 expect an aluminium frame with a lower-end groupset (like Shimano Sora), carbon fork and a nine-speed transmission. Bikes around £1,000 are capable of being raced so expect an aluminium frame with carbon fork, and a 10-speed groupset (Shimano Tiagra/105). Bikes over £2,000 are race-honed and their full carbon frame and 10- or 11-speed groupset (eg, Shimano Ultegra/SRAM Force/Campagnolo Chorus) will reflect this.

CUTTING-EDGE TECH
From aerodynamic frame detailing to electronic shifting, power meters and specific aerodynamic tube profiling and manipulation, cutting-edge race bikes are the testing ground of new tech. Of course, all that tech ups the price and, for all but elite racers, a £6,000 bike may well be more cachet than anything else. The good news is that after a few years the proven tech will trickle down to lower price points for the benefit of all.

LIGHTWEIGHT

Weight saving is key for race bikes as the less they weigh, the less effort the rider has to expend to pedal at a certain speed. Chasing the grams out is done by using space-age materials and manufacturing techniques in the frame, but also in all other key components. The sky's the limit - but the more exotic tech on display, the higher the price tag, too.

How bikes can make you go faster...
Pure and simply, race bikes are built for speed. They're built in the same vein as pro riders' bikes, where lightweight, agile handling and aerodynamics are crucial. The geometry of race bikes is no-compromise: they're about performance and the rider's position reflects this - low down and tucked in for minimal wind resistance. The downside is that normal riders may find race bikes aren't that comfortable, although carbon bars, stems and seatposts can be used to add comfort. Short wheelbases are the norm as they allow for responsiveness.

However, there is a great variance in geometry - the devil is most certainly in the detail. So try as many bikes as you can until you find the one that works best for you.

Spend at least £400

Weight range Entry level 11kg down to 6kg for a thoroughbred

25

FRAME DESIGN

Oversized and tapered headtubes and fork steerer systems (44mm at the bottom tapering to 34mm at the top) are stiffer than standard 34mm head tubes, boosting steering precision. Curved seatstays retain the rigidity of the rear triangle for power delivery while increasing comfort. Oversized tubes maintain frame strength and rigidity but require thinner wall thicknesses - therefore, less material and weight.

WHEELS

Wheels can adversely affect the way a bike feels and responds as rotating mass (ie, wheel edges - rims and tyres) can make the biggest single difference to how zippy a bike feels. The heavier the wheel rims and tyres, the more effort they'll take to accelerate and the more they'll need to change direction too, so make sure that a bike's wheels are good and suitable for its price tag.

SPORTIVE BIKES

Fast, efficient bikes for getting the miles in - and comfortable for the long haul

Riding a sportive (or a 'gran fondo') is the closest many riders will come to competing in a real race. If you want to finish among the leaders you'll want your bike to be fast, but as events can be 100 miles or even longer – and be extremely challenging – you'll be spending hours in the saddle, so day-long comfort is just as crucial.

FRAME MATERIAL
The majority of sportive bikes have aluminium frames. These are stiff and hardwearing, but can offer a slightly harsher ride than carbon – which is why some brands will use carbon seatstays and chainstays to add comfort. Higher-end frames will use full carbon fibre as it's light and strong and the perfect compromise between comfort and performance. However, it requires more care to avoid general knocks and scrapes damaging the integrity of the frame.

GEARING
Sportive bikes often get compact gearing rather than standard gearing. Compact refers to smaller front chainring sizes (number of teeth) than standard ring sizes. Standard non-compact rings are usually 53-39T these days, while compacts are generally 50-34T or 50-36T. Compacts result in lower (easier) gearing, with a like-for-like rear sprocket, for lesser mortals than Tour De France pros - perfect for longer, hillier rides.

GEOMETRY

Sportive frames tread the line between all-day comfort and speed. The riding position is more upright than on a race bike – typically aided by a longer headtube and shorter top tube. Longer wheelbases and relaxed seat and head angles add stability and make the handling more neutral.

What is a sportive?

Like many cycling terms the word 'sportive' hails from France – where a long-distance cycling challenge is a called a randonnée cyclosportive. Hence 'sportive'. In Italy – and sometimes the USA – the term is gran fondo.

These are well-organized events and can have thousands of entrants – 15,000 in the Ardechoise. The two best-known French sportives are the Etape du Tour, run annually over a mountainous stage of the Tour de France, and the Marmotte, featuring over 5,000m of climbing.

You can ride any bike on a sportive, but you'll want lightish weight and loads of comfort – carbon or titanium if the budget allows. Drop bars give you the most riding positions and you'll need low enough gears to cope with hills – so check the route profile beforehand.

Spend at least £600
Weight range Entry level 10kg

27

FRAME FITTINGS

Sportive bikes are more versatile than race bikes. Many come with fittings for mudguards, eyes for mounting pannier racks on for carrying luggage for touring and commuting, as well as bottle cages for water bottles or battery packs for lights. These increase the bike's versatility.

GROUPSETS

The groupset is the transmission and brakes: look for established brands like Shimano, SRAM or Campagnolo. Recently there has been a 'trickle down' of technologies from the high-end groupsets to those lower down. This has meant improved shifting performance – across nine, 10 and now even 11 speeds for Campag.

SIZE AND FIT

It's important to remember that different brands size up differently: one brand's 56cm may be smaller than another's, and vice versa. So before you buy, pay the utmost attention to finding the right size for you for both comfort and performance. A good shop can take you through a bike fitting process to determine what size is right for you. See the Bike Fit feature on p30 for more information.

WOMEN'S BIKES

Fast rides that prove this is not just a man's world

Women's road cycling a is fast-growing sector of the sport, with more riders and more high-profile races than ever. Appropriately, today's female riders have more choice than ever when it comes to buying a road bike. Whether women actually need a bike with female-specific geometry is a moot point, but there's no doubt that women cyclists do require female-specific components for comfortable and efficient cycling – and buying the correct size bike is just as crucial for women as it is for men.

ADAPTATION
When looking for a new steed, don't rule out anything. Instead, test bikes aimed at women and men from different brands to find what works for you. A man's bike - with a few tweaks - may work better than a women-specific bike, especially if you're after a performance bike for racing. You can always change the saddle, swap the bars to reduce width (38-40cm is typical), shorten the reach to the hoods and reduce the drop. A change to a slightly shorter stem may be of help - just don't go too short or too long.

MAKING CONTACT
Geometry aside, the most obvious differences between men's and women's bikes are the main contact points: the saddle and the handlebar. Saddles are generally wider to support women's sit bones, but saddle choice is very personal so try as many as you can. When it comes to the handlebar, a good rule of thumb is that the width of your bar should match the width of your shoulders. Bear in mind, however, that the wider the bar, the more stable the ride, while narrower bars will give the bike a fast, responsive feel.

NEED TO KNOW

What women want...
There's no simple definition in labelling a product as a woman's bike - it can mean many different things. Also, while there might be fewer women riding, there's just as much variety physically. Try before you buy and don't discount a man's bike - you might find the fit more suitable.

When bike geometries are tweaked for women's bikes, this often leads to a more upright riding position. The oft-stated reason for this is that a woman has a shorter torso and longer legs. Bike maker Cervélo has declared it a myth and insists that women need the same geometries as men. Some riders might prefer being more upright, but if you're planning on faster riding, you could be better off with a more stretched out - and thus more aerodynamic - riding position.

Spend at least £650
Weight range Entry level 12kg

LEVER REACH

If you have small hands - and this goes for men too - you might need to bring the levers closer to the bar. A lot of Shimano-equipped bikes are supplied with shims to do this and Specialized produces an aftermarket product that works in the same way. Both the shift paddle and brake lever can be adjusted for reach on SRAM-equipped bikes by rotating a cam and a bolt respectively. Campagnolo takes a different approach, with plastic shims that can be used to increase the reach, but it can't be reduced. A good bike shop should be able to advise you on fit and swap components if needed.

SIZE MATTERS

While there's little evidence that women's bodies have proportionately longer legs than men's, what is true is that women are on average shorter - and have smaller hands and narrower shoulders. If you are around 1.5m tall you'll be looking at frames around 44-46cm. This shouldn't be a limiting factor - Giant makes a 43cm women's bike, Specialized 44cm, while specialist frame makers could go even smaller.

BIKE FITTING

A properly set-up bike is a joy to ride – here's how to get it right

Riding a bike that doesn't fit properly is no fun. The handling is compromised, it'll likely be uncomfortable and you risk injury from over-reaching or being too cramped.

There are no cast-in-stone rules for how to set up your bike, but there are general principles. The correct set-up simply means that your bike fits you for the type(s) of riding you do. This could mean it has been set up for more speed, better aerodynamics or increased comfort.

Getting the right fit means more than just having the right size frame; it means that your bike fits you at all the main contact points – handlebar, saddle and pedals – so you don't have to adopt an uncomfortable position.

Here we look at the set-ups for general road riding, touring/commuting, and time trialling. We're not all the same, so this is a guide only. A good rule is that if it feels right, it probably is – unless your body has adapted to a bad position and this now feels normal.

After you have chosen the right size frame, it's time to fine-tune. This starts when you choose the length of the stem and the width of the bar, and is completed by setting the bar and saddle height. If in doubt, consult a good bike shop or arrange a bike fitting session – a decent cycle shop should help you achieve a perfect fit. They should put you on a fixed trainer to check your position once you're warmed up. Make sure you're kitted out in your normal riding shoes, pedals and shorts.

With experience, you will find that a correctly sized bike will look in proportion when set up. Compact frames (with sloping top-tubes) are meant to look more radical than conventional level top-tube frames, so expect to see an extra two to three inches of seatpost showing compared to bikes with horizontal top-tubes. The contact points should be exactly the same – a compact should feel exactly like your conventional road bike with respect to riding position.

SIZE WISE

The dominant dimension on a road bike is the reach to the bar. The reference measurement from your frame is a horizontal line from the centre of the headtube at the top to the centre of the seat-tube (or seatpost on compacts). If you're 5ft 3in to 5ft 6in tall, you need a frame with a 52 or 53cm top-tube. Riders in the 5ft 8in to 5ft 11in range need 54 to 56cm top-tubes, and riders from 6ft to 6ft 4in need 56 to 58cm.

Getting the right fit at the contact points is the primary aim of a well set-up bike – you want to feel well balanced and have good handling in all circumstances. Although the reach to the bar on a road bike is both forward and down, a correctly set-up road bike will let the rider reach all parts of the bar without any stress. You should be able to reach the top of the bar with your arms not quite straight and your back at an angle of around 45°.

◀ Taking time to get the right set-up can pay dividends

1 Set up your bike and wear your normal cycling shoes and shorts. Measure your actual inside leg with socks on or to the top of the sole of your shoe at the heel. Do this by holding a level up in your crotch or just by pushing the end of the tape measure into your sit bone where you rest on the saddle.

2 Multiply this by 109% to get your saddle top-to-pedal distance. This may need to be modified up to 15mm either way to compensate for different riding styles. Set the saddle flat with scope to put the tip slightly up for men and slightly down for women (+/-8mm from the level). Set the saddle height to your 109% length.

3 Warm up enough so that you start pedalling naturally, then stop with your leg at full extension. Your foot should be flat or slightly toe-down, but make sure you don't change your natural style for the set-up – things will immediately change back when you get out on the road. Once you're happy with the saddle height, concentrate on the reach to the bar. On the tops, you should be relatively upright and comfortable. Similarly, you should be happy to spend lots of time on the brake hoods or tri-bars. Adjust the reach by either swapping the Ahead stem for a shorter or longer one, or use an Ahead adapter if your existing stem is a quill type.

4 The drop portion of the bar should not be out of reach, so spend time in this position to make sure that the brakes and gears are accessible. If they're not, take time to move the levers. A good starting point is to create a horizontal platform from the shoulders of the bar onto the hood of the brake levers. This provides a comfortable cruising position while still allowing access from the drops.

5 Check the handlebar width by comparing the measurement across your shoulders with that across the bar, and be prepared to go wider or narrower accordingly. Remember that wide bars open your arms and have the effect of dragging you forward, which is not good news for smaller, slighter riders. Measure the bar across the centre of the ends – 38cm is narrow and 44cm is wide.

6 Dropping a plumb line down from the kneecap will give you a fix on your cleat position. The plumb line should drop through the pedal spindle – if it doesn't, move the saddle fore or aft to correct. The ball of your foot should be over the pedal spindle for balanced pedalling. You may have a preference for lifting and dropping your heel when pedalling (called 'ankling') or you might prefer to push bigger gears with a stiffer ankle action. In the first instance, move the cleats forwards for more ankle freedom and backwards for big gear crunching (the latter is not generally recommended).

The reach to the hoods should be longer and lower but still comfortable for extended periods. You should be able to maintain the position on the drops for long periods and it should be comfortable on fast downhill sections to afford you the strongest grip on the brakes. A common error is to have the reach too long and too low, especially for people with shorter torsos. Avoid this by flipping the stem to raise the bar, or fitting a shorter stem to lessen the reach.

FANCY FOOTWORK

The adjustment should all go on at the front end of the bike. A quick fix is to move the saddle forward or back along its rails to make up for a long or short reach, but this forces the rider out of the classic saddle-to-pedal position that gives maximum power (see 6, above).

Finally, pay attention to the position of your feet on the pedals. Poorly placed feet can lead to all sorts of difficulties for cyclists, from hotspots – where the pedal or cleat digs into your foot and cuts off the circulation – to knee and leg problems. For performance riding there is an ideal position, but if you don't feel right be prepared to make further adjustments. Remember, though, to keep each one small and to give yourself time to get used to it before adjusting again. For more information on adjusting your cleats see page 40.

BIKE ESSENTIALS

Here's a guide to the basic riding wardrobe, tools and accessories you need to keep smoothly spinning the miles

HELMET

Helmets can help protect you in the event of unfortunate accidents or collisions. Plus, you might find that if you wear one and follow sensible precautions on the road, you'll feel more reassured about your safety on the bike. This means you can concentrate your efforts on developing your technique and handling skills and, of course, simply enjoying the ride. They are also required when riding most events.

There's a huge range of lids on the market, with styles, colours, materials and sizings varying dramatically. Wearing a helmet no longer means sweltering inside a heavy casing – light and well vented options are the norm these days.

As with your bike, try different models out at your local bike shop before you buy. If a helmet's going to be effective at all it needs to be properly fitted and securely attached to your head, which means it should sit level, cover your forehead and have snugly fitting straps.

BASE LAYER

If you're riding year-round and the temperature drops it can be hard to know what to wear on the bike. Go for a snug jacket or jumper and you'll soon find that you overheat and sweat. The solution is to wear layers made from wickable materials that are specially designed for athletes.

Start with a tight base layer, which sits next to your skin and should fit easily under a jersey and jacket. Base layers can be thermal, windproof, long-sleeved, high-necked... the choice is yours. The main thing is that the weave of the fabric wicks sweat away from your skin quickly, keeping you dry and warm.

PEAK OR NOT?
Many roadies opt out of using a peak to make them more aerodynamic, but peaks can provide shade in summer and shelter from the rain in winter.

CHECK ADJUSTMENT
Most helmets have some sort of widget that allows you to adjust the fit of the rear cradle. Look for vertical tweaking options for the cradle too, for the best fit.

GOOD VENTILATION
The best helmets are cool and comfy even on the hottest days. Look for big vents, plus some deep channels inside the helmet.

SHORTS

For riding in the depths of winter you'll need to invest in a pair of cycling tights to keep your legs toasty, but come milder weather you can switch to cycling shorts. These will be made of tight-fitting stretchy panels to allow freedom of movement without excess material to bunch or chafe.

Shorts come in lots of shapes and sizes, so find what works for you and the weather you're riding in. For spring and autumn, slightly heavier material paired with knee warmers can work well, whereas you'll want lightweight fabric in the heat. Poorly fitting shorts can lead to chafing and discomfort, so choose carefully.

MITTS

While full-fingered gloves are essential for keeping your hands warm and mobile when it's cold, they become a hindrance when the mercury rises. That's where mitts, or fingerless gloves, come in.

Designed to give you the protection of gloves without the heat, they have palm padding that absorbs road vibrations through the bar and will act as a shield if you hit the tarmac. Pairs with mesh backs will keep you extra cool, and towelling sections can be handy when you need somewhere to wipe your runny nose (it happens to everyone). Look for tabs, which are helpful for removing gloves.

TOWELLING-BACKED
The back of your mitt is often the most convenient way of wiping sweat or a runny nose.

GLASSES
Almost an essential, especially if you're prone to streaming tear ducts or like summer rides in the country, where getting a fly or grit in your eye is no fun at all. Choose glasses with as much coverage as possible and look for photochromic or interchangeable lenses, so you can adapt them to the conditions – dark for sunny days, clear for night and yellow or orange to make overcast days look cheerful! You can get a basic set with three lenses without breaking the bank.

ARM WARMERS
The ultimate accessory for transitioning between the seasons, arm warmers should be worn with short-sleeved jerseys. They'll keep you insulated but are designed to be removed easily and, if you're confident enough, on the move. Just pack them into a pocket for use later on. In terms of clever materials we'd recommend ones made out of Roubaix fabric for the ultimate in breathable windproofing. Gummy grippers are also helpful for keeping the warmers in place.

BIB TIGHTS
As well as providing three-quarter or full-length coverage to keep your legs warm, bib tights have a high front that extends up to around your navel. This gives your core added protection against the elements and means no waistband to dig in. Bib tights should be tightly fitted and are held up by a pair of elasticated braces. It can be worth looking for bibs with wider shoulder straps, which will help prevent pinching.

33

WATERPROOFING
Often expressed as hydrostatic head – how high a column of water in mm could be supported by the fabric before it leaks. 5,000mm is okay, 20,000mm top of the range.

SEAMS
Can be stitched, stitched and taped, or just taped – a seam of any kind is a waterproofing weak point. Avoid irregular or loose stitches, misaligned tape or over-bumpy tape where several seams meet.

MATERIALS
There's always a pay-off between water-proofing and breathability. Vents help regulate temperature and humidity so the more numerous and adjustable they are the better.

VISIBILITY
If you can't stomach fluoro, choose bright colours with white panels and reflective logos, piping, decals, zips and stitching. At night, white is more visible on the road than fluoro.

OPENINGS
Cuffs need to keep wind and rain out so a tight fit is crucial, as is adjustability. Collars need to be high and close enough to keep rain and draughts out, especially when you're bending forward.

ZIPS
Should be free-moving, durable and usable one-handed; big zip-pulls help. Zips are a waterproofing and draught-proofing weak point so look for waterproof ones or those protected by a storm flap.

JACKET
The type of jacket you buy depends on what other cycling clothing you're investing in. Look for a cycle-specific cut with a longer back (or drop tail) to keep you covered when you're leaning forward on the bike. If you've got base layers and warm jerseys to layer up in the cold, then a lightweight windproof and/or waterproof shell will sit over them nicely. The beauty of this is that the same jacket can be thrown on over a top if you're heading out on a summer's day that's threatening rain or wind. Just pack it into a pocket or cut-off water bottle if you don't need it.

Heavier-duty jackets can be worn over one layer and still protect you in the cold. Look for breathable fabrics and zipped vents to stop you getting too sweaty. If the material is waterproof then make sure you check the washing instructions before throwing it in the machine.

LOCK

If you leave your bike unattended at all then you're going to need to lock it. This is one area where you truly get what you pay for: good locks aren't cheap but the best will resist anything short of power tools and make a thief look elsewhere. It's impossible to be sure how good a lock is just by looking at it, but tests have shown that the best protection comes from D-shaped shackle locks with hefty armouring around the lock mechanism. The U of the lock should engage at both ends and the key should be flat – not a cylinder, which is easier to attack. If you're keeping your bike in the garage, consider a strong wall lock.

PUNCTURE REPAIR KIT

With punctures always a possibility, carry a spare inner tube with you so you're covered. If that then blows, a puncture repair kit will be invaluable. They include pre-glued patches or those that require some liquid latex for sticking everything together – all you need to get home. Take the instructions too if you're not sure what you're doing.

FRAME PROTECTION

There's no point buying an expensive lock just to damage your bike when you drop all that weight on it. Look for a thick, rubberised coating on the shackle to protect against frame damage.

SHACKLE

The U-shaped bit that fits into the barrel. If the slot for the mechanism is square cut it can be weak. Check how much of the barrel swings into place when locked - ideally, more than 5mm.

SECURITY RATINGS

The most consistent is the Sold Secure Rating. Gold, Silver and Bronze show how long a lock will hold out. Bronze is 1 min with basic tools, Silver 3 mins with a wider array of tools and Gold 5 mins with more sophisticated kit. The Dutch ART standard (rated 1 to 5+, the higher the better) is also a good guide.

LOCK BARREL

The cleverest designs have the lock mechanism in the centre of the barrel, which makes it harder to attack with a drill (unlike end-mounted locks). Weight matters too. If a lock is heavy it's a sign that it's probably armoured. Look for brands like Kryptonite, Abus, Squire and OnGuard for armoured locks.

LIGHTS

Essential if you're going to ride after dark, lights do two jobs: make you visible and illuminate the road. In the city there's enough ambient light that you just need small, fairly bright units that other road users can see. They can be combined with reflectors to increase your profile.

For unlit roads you need something more powerful. Efficient, bright LEDs and lithium-ion rechargeable batteries mean compact lights can now pack an incredible amount of power. They're great for long-distance commuting.

MINI PUMP

Any seasoned cyclist will tell you that if you're riding more than a kilometre or so from home on your bike you should be prepared to fix punctures. Whether you swap your inner tube or patch the damaged one (see 'Puncture repair kit', page 35) you'll need to reinflate before you can be on your way. A lightweight mini pump will be barely noticeable in your pack or attached to your bike's frame. Don't scrimp on size too much though, as the smaller the pump the harder it will be to inflate your tubes to 7 Bar, the typical pressure for road tyres. A built-in pressure gauge is an advantage, as is a comfortable handle.

SWITCH AND MODES
The switch should be easy to use but hard to turn on accidentally, to prevent flat batteries. It also needs to be well sealed, and offer at least one flashing mode and one constant.

FRAME SIZE
If you're buying a frame-fitting pump to go under the top-tube or against the seat-tube then make sure it fits your bike.

MOUNTING
Needs to be strong enough to hold the light over bumps but also offer a quick-release-style system for removal. Mounts that require no tools to fit are a bonus but by no means necessary.

BEAM PATTERNS
Some lights feature a beam similar to that of a car or motorbike. This means the top of the pattern is essentially cut off, allowing a bright light to be used without it dazzling road users.

HOSE
Either separate or extending from the pump. They take longer to fit to a tube's valve but stay on and let you pump in a more comfortable position.

LIGHT SOURCE
Most bike lights use Light Emitting Diodes (LEDs), which emit light by being switched on and off quite quickly. If you switch them on and off for different lengths of time you can boost or reduce output.

PRESTA/SCHRADER
Presta is the skinny valve with a locknut, usually on high-pressure tyres; Schrader is the chunkier car-type valve.

TYRE LEVERS

Tyres are made of tough rubber so if you need to change the inner tube it can be hard to remove them using your hands. Tyre levers are made of shaped plastic – buy quality ones as cheap ones can snap. Simply hook them under the tyre bead and pull out and down to separate rubber from rim. Hook the other end of the lever around a spoke to hold the tyre in place while you loosen it in another place.

BUFF

For such a cheap accessory a Buff can make a remarkable difference to your comfort in the cold. Made out of polyester, the lightweight tube can be worn as a snood, pulled up around your mouth and nose or tied on your head to act as a buffer against icy gusts that get through helmet vents. Don't forget about Buffs in the summer either – if it's baking hot or you're taking part in a big event, try soaking one in cold water and wearing it on your head.

CLIPLESS PEDALS

Buy a basic road bike and it will most likely come with standard flat pedals. These are fine for short trips, but as your skills improve, pedals that attach you to the bike via the soles of your shoes are worth considering. Contrary to what the name suggests, you clip into clipless pedals using cleats. Pedals are the points at which your power is transmitted to the bike, and clipless models allow you to transmit force without your feet slipping off the pedal.

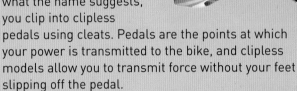

SHOES

Road shoes have stiff soles for efficient power transfer; also your feet won't flex over the pedals. Most cycling shoes have threaded holes in the soles so that you can bolt on the cleats you need to use with clipless pedals. It's quite difficult to walk in road cleats so some commuters prefer trainer-like cycling shoes with embedded cleats. These are used with the SPD pedal system pioneered by Shimano, and can be worn both on and off the bike.

TRACK PUMP

To keep annoying punctures and rolling resistance to a minimum, you need to pump your tyres up regularly. While mini pumps are excellent for roadside emergencies they require quite a lot of effort to get a standard 23mm road tyre up to 7 Bar. Track pumps are larger and much handier for home use. Look for a heavy, stable base; fold-out feet are handy if you want to pack the pump and take it to events. A decent model should have a pressure gauge, possibly a digital one. Most road tyres have Presta valves, but pumps with Schrader heads too are useful.

37

GOING CLIPLESS

Upgrading to clipless pedals can make a huge difference to your riding. Here are the advantages - and the pitfalls

Pedals are a fundamental part of any ride and getting the right ones can have a massive impact. The improvement in performance with a pair of clipless pedals is undeniable, but the idea of careering through traffic buckled to the bike leaves some riders feeling a little uncomfortable. Luckily, as with most things bike, there's something for everyone and if you're in two minds as to which pedals you need to complete your perfect build then look no further.

CLIPLESS TECHNOLOGY
The term 'clipless' is misleading. The name refers to the mechanism of cleats and bindings that lock your shoe to the pedal, but stems from the toe-clips that this system replaced, where leather straps kept riders' feet in position.

Although the first clipless pedals date back to the late 1800s and various designs were patented during the 20th century, none gained any notable success until the seventies, when Cinelli brought out the M71. Affectionately nicknamed the 'death cleat' by American riders, the M71 system involved a hand-operated lever that needed to be pulled before your shoe would release. Needless to say this meant for a sluggish dismount and the crashes that inspired its morbid moniker meant that few riders adopted clipless pedals until the next decade.

In 1983 French company Look released its first commercially successful clipless road pedal. Anyone who needed evidence of the benefits of Look's clipless system got just that in 1985 when Bernard Hinault won the Tour de France using the pedals. From here the clipless bandwagon picked up a host of manufacturers, most notably Time and Shimano. Any road rider worth his salt was soon using one variety of clipless pedals or another, and even off-road riders started clipping in.

WHY GO CLIPLESS?
So what do you gain from having your shoes attached to the pedal? With your feet clipped in you're utilizing your hamstrings – which pull up – instead of solely relying on your quadriceps pushing down. This spreads the load between your upper leg muscles, increasing pedalling efficiency and exerting up to 25 per cent more power. The balls of your feet will remain rooted to the centre of your pedals, which is the most efficient pedalling position, enabling your calves to shoulder some of the burden as well.

The effort exerted on a ride is reduced and it takes longer for fatigue to kick in. As well as increasing power and efficiency, you also benefit from increased control. There's nothing worse than wet trainers sliding around on a pair of flat pedals, especially when climbing out of the saddle. Being attached to the bike also helps you manoeuvre out of tight spots more easily, hopping up onto kerbs or over obstacles. Cycling shoes are also a lot stiffer than regular footwear, which reduces flexion and further improves the transition of power from leg to pedal.

PITFALLS
Unfortunately the haunting image of Cinelli's 'death cleats' still looms large over a lot of riders and the idea

---

TOP FIVE CLIPLESS BRANDS

Look
The original clipless brand, Look produces simple but very effective road pedals. They famously helped Bernard Hinault to his fifth Tour de France victory in 1985 and haven't looked back since.
CHECK OUT: The Keo Classic is a great entry-level road pedal with a simple design, enabling easy clipping, both in and out.

Time
Time entered the clipless market with the help of former Look engineer Jean Beryl and shot to fame when Miguel Indurain used its pedals while winning his five Tour titles in the early 90s.
CHECK OUT: The I-Clic2 is a great pedal with a reliable mechanism and durable manufacturing.

SPD SL
Shimano's road-ready breed of clipless are sleek and easy to use. They're built for perfect power transfer and there's a pedal for all pockets.
CHECK OUT: Shimano's R540 Light Action pedals are a great choice for beginners. They're easy to clip in and out of, have a wide platform and are reasonably priced.

CLIPLESS SYSTEMS

Stack height

Stack height is measured from the middle of the pedal axle to the sole of the shoe. A lower stack height is more efficient because it places your foot closer to the centre of the axle.

Bearings

Pedals have either loose or sealed bearings. Better-quality pedals with sealed bearings have a longer life expectancy, but the life of loose bearings can be prolonged by giving them a regular service.

of slowly toppling over at a set of traffic lights is too much for some people to bear. Releasing can be a bit disconcerting at first but most pedals can be adjusted to reduce the release tension, allowing you to bail out with ease should the need arise.

Newbies also voice concerns over the added strain on the knees that comes from having your feet in a fixed position, so it's best to get your cleats set up properly. Most pedals come with some degree of what's called float, which can be adjusted to allow your foot to move slightly as your body shifts on the bike.

Another slight annoyance is having to wear cycling shoes and cleats that are uncomfortable to walk in and make you sound like you're auditioning for *Riverdance*. If you think you'll find this a particular problem, you could opt for mountain bike pedals – Shimano and Crank Brothers being two popular brands in the MTB clipless world. The shoes generally have more recessed cleats, which don't clatter on the floor as much as road shoes. They also have soles with better grip so are more suited to walking around off the bike. Some MTB and touring pedals also have a larger cage, which allows you to pedal while unclipped.

WHAT ABOUT FLATS?

If the idea of being bound to your bike is too scary, or you're just too fond of your daps, then there are some great flat pedals to choose from. Although you lose out on the energy efficiency and control of a clipless set-up, you do gain the freedom of being able to jump on and off the bike without so much as a second thought.

Your choice of pedal will boil down to what kind of riding you want to do, but pedals can be swapped very quickly if your commuter bike becomes your sportive machine at the weekend. If your mind isn't made up then speak to your friends, seek out some experts and see if you can have a go on a pair that takes your fancy.

CLEAT SET-UP

Correct cleat set-up means comfort and pedalling efficiency. Get it wrong and you won't be happy at all

Badly positioned cleats not only stop you getting maximum power through the pedals, but they can also lead to muscle or joint pain all over.

It's vital, then, to get the set-up right. One foot at a time. Don't just mirror the cleat position on each shoe as there is often a difference in the length of your feet, or the angle that's comfortable for each leg, so set them up independently.

MAKE YOUR MARK

The correct fit is about positioning your foot in relation to the pedal: the pedal axle should be 5–7mm behind the ball of your foot. You can find the ball – which is at your first big toe joint – by putting your thumb on the side of your shoe and wiggling your toes. Mark that point with a piece of white tape on the outside of the shoe, and put the centre of the cleat 5–7mm behind that point.

Most cleats have the fore/aft centre of the cleat marked with a line. But SPD SLs, for example, have their centre point where they start to taper. Many shoes have helpful marks on the sole too, but it's still best to check.

START NEUTRAL

To start with, set your cleats in the neutral position – pointing straight up the centre of the shoe – and change them only if necessary. Most cleats have a degree of 'float'

– a small amount of lateral play for your foot to swivel on the pedal – which can help prevent putting extra pressure on your ligaments and joints.

TEST RIDE

The best way to tell if you need to move your cleats from the neutral position is to cycle in them, and adjust them slightly each time until you find a comfortable position.

Sometimes it helps to get another experienced rider to watch you riding. They can tell you whether your knees are pointing in or out too much, how close to the crank your heels are, or whether you look like you're extending your leg too much – something your saddle height also affects in a big way. Alternatively, get a friend to film you on their phone or camera, from the front and side, so you can analyse your pedalling yourself.

CHECK THE ANGLE

If after the test ride you decide you need to change from the neutral position, there is a tried and trusted way of finding your cleat angle for each foot. Perch squarely on the edge of a table with your legs dangling off the side, so your cycling shoes rest on a square piece of paper, the edge of which is perpendicular to the table edge.

Draw around your shoes, then place the cleats within the outlines of your shoes so that they too are square to

SLIP-LASTED OR BOARD-LASTED?

When making the inside 'last' section of a shoe, there are two main technologies. You should be able to remove the insole from any shoe to expose this. The cheaper slip-lasted method involves sewing the upper together down the midline of the inside of the shoe. This creates a more rounded profile to the inside of the shoe, and is often more flexible. The more traditional board-lasted shoes, on the other hand, have a separate 'board' along the base, and are sewn around the sides of the sole. They have a more box-section appearance that's generally more stable and better accommodates custom orthoses and other in-shoe modifications such as heel lifts.

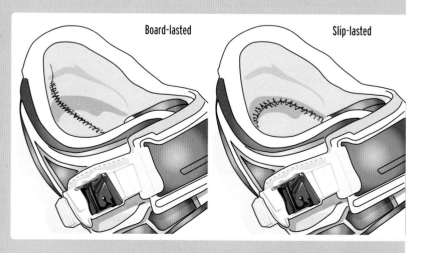

Board-lasted   Slip-lasted

PAIN POINTERS

Bad angle
If your heel is forced too far out when you're pedalling it will put pressure on the medial ligaments in your knee and the ligaments on the outside of your ankle. The reverse would happen if your heels are too close to your crank arm, resulting in pain when walking or running, even if you cannot feel any problem when pedalling.

Heels up too high or down too low
If your heels are pointing down when you're cycling then you are stretching the anterior tibialis muscle, which could cause shin splints. If your toes are pointing downwards, then you are contracting your calf muscles too much, and that can effectively shorten your Achilles tendon. This will cause an imbalance through your ankle, knees and hips, which may be a problem when you get off the bike.

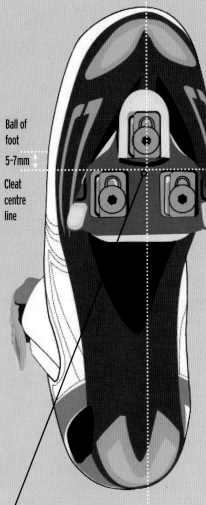

Ball of foot

5-7mm

Cleat centre line

CLEAT ALIGNMENT
The neutral position is the best starting point for finding your ideal cleat alignment, where the centre line of the cleat lines up with the centre line of the shoe. At this point the cleat angle is zero degrees.

STOP HOT SPOTS
Long hours in the saddle can lead to a burning sensation on the balls of your feet, but there are ways to prevent it.

Shoe size
If your shoe is ill-fitting it can place extra pressure on your metatarsals (long bones in your feet) which could cause hot spots. Try out a few shoes before you buy. Make sure the width is right – snug without pinching. Length-wise, your toes should only be a couple of millimetres from the end of the shoe to keep your foot in place.

Inserts
If your shoe fits well but you still get that burning sensation, you might need extra support, depending on how arched your feet are. Specialized offers three footbeds for flat feet, standard or high arches; and Bont is the master of heat-mouldable insoles.

Cleat position
It could also be that your cleats are in the wrong position. Moving them back a couple of millimetres should help relieve the pressure on your forefoot. If this doesn't work, try moving the cleat forward so it's just slightly ahead of the ball of your foot.

---

the edge of the table. Hey presto! The angle between a centre line drawn through the length of your shoes and the vertical edge of the paper is your all-important cleat angle.

TIME TO RETIRE
Unlike other shoes, it's harder to know when cycling shoes are past their best. Training shoes, with regular cleat replacements, should last many years before wear and abuse has them splitting at the seams. When they no longer tighten snugly and work loose when you accelerate, it's time to say goodbye. Or at least, au revoir – they can still do duty on winter turbo trainers, where spinning rules over sprinting.

Racing shoes, however, should be rigid and supportive in order to optimize performance. Their cleats should never be allowed to wear thin – this endangers you and your fellow riders. Carbon fibre soles resist fatigue and so offer continued performance for many years, but any proper racing shoe that can be significantly flexed by a pair of unkind hands is really no longer up to the job, and should be demoted to training use.

▶ Worn-out shoes: discard or use for training

THE PERFECT RIDING POSITION

Comfortable cycling starts with a bike that puts you in the right position. Discover exactly what that is and how to find yours

◀ Set your bike up right and you'll ride efficiently and comfortably all day

The secret to cycling happiness is setting up your bike so that it puts you in your perfect position for riding all day with optimal efficiency and comfort. Let the bike contort you into the wrong position and you risk compromising a bike's handling and safety, suffering postural pain or causing yourself overuse injuries.

"The bike is a fixed machine, which is adjustable, whereas the human body is only adaptable over time," says bike fitting pioneer Dr Andy Pruitt, founder of the Boulder Center for Sports Medicine in the US, and bike fitter to pro cycling stars such as Tom Boonen and Tony Martin. "So you're far safer adjusting the bicycle to the human than making the human adapt to the bicycle." Modern professional bike fitting theory and practice centres on finding a rider's 'neutral' riding position – one that "minimizes the stress and strain on the musculoskeletal components to optimize comfort" as Pruitt puts it.

It does this by analysing the three areas of contact between you and your bike – the pelvis, feet and hands – and evaluating the joints that link them for biomechanical dysfunction as you pedal, before moving the relevant bike components to their optimal position according to each individual rider.

STEP 1: PICK A SEAT

As the one component on the bike supporting most of your weight, the saddle is also responsible for a great deal of your comfort – or discomfort if you get the shape, width, structure or alignment wrong. But because the one you choose will affect your saddle height, as well as pedalling biodynamics, it should be the first thing you choose. Which is difficult because there are so many different options...

German company Gebiomized might now be able to help you quantify – and visualize – what suits you best. Its pressure-mapping saddle cover fits over any saddle and has 64 sensors linked to software that displays a live colour-coded graphic of pressure levels and distribution on the saddle – and therefore on your behind.

Whether you can see it or not, the consensus for saddle choice – as set out by the Medicine of Cycling Bike Fit Task Force, made up of bike fit experts such as Serotta, Specialized, Bikefit.com and Retul – remains the same: it should be within 2.5 degrees of level front to back, support most of your weight on your ischial tuberosities (sit bones) and minimize pressure on your perineum – where your pelvic floor muscles, blood vessels and nerves are concentrated. Matching saddle width to the width of your sit bones is the best place to start.

STEP 2: SADDLE UP, OR DOWN

After a good warm-up – all physiological bike fit measures need to be taken during or shortly after real levels of riding effort – sit on the bike on a turbo trainer, hands at the back of the brake hoods, unclip your feet and pedal backwards with just your heels on the pedals. At the right saddle height the heels should stay in contact with the pedals even at bottom dead centre (BDC) – but only just. Don't let your pelvis rock.

Once you've set this height and clipped back in you should find you have about 30 degrees of flexion in the knee at BDC – about right for an average recreational rider without injuries or issues. "The backwards heel pedal is an excellent starting place," says Pruitt, "as it takes into account hamstring flexibility at the bottom of the stroke."

There are many more methods for working out saddle height but, as Pruitt indicates, what you're looking to create is the right amount of knee flexion – bend in the knee – at the bottom of the pedal stroke – BDC.

The accepted ideal is about 25 degrees, which will ensure that the powerful quad muscle is at its optimal length for as much of the downstroke as possible.

STEP 3: BAR COUNSEL

"One of the most common set-up mistakes is a reach that's too low and too long," says Pruitt. "The old Italian rule was 'never set the bar lower than a fist width below the saddle' and that's still a good starting point."

Modern bike fitters start with around a 5cm drop and then adjust the length and height of the stem informed by the rider's functional movement screen. The optimal distance and drop of the bar from the saddle depends on your hamstring length, lower back flexibility and functional core. The less core strength and flexibility you have, the closer and higher the bar needs to be.

"In terms of reach, start with a 90-degree angle at the shoulder, your hands on the hoods and arms slightly bent at the elbows. The angle of your torso when riding on the hoods should be about 45 degrees, ranging to about 40 for the most flexible and 50 for the least flexible.

"Bar width should roughly match your shoulders (though a change in width will also change reach). If you ride on the hoods most of the time, rotate the bar so the tops are level, not the drops. You should be able to comfortably ride in all hand positions on the bar and specifically have easy and comfortable access to the brakes and shifters."

If the drops feel too low or stretched out, try a compact bar with shorter forward 'throw' and shallower drops, as you really shouldn't be doing long, fast descents on the hoods. The shifters can be moved for better access or comfort too.

STEP 4: FLEXI-TIME

Having 25 degrees of knee flexion won't suit everyone. Many riders – especially juniors whose big bones are still growing, and the 40-plus, who might be starting to stiffen up – are not flexible enough to pedal with this much leg extension. This is where a functional movement screen comes in – a series of range of movement checks that are now at the heart of every good professional fitting process.

If you get a professional bike fit, the first thing the fitter will do, after the initial interview and measures, is study your standing posture for imbalances and assess your range of motion, paying particular attention to your

TOP TIPS

Position change
A bike fit is only a snapshot. As you get older and your fitness changes your ideal position will change

Bar height
Never setting the handlebar lower than a fist width below the saddle is a good starting point for bar height

Knee-bend angle
The bend in the knee at the bottom of the pedal stroke is likely to be around 25-30 degrees

INSTANT UPGRADE

If you want to adjust your position on the bike, such as raising the saddle to get more power or lowering the bars to get more aero, do it incrementally in order to allow your body to adapt and avoid injury.

hamstring and hip flexibility. The more flexible you are, the more leg extension you can tolerate and the longer – potentially more forceful – downstroke you can produce.

One of the best ways to assess hamstring length is by performing a locked-knee standing toe touch.

STEP 5: TO AND FRO

The saddle's fore and aft position affects your weight distribution, which according to tradition should be about 55 per cent rear, 45 per cent front. Most of the body is supported by your saddle, feet and core, so you should rest lightly on the hands.

Although saddle 'setback' is expressed as the horizontal distance from the centre of the bottom bracket to the front of the saddle, the Knee Over Pedal Spindle (KOPS) method is a good technique for starters.

To check it, rotate your pedal to the 3 o'clock position and get someone to drop a plumb line from the bony lump below the front of your knee – your tibial tuberosity. Check the line passes through the forward pedal spindle. Spin your other pedal round to the 3 o'clock position and repeat the check on that side.

Move the saddle backwards or forwards if needed, then recheck your knee flexion and readjust saddle height if necessary.

STEP 6: AND REPEAT

Given the importance of the functional movement checks to the final set-up of your bike, it is important to remember that a bike fit is only a snapshot of the rider and bike at one particular moment in time.

As you get older and weaker – or possibly even stronger and more functional – you need to revisit your bike fit in order to discover your new optimum riding position.

This can also be a motivational tool. Back and hamstring stretches, for example, can have a big payoff by letting you lower the front end and reduce wind drag. A six- to 12-week programme to lower the front end of your bike by a centimetre is a great goal – just don't sacrifice physiological comfort in order to achieve it.

" You should be able to comfortably ride in all hand positions on the bar "

GET THE MEASURE...

Before you go changing your bike set-up, measure and record its vital stats, so you can put it back if you need to

Seat height - from centre of bottom bracket to top of centre of saddle (not simply to top of saddle in line with seat-tube)

Reach - from front edge of saddle to back of the brake hoods

Seat to bar drop - vertical distance from top of saddle to top of handlebar

Saddle setback - horizontal distance from tip of saddle to centre of bottom bracket

Stack height - vertical distance from top of bar to the ground

Handlebar width - measured from bar centre to bar centre behind brake hoods

Knee flexion - this can be measured statically with a goniometer, to find the angle between the centre of the ankle bone and the greater trochanter at the hip, using the end of the femur on the outside of the knee as the joint axis

Dynamic measuring - due to the influence of pedalling technique on your ankle, hip and knee angles, modern bike fit prefers to measure these angles with motion capture technology, such as the Retul system

Many of the measurements are hard to take, but... there's an app for it! Bike Fit Fast for iOS will help you take the measurements, and do your own video analysis, within the app.

JOIN A CLUB

Meet new buddies, get help with motivation and ride new routes - just some of the benefits of belonging to a cycling club

▼ ▶ Many clubs now offer different rides for different levels

What do you think of when someone mentions cycling clubs? Ultra-competitive elite cyclists hell-bent on crushing the opposition at all costs? Happily, while many clubs no doubt have a rich and extensive racing history, the landscape is certainly changing – and for the better.

In the past, cycling clubs presented an image of riders grinding out hours of miserable training. These days, clubs offer everything from BMX to mountain biking and they are actively encouraging novice racers and even beginners.

It's now possible to join a club without ever racing, without finding the relative merits of shifter internals and lactate thresholds fascinating and without – unless you'd like to – giving up your whole life to the cause.

A cycling club can help you get what you want from your rides; if you want to get race ready, maintain your fitness or just go for a ride with some like-minded people, there is a club out there for you.

HOW TO CHOOSE
We're all different. And every cycling club is different, so choosing the one that's right for you isn't as simple as picking the one with the prettiest jersey (well, it can be, but we advise a little more research...) Here's a checklist to help you find your perfect match.

DOES IT CATER FOR YOU?

One thing that puts off potential members from joining a 'serious' club is the thought you won't be able to keep up and you'll be left in the middle of nowhere. Don't worry, club etiquette makes this an unlikely event: they look after their new riders. Many clubs also offer specific beginner rides or groups of varying abilities, so everyone can find their own level. The bigger the club, the more variation it should provide.

Once you're in: If a club offers different levels of riding, you get an enormous sense of achievement as you progress through the groups. You'll benefit from the experience of the other riders around you and, eventually, you'll even be able to help new members when they join.

DOES IT DO MORE?

A good club is more than about just having good cyclists meet up to ride once a week. You may be able to find a club offering core fitness classes, experienced coaches to help with technique and strategy, 'bike fit' experts, sports physicians and mechanics.

Once you're in: Try offering your own skills. If you're a dab-hand with the puncture repair kit and torque wrench, you can help out any less mechanically minded club-mates. And if you make to-die-for flapjacks, well, you'll be up for Club Member of the Year...

IS IT RELAXED ENOUGH?

A good club offers a sense of community. The post-ride café or bar 'de-briefings', the second-hand sales and the summer gatherings help to make the club special. There you can make friends, plan rides, determine cycling groups within the club and discuss issues with other riders and coaches.

Once you're in: It's simple really – hanging out with like-minded individuals is good for you! For starters, guys, you won't have to explain why there's no hair on your legs... and we know people who've met their partners – and their plumbers – through their clubs.

CAN YOU TRY IT OUT?

A club might claim to be friendly and all things to everyone on its website, but we've all had our fingers burnt by organizations that simply don't deliver on their promises.

Be clear about what you want from the club and if you can't get the answers you need, turn up and speak to members in person. First impressions aren't always right and the best way to see how a club runs is by giving it a go without committing yourself. Try before you buy. Most clubs will allow you to join them on a few taster sessions before asking you to sign up.

Once you're in: You shouldn't buy a bike without a test ride and the same goes for your club. By joining for a few rides before signing on the dotted line you'll be sure it's right. Likewise, it'll give the club the chance to find out if it likes you.

CAN IT GROW WITH YOU?

While you might not know your bar plug from your bottom bracket when you join, once you've caught the bug it's good to know your club can move with you. Everyone will be focusing on the same local races, so your training should be automatically tailored to fit that without having to slog through countless text books and come up with your own schedule.

Once you're in: Choose wisely and you'll find a club that'll be your home-from-home. As you get faster, so will your club-mates. Just hope they don't get too fast...

RULES OF THE ROAD

If you're new to road cycling then follow this advice to stay safe and ride with confidence.

OWN THE ROAD

Don't be afraid to occupy the moving traffic lane. You should ride roughly in line with where the nearside of a car would be – ensuring that you can be seen and that drivers have to manoeuvre to overtake – or in the middle of the lane. The latter position means you should be able to prevent vehicles from overtaking you so that you're free to turn, overtake or change lanes. These riding positions are variously known as 'normal' and 'taking the lane' or, technically, 'secondary' and 'primary'.

NO ALARMS, NO SURPRISES

It might seem obvious, but be predictable. Make sure that you hold your line and position in the road and don't weave from side to side. When you do need to change direction or your position in the road, always look first to check it's safe to do so – a 'lifesaver' glance over your shoulder – and then, where applicable, make a clear signal to alert others what you're about to do.

WHITE LINES, DON'T DO IT

Road markings apply equally to you as a cyclist as they would if you were in your car. That means you should never cross solid white lines in the middle of the road and always obey stop lines at junctions.

THINK AHEAD

Always try to look ahead down the road and anticipate any potential problems or dangers. If you know you need to change lanes or have a turn across the traffic approaching, look and move early.

DON'T OFF ROAD!

Unless clearly marked as a shared cycle/pedestrian lane, cycling on the pavement or any footpath is illegal and dangerous both for you and pedestrians. If you're not confident about riding on the road then consider attending a suitable course.

GET IT COVERED

Keep your hands in a position where you can easily and quickly operate your brake levers in a safe manner. Avoid sudden braking and locking up your wheels, especially if riding in a group.

SEE THE LIGHTS

Cyclists are required by law to obey all traffic signals. Stop at all red lights and remain behind the solid white stop line. There are sometimes marked boxes for a cyclist but, if not, do not be tempted to creep forwards. Even if the way ahead, such as when turning, appears to be clear, wait for the lights to turn to green before moving off.

For more expert advice on all things cycling, visit British Cycling's Insight Zone – an online resource of tips and techniques from the experts at British Cycling: **www.britishcycling.org.uk/insightzone**

To find out more about Bikeability and Cycle Training, please visit **https://bikeability.dft.gov.uk** and **www.britishcycling.org.uk/cycletraining**

CARS PULLING OUT

There are a million and one things that can momentarily distract a driver. All it takes is one screaming child, barking dog, ringing phone or trapped bumblebee for a car to pull out at a junction or from a kerb without noticing you on a bike. Limit the chances of this happening by riding in a prominent position on the road, not hiding away by the kerb, and always be vigilant at junctions in case you need to make a last-minute swerve.

OIL SPILL

Oil spills, rain-covered road markings and drain covers, damp leaves... all of these may send you skidding into the path of an oncoming vehicle. Try to ride around them, but if this isn't possible ride straight through them, slowly, and do not brake, as this could cause you to slip.

DOGS

Dogs without leads can be a problem - even the best behaved are liable to charge across the road if they see a particularly appealing cat to chase. But dogs on leads can also be a problem - a tense lead can act like a trip wire. Cycle into it and you could be catapulted into the air! Watch out for rogue puppies and careless owners too.

CAR DOORS

A parked car is still a hazardous car. If it's parked in a cycle lane you may need to overtake in traffic. Always do so with caution, signalling and checking in advance. A thoughtless passenger swinging open a car door directly into your path could cause a collision too, so always give them a wide berth so you don't have to swerve out at the last minute.

USE HAND SIGNALS

Riding in a tight pack is fun, but with the riders behind unable to see ahead, you all need to communicate - especially when it comes to hazards. Here are five simple hand signals to help keep you all riding safely

ROAD SURFACE HAZARD!

1 In a close riding echelon, the front rider is the only one who is likely to see most of the hazards on the road surface itself directly ahead. Point at the offending hazard as it appears ahead and as it rolls past. This is good for potholes, drainage grates, sticks and stones. Keep the message going throughout the group.

ELBOW FLICK

2 A common signal for the club chain gang. If you see the rider powering away on the front ahead of you start to waggle his elbow, without taking his hands off the bar, he wants you to come through and overtake on the side of the wagging elbow, then he can take a rest on your wheel as you do a turn pulling on the front.

STOPPING!

3 Either hold your hand up as above or hang it down with your palm facing backwards. With a shout of "Stopping!", this will tell the riders behind that you are about to come to a standstill. Good for approaching traffic lights and junctions. Don't leave it too late, though, as you'll need both hands on the bar to brake properly.

SCATTERED HAZARD!

4 Unlike pointing to single road hazards, this open-handed 'waving at the ground' lets riders behind know there is a widespread hazard across a significant part of the road. This could be broken glass, loose stones, mud or even nails. Riders should understand they need to proceed with care rather than swerve around the hazard.

MOVE OUT!

5 This can look like the rider in front is giving a good waft to dispel a bad smell! It's most often used to tell riders behind that there's a parked car, pedestrian or obstruction at the side of the road, and you're about to move out around it in the direction of wafting. Can be a pointed finger instead, jabbing in the relevant direction.

ON THE ROAD

You've got the bike set up, you're wearing all the right gear; it's time to get out on the road. We've got the skills, techniques, tips and tricks to help you ride safer and faster. But the road ahead isn't flat - you're going to have to conquer those climbs and master the descents...

BEAT ANY HILL

Going up? It's all in the mind - and the lungs and the legs...

The hill or even the mountain is one of cycling's great challenges. Get it wrong and you can find yourself cracking long before the summit; get it right and you can leave your rivals panting in your dust. Here's a few tips to take the fear out of those gradients...

SPIN TO WIN

Using lower gears and a higher cadence (cadence being the speed at which you spin your pedals) is the single most important rule in climbing. Some might brag about tackling climbs in their top ring, but the clever riders twiddle their way up a hill rather than grinding and zig-zagging their way to the top.

On longer climbs you should always aim to spin smaller gears from the saddle. This doesn't mean continuously spinning at 120rpm (revolutions per minute) like some of the pros in the Tour de France, but a steady cadence of around 85–95rpm in a gear that feels relatively easy. You should aim to sustain your cadence and level of effort for the entire climb by adjusting your gears to suit the gradient – and key to that is doing some homework about the climb so you're familiar with its length and gradient and can judge the level of effort you can realistically sustain.

If you do have to get out of the saddle – to overcome a gradient change or to ease aching muscles – keep pressure on the pedals and rise up a gear to maintain speed and momentum.

TAKE A SEAT

Although there might be times when you need to stand, sitting is more efficient than standing up. Standing up wastes energy, because you're having to support your body weight as well as propelling yourself skywards.

INSTANT WIN

Standing up on the pedals and pushing a hard gear going uphill is less efficient than sitting in the saddle and spinning an easier gear. The speed gained does not justify the effort and uses up valuable glycogen reserves.

> **So much of climbing is psychological. On longer rides particularly, it's important to break a hill down into sections**

Studies carried out by the University of Franche-Comté in France found that standing was less efficient when intensity is lower than 75 per cent VO2 max, while a Utah State University study reported that on a 5 per cent incline sitting down is 3.7 per cent faster than standing at a high-intensity power output of 400W. However, the US study went on to report that the speed difference between standing and sitting is negligible above an incline of 15 per cent.

SMALL STEPS

So much of climbing is psychological. On longer rides particularly, it's important to break a hill down into sections, to see it as a series of minor victories rather than get daunted by the scale of the whole ride.

Focusing too far into the future can shred your nerves. The weight of the task in front of you makes you nervous, burning huge amounts of precious glycogen and taking you away from the calm zone where elite cyclists perform best. It is better to play it out gradually, changing your focus on each bend and to think about what's going to happen 10 metres – not 10 km – ahead. Some experienced riders count revs as they are pedalling to stop their mind panicking, especially when it gets really steep. It can keep you motivated at the same time as focusing on a genuinely important factor.

BREATHE DEEP

To combat nerves, practise belly breathing. Hold the brake hoods with a wide grip to open your chest for better air intake, breathe in through your nose to a count of three, pause, then slowly exhale through your mouth for a count of four.

It is a similar principle to using a paper bag for panic attacks. The excess of carbon dioxide in your system is

54

caused by the short, staccato breathing, and that means your brain and other muscles simply don't have the oxygen they need to function properly.

The longer breaths activate the parasympathetic nervous system and slow down your heart rate, which helps you develop a more normal breathing pattern.

EXCUSES, EXCUSES

Too many riders think it's impossible to get the training in to be a good hill climber if they either don't live near a mountain range or have a full-time job. But climbing is just power output, and that can be achieved on the flat too. Short, intense intervals, 30 seconds at over 30mph, ease off, then repeat can substitute for a personal VO2 max test.

Jump squats are also useful for improving power output. Take a pair of dumbbells that add up to about 30 per cent of the weight you can squat in one go. Stand with your feet hip-width apart, holding the dumbbells at arm's length next to your thighs, your palms facing each other. With your chest out and your shoulders back, assume a squat position by drawing your hips back and bending your knees so that your legs form a 90-degree angle. Now, jump explosively while exhaling fully to straighten out your body up and into the air. Keep your arms by your side, lifting the dumbbells as you rise. On your descent, inhale and draw your hips back while bending your knees to softly land into the starting position.

Pause momentarily before you begin your next jump to get your muscles firing as quickly as possible. Try five to eight jumps in a row and concentrate on achieving maximum height in each, landing as softly as possible.

In a study published in the *Journal of Strength and Conditioning Research*, researchers found athletes who did jump squats improved their 20m sprint times by 17 per cent in eight weeks.

LOSE POUNDS, SAVE CASH

If you are going to get up those hills faster you need to look to your power-to-weight ratio. You have to improve one or the other – if you've got a couple of stone to lose, you're better off dieting or spending cash on a personal trainer than on a lighter bike.

It might sound obvious, but think how much you spend on lighter components without looking at your body. Take a 90kg, 1.78m cyclist – applying 200 watts of power on the flat, they'll do about 20mph. If they dropped to 73kg and applied the same power, their speed would be 21mph. Transfer that to a 10 per cent hill and their speed would increase from 4.2mph to 5.1mph.

The key to weight loss has to be gradual and healthy. Incorporate gradual changes to your diet. Start by increasing your intake of nuts – 70 almonds per day, to be exact. That's the number that people in a City of Hope National Medical Center, California, experiment ate daily for six months to drop eight per cent of their body weight. "They're a nutrient-dense food with healthy monounsaturated fat, protein and fibre, and make you feel full." Grab a handful when you're feeling peckish – you'll be less likely to overeat at meals.

Swapping a steady training ride for intervals will shed pounds too, say researchers at the University of New South Wales. Over 15 weeks, men who cycled hard for eight seconds then lightly for 12 seconds for 20 minutes, three times a week, lost 6lb – three times more than those who exercised steadily for 40 minutes.

So there you have the secret formula to hill climbing prowess: spin, sit, sprint, diet... and you'll fly up those hills.

TACKLING ALPINE-STYLE CLIMBS? GET THE LOWDOWN ON GOING UP

Sit down...
Sitting in the saddle for as much of a long climb as possible is the most aerobically efficient way to the top. Sitting gives the large muscles at the back of your thighs more leverage to pedal. Standing is more powerful but will use vital glycogen stores faster. Even so, getting out of the saddle occasionally is essential to give your bum a rest, get circulation flowing, and vary the muscle groups that are doing the work. When you are out of the saddle, resist rocking the bike too much, as it is inefficient.

...And relax
It's a waste of energy and tiring to grip the bar tightly, consequently tensing your upper body as you climb. Work on climbing with your back straight and shoulders back, with your hands resting on the bar tops. This will open up your diaphragm, making more space for your lungs to expand into and improve your aerobic efficiency. Changing your hand position will help prevent any pressure or repetitive strain injuries such as ulnar neuropathy.

Chase me, chase me!
Despite the motivational advantages of sitting on another rider's wheel up a climb, there is little aerodynamic advantage to be had from drafting at climbing speeds. If you can find similarly paced riders, climbing in a group is more social and may offer protection from crosswinds or headwinds. Beware of riding too close to the wheel in front of a rider who is climbing seated, as when they get out of the saddle they may slow enough that you ride into them. When tackling hairpins, remember that the shallowest gradient is always on the outside of the corner.

Gears ideas
A cadence of about 90rpm is ideal. Don't let a gear get too far 'on top' of you before you change down. This will

sap your glycogen reserves and changing down at too slow a cadence puts a lot of pressure on mechanicals. Just before you stand on the pedals, change up to a bigger gear to compensate for your lower cadence and keep your power consistent. Change back down when you sit down again. If you are consistently struggling on hills, fit easier gears.

Pace, don't race
Pacing is crucial to deliver your best effort on a long climb. Some mountainous European events have several climbs that can take up to an hour to ascend. So if you go too hard, too early, there's a good chance you could blow before the top or irreparably damage your whole ride performance. The key is to stay aerobic as much as possible until you're ready to give it your all - perhaps in the last few miles of the event's summit finish. If you're using a heart rate monitor, this threshold figure will typically be at about 65 per cent of your maximum heart rate. If you're riding on perceived exertion alone, you need to back off when holding a normal conversation is no longer possible.

Forget-me-nots
➜ Practice makes perfect – there's no shortcut to better hill climbing. If you want to get better, not to mention fitter, you need to do it again, and again, and again, and again... A regular hill climb will also gauge your training progress.
➜ Don't forget to fuel as you climb. An energy gel in the preceding miles will also help you arrive better prepared for the effort.
➜ Lose weight: power to weight ratio is everything for climbing, and every extra gramme of body fat will make it harder work - and hotter too, because fat insulates more than muscle.
➜ Don't let your body overheat: make sure you undo zips and remove outer layers so that your body can maintain the constant temperature it needs for metabolic efficiency.

◢ Climbs can be an hour long - so don't go off too fast

DESCEND LIKE A PRO

Exhilarating descents are cycling's way of saying thank you for the climbs. And they can be more fun than scary with these tips.

STAY LOOSE

Relax your death grip on the bars and release the tension from your arms and shoulders. A stiff body will move with the bicycle as it reacts to bumps and correcting all that unwanted movement is tiring. Put weight on the pedals, soaking up bigger ridges by keeping pedals straight and using your legs as suspension.

KEEP PEDALLING

Most long descents come after a hard climb, so suddenly relaxing your legs will make them stiffen up. To avoid this, make sure you keep your legs turning on the way down.

KEEP YOUR DISTANCE

Remember that the rider in front has no brake lights; you'll get no warning if they have to suddenly brake. So make sure you look well ahead down the road – not just at the wheel of the bike in front – and always leave enough room for your reaction time.

" The lower you crouch, and the more you tuck in your elbows, the lower your frontal area and wind resistance – and the faster gravity will propel you "

READ THE ROAD

Correctly anticipating dangers – corners that tighten, changes in surface, wet patches, manholes, riders behind or in front of you and cars in side roads, for example – comes from constant observation.

Focus well ahead and leave your peripheral vision to pick up movement. Covering your brakes at all times, even with a forefinger of each hand, will help you react quickly.

TUCK IN FOR SPEED

The lower you crouch, and the more you tuck in your elbows, the lower your frontal area and wind resistance – and the faster gravity will be able to propel you. Try to keep your head up and look where you're going too.

To get extra pace, ride with your hands on the lower handlebar drops and dip your torso down towards the top-tube. Keeping the chain on the big ring on the front will keep a decent amount of tension in your chain and avoid the chances of it jumping off if you hit a bump.

SIT UP TO SLOW DOWN

Just as going aero will make you descend faster, if you want to wipe some speed off a descent without having to resort to protracted, rim-wearing braking, then sit upright and catch some wind. It'll help cool you down after that long climb too.

Switching your hands to the hoods or tops helps add drag, as does sticking out your elbows and knees. Using your body as a natural brake also helps add control, as it's a much more stable position should you lock a wheel, and an easier position in which to support your body weight while braking hard.

INSTANT UPGRADE

To get up those hills that demand you climb out of the saddle, practise on steadier drags first. Select a gear that feels too high to ride seated, then stand, so power from your upper body assists your legs. Keep standing for as long as you can, roll back down and repeat. This will strengthen your core.

WATCH THE EXIT

Check around you on the approach for other riders and traffic. Keep your head up throughout the corner, looking ahead through the apex to where you want to be on the exit. This isn't the time for checking out the scenery or the front wheel, because bikes will head where you're looking.

KEEP IT DOWN LOW

Your shoulders should be relaxed and your elbows bent – stiffening up will make you over-correct and over-brake, and less able to deal with mid-corner problems. For the lowest centre of gravity and best weight distribution, corner with your hands on the drops. That way, you'll easily cover the brake levers with one or two fingers too.

LEAVE THE LEVERS

Cover the brakes throughout the corner but do all your braking before you turn in. Freewheeling through the corner will make you smoother, safer and faster, since the tyres only have to deal with cornering forces and not braking forces as well. Over-braking during the turn is likely to make your bike slide out underneath you, with potentially painful consequences.

KNOW YOUR LINES

The aim is to take the smoothest, most constant and least acute path through any corner. Starting alongside the kerb for a 90-degree right-hand bend, apexing mid-corner on the white line and drifting to the kerb is the ideal, but dirty gutters and approaching cars can limit this. Apply the theory wisely, and try to visualize one smooth line.

CORNER AT SPEED

There's nothing better than a perfect line through a downhill corner. Here are six top tips for tackling the bendy.

WEIGHT OUTSIDE

Just before you turn in, lift your inside foot so the pedal is at 12 o'clock. As well as avoiding grounding the pedal as you lean the bike over, this will help transfer weight to the foot on your outside pedal, which will lower your centre of gravity (your weight is on the pedal, not the saddle) and help push the tyres into the road. Don't put too much weight on your hands, but a little more pressure on your inside hand will help your bike turn in and track the corner well.

POWERING OUT

Don't start pedalling until you're through the corner and almost upright. You might not need to do much catching up if the descent is steep, but if you do, you should have changed into the right gear before the corner. Start looking for the next turn and repeat – and above all, think smooth!

RACE GROUP DYNAMICS

It's easier and faster riding in a group, but everyone needs to know the rules.

MANNERS
Nose blowing, eating, drinking and chatting are best saved for further back in the group – not out front. Remember this and others will respect you more.

HOW CLOSE IS TOO CLOSE?
If you're riding with someone you draft regularly, your front tyre needs to be inches from their back tyre to get the most benefit. On sportives, most accidents happen where large groups ride close together.

ON THE WHEEL
If you find yourself in the middle of a strong, smooth chaingang, enjoy the rest but don't lose concentration. Ride slightly offset, so you can keep an eye out for any potential problems further up the road.

ON THE FRONT
Pedal smoothly and efficiently on the flat, and if you do have to get out of the saddle, try your utmost not to shoot your bike backwards as you stand up.

STEADY AS SHE GOES
One of the biggest mistakes people make is overreacting to hazards. Remember there are people riding close to you; brake softly and don't make sudden movements. The further back you are in a chaingang, the less time you'll have to react.

KNOW YOUR LIMITS
If the group starts pulling away, don't destroy yourself keeping up. In a sportive, you're better off conserving energy and waiting for the next group to come through to ride with them.

SITTING UP AND MOVING
When you've done your turn at the front, don't stop pedalling or sit up suddenly. Keep your pace while you pull out. That way the rider on your wheel can get a pull onto the wheel you've been drafting. Once you're out of the way then you can sit up.

LOOK WHERE YOU'RE GOING!
Before you move, put in a 'life-saver' glance in the direction you want to go. Following riders will see your head movement and know you're about to move.

INSTANT UPGRADE

When riding through and off with your friends, try to get as close to their back wheel as you can. But look over their shoulder at the road ahead, rather than stare at that back wheel, as it will help you anticipate any action they may need to take.

INSTANT UPGRADE

A climb is the perfect place to drop your rivals. Settle into a climb and then sprint for a landmark, settle back down, then sprint again. Repeat as often as you can, then apply and watch them crack.

GO FASTER FOR FREE!

Put your wallet away, this one's on us...
Your guide to going quicker for no cash at all.

Lightweight and aerodynamic kit may make your bike lighter, but your wallet will slim down too. So, why not go faster for free?

ZIP UP TIGHT

It's no good having an aerodynamic steed if your waterproof is billowing about like a parachute. Equally, an unzipped jersey could be slowing you down. So zip up and safety-pin anything especially baggy into a more figure-hugging shape.

USE GRAVITY!

It's pointless being a great climber if you can't get down the other side quickly. Practise your descending and concentrate on building a relaxed, smooth flow and use a twisty climb to practise your cornering/descending on the way down. Don't trail the brakes into bends – you'll be using grip that would otherwise be speeding you through the corner. Change down a few gears if necessary too, so that on the exit you're ready to power away. Arcing a smooth, straightened-out line will also let you carry more speed.

TUCK IN

By keeping your upper body still and your pedalling stroke efficient, you'll save energy and create less drag. Use a full-length mirror to watch how your body moves as you pedal on a turbo trainer. Also watch how your knees track. Flared-out knees can lead to higher drag and a slower top-end, losing up to 90 seconds over 40km.

OIL AND CLEAN IT

Muck adds unnecessary weight and can easily negate the gains of lightweight kit. Pay particular attention to your chain, because energy lost through friction is wasted.

SLIPSTREAM OTHERS

The energy savings of riding in a group are massive. Research by Dr James Hagberg at the University of Florida has shown a cyclist can use 30–40 per cent less energy while drafting than those leading the pack. To get the most from drafting you must learn to ride comfortably within 20–25 cm of the wheel in front of you.

DON'T BUY PIES...

Shaving a few hundred grammes off your bike is pretty futile if you're holding a few thousand around your waist. It should come as no surprise that as a rider loses fat, their frontal area decreases and their drag is reduced. Drop 3kg and you just might gain more speed than you would by upgrading to an aero helmet, which can equate to a minute over 40km.

GET A DRINKING HABIT

Being dehydrated severely compromises performance. Even on cooler days, it's vital to replace fluid lost through breathing, sweating and urination. Drink one or two cups of water before exercise and then sip throughout; you should aim to take in 500–1,000ml per hour. This might seem a lot, but sweating alone can account for it. A fluid loss of only 2–3 per cent (1.5–2kg in a 70kg rider) will result in performance dropping by 3–7 per cent.

USE YOUR DROPS

Ride in the drops on long, flat roads, long descents or into stiff headwinds. Wind tunnel testing has shown that a 70kg cyclist putting down 200 watts of power would be travelling at 32.4kph on the brake hoods, but 34.4kph on the drops.

PUMP UP YOUR TYRES

An under-inflated tyre increases rolling resistance, is more prone to pinch flats and handles badly. An over-inflated tyre gives a harsh ride and less traction. Most road tyres require 5.5 - 9 Bar, but your front tyre needs roughly 10 per cent less pressure than the rear. If a 75kg rider uses 7 Bar on his road bike, a 90kg rider should run around 8.3 Bar and a 60kg rider could get away with 5.5 Bar.

BREATHE BETTER

Most cyclists overuse their rib muscles for inhaling and exhaling but your abs can do the work more efficiently, so be sure to breathe from your stomach. Hunched shoulders reduce lung capacity, so your handlebar width should at least equal that of your shoulders. Finally, flush carbon dioxide from your blood prior to hard efforts by taking 15 deep breaths beforehand.

FIT TO RIDE

Training is the key to successful cycling. The hours and effort you put in on the bike during training rides and off the bike in fitness training will determine how you perform on the big day. This chapter takes you through the rides, fitness regimes, muscle-building exercises, technology and mental attitudes that will transform you into a stronger and faster rider...

WINTER TRAINING

Varying your fitness training will improve your performance and give you many other benefits.

For most, cycling is about the pursuit of fun and fitness in the great outdoors. Winter, however, is often a deterrent, bringing fewer daylight riding hours and nasty road conditions. But don't hang up the bike and kiss goodbye to a season's worth of hard-earned fitness. Stay at home, get your kit on and start laying the foundations for next year's personal bests.

1 HIGH CADENCE

High cadence intervals allow you to improve endurance and speed. The ability to maintain a good cadence of 80–100rpm is essential to maintain your speed for longer, as pedalling an easier gear at a higher cadence fatigues the muscles less than a harder gear in a lower cadence. It stresses your cardiovascular system more but your muscles less – which means staying fresher for longer. These intervals are a must for time triallists.

Do this

Warm up for about 10 minutes, then perform 4 x 4 minutes @ 100rpm and 6 minutes @ 80rpm. Stay in zones 1 and 2 (see Zoning In, on the opposite page, to work out zones based on your heart rate). Select an appropriate gear so you are able to use these cadences while remaining in the correct zones. Stay seated with hands on the drops. Relax, look forward and don't rock your hips.

2 ONE-LEGGED DRILLS

One-legged drills are much safer on a turbo than the road. They're also great for technique as they make each leg work throughout the entire pedal rotation.

Do this

Warm up for 10 minutes in a low gear, then perform a single 25-minute block at a low intensity in HR zones 1 and 2. Every 5 minutes take one foot off the pedal and continue pedalling with the other foot for 30 seconds. Change legs and pedal one-legged for another 30 seconds. Put both feet back on the pedals and pedal for 5 minutes until the next

set. Warm down for 10 minutes with easy pedalling and no resistance on the turbo trainer.

3 CADENCE STEPS

Focusing on cadence, this 'Leg Ripper' workout brings your leg speed up rapidly. On the turbo trainer its main use is to keep you busy, because it demands constant concentration. All blocks are 3 minutes long, and recovery between each block is always 90 seconds at recovery pace. Heart rate should not reach the goal zones until you're 30–60 seconds into each block.

Do this

Warm up for 5 minutes in recovery zone 1
*   Ride in zone 2 at a cadence of 100rpm
*   Ride in zone 2 @ 110rpm
*   Ride in zone 2 @ 95rpm
*   Ride in zone 2 @ 115rpm
*   Ride in zone 2 @ 110rpm
*   Ride in zone 3 @ 115–125rpm
*   Ride in zone 3 @ 110rpm
*   Ride in zone 3 @ 120rpm+
*   Ride in zone 4 @ 95rpm
*   Ride in zone 4 @ 105rpm+
*   Cool down for 5 minutes in recovery zone 1

4 OVER-GEARED INTERVALS

This workout adds strength training to an endurance session. Use it in the second phase of the endurance cycle (4–8 weeks), once you've built a small endurance base. The strength component of the fitness gained from this session is good for climbing or distance riding at medium intensity.

Do this

After a good 10-minute warm-up, perform 40 minutes in zones 1 and 2 with the following cadence changes:
*   10 minutes @ 80rpm (easy gear)
*   5 minutes @ 60rpm (big gear)
*   10 minutes @ 90rpm (low gear)

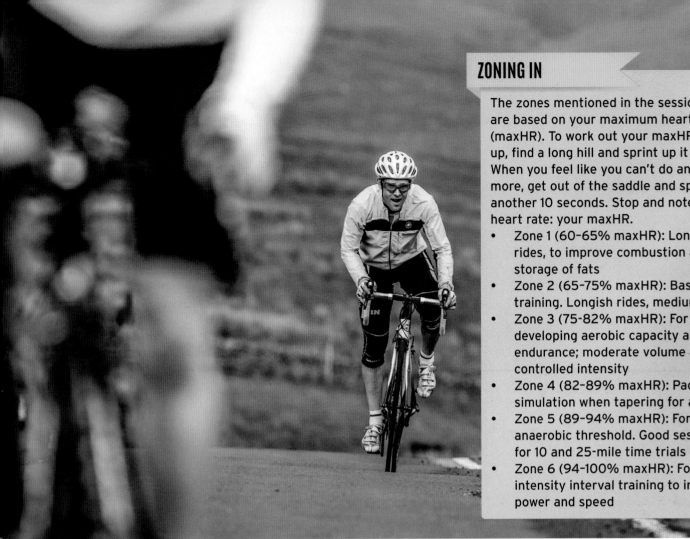

- 5 minutes @ 60rpm (big gear)
- 10 minutes @ 80rpm (low gear)

Warm down with 10 minutes of easy pedalling. Stay seated throughout with hands on the drops.

5 STRENGTH AND CONDITIONING

Your body can get so efficient at cycling that other muscle groups can get ignored, leaving you vulnerable to injury. This off-bike routine, which includes strength and conditioning exercises, core work and stretches, sounds a lot but only takes about 20–30 minutes. These sessions will improve your neuromuscular pathways through repetition and improve muscular endurance.

Perform both exercises in a slow, controlled movement – holding onto a chair for balance if you need to.

Do this

Single-leg squats Stand upright with one leg supported behind you on a chair. Squat down by bending both legs until you have about an 80-degree bend in the front knee, then straighten up again. Keep your abdominals clenched and chest out throughout. Repeat 20–30 times then change legs. Perform 2–5 sets, with 30–60 seconds' rest between sets. Start off gradually and progressively build up the duration, number of sets and repetitions as well as intensity by carrying weights.

Single-leg step-ups Find a step that will give you about a 90-degree bend in the knee at the starting position. Exhale, clench your abdominals and step up, keeping your torso upright, so both feet are on the top step. Inhale as you step back down again with the same foot. Change leg and repeat 20-30 times per leg. Again, build up progressively.

6 TECHNIQUE AND LACTATE THRESHOLD

If you only have 40-50 minutes to spare, this turbo session is a great workout. Focusing on pedalling skill development and lactate threshold training, it boosts fitness and efficiency. Aim to do these a couple of times a week in winter.

Do this

- Warm up for 5 minutes (small ring, 15t sprocket) @ 90–100rpm to gradually increase your heart rate
- Start with 3 x 30-second hard tempo efforts (big ring, 15t sprocket) @ 85-95rpm to increase heart rate
- Pedal easy in small ring for 1 min
- Leg speed drill: 6 x 20-second fast legs intervals (small ring, 15t sprocket) @ 110–130rpm, with 20 seconds recovery, gradually increasing cadence with no bouncing
- Pedal easy in small ring for 1 min

- Pull-up drill: 6 x 20-second intervals (big ring, 12–13t sprocket) @75–85rpm, focusing on the upward pulling phase of the pedal stroke, engaging the hip-flexor muscles. This can also be done one leg at a time. Pedal easy for 20 seconds between efforts
- Pedal easy in small ring for 1 min
- Stand-up drill: 6 x 20 seconds (big ring, 15t sprocket) @ 85-95rpm. Start each interval in the saddle for 10 seconds, then transition smoothly to a standing position for 10 seconds. Pedal easy for 20 seconds back in the saddle between each effort
- Pedal easy in small ring for 1 min
- Lactate: 3 x 4-minute tempo intervals at lactate threshold (85 per cent HR max) @ 75–85rpm (big ring, 12–14t sprocket), with 1-minute easy-pedalling recovery between each effort
- Cool down for 5–10 mins in zone 2

7 BASE BUILDER

This endurance and cadence workout is good for building your aerobic base and pedalling technique throughout the winter. For base building keep in zones 2 and 3. For building technique and core stability you need to avoid bouncing at higher cadence work.

TOP TURBO TIP

Staying hydrated before, during and after a turbo session is vital if you want to get the best out of it.

Do this:

- Warm up for 5-10 minutes with 3 x 30-second intervals in the big ring/15t sprocket, and 30 seconds soft-pedalling recovery in between
- Pedal easy for 1 minute
- Perform 8 x 20-second high cadence intervals (small ring, 15t sprocket @ 100-120rpm), with 20 seconds rest between. Focus on keeping your upper body relaxed and not bouncing in the saddle
- Pedal easy for a minute
- Do 4 x 7-minute aerobic tempo intervals (big ring, 17t sprocket @ 80-90rpm), with 30 seconds rest after each effort. Focus on keeping your heart rate in zones 2 and 3.
- Pedal easy for a minute
- Finally, do 6 x 20-second high cadence intervals (small ring, 15t sprocket @ 110-130rpm), with 20 seconds rest between each. Keep your upper body still and let your legs do the work

8 CORE STABILIZERS

Increasing the stability of your core muscle will brace your spine, and give you a solid and more efficient pedalling platform. These two exercises will strengthen your rectus abdominals (six-pack), external obliques and TVA (traverse abdominals). For more core exercises see page 124.

Do this

Glute bridging Lie on your back with your knees bent, feet flat on the floor and your arms out to either side. Start the exercise by clenching your abdominals and squeezing your glutes, then raise your hips until there is a straight line from your shoulders to your knees. Hold for 15–60

seconds, then slowly lower your hips to briefly touch the floor before repeating. Start with two sets of 20–30 repeats, with 30–60 seconds recovery between sets.
Plank Start at the top of the press-up position, engage your core muscles, then bend your elbows and lower your weight onto your forearms, so your body forms a straight line. Keep your abdominals and glutes clenched and your spine in a neutral position, and hold for 15–60 seconds.

9 STRETCHES

Cycling uses a limited number of muscles in a restricted range of movement. This can cause the over-used muscles to tighten and work against their opposing muscles, reducing joint mobility. Repeat each of these stretches two to four times after a workout, and don't forget to breathe throughout the stretch.

Do this

Cossacks stretch Start standing with feet just wider than a shoulder width apart. Crouch down onto the ball of one foot, bending one knee while the other leg stays straight, supported by your heel. Now stretch your inner thighs. Next, twist your body to face the straight leg's toes and lean forwards to stretch your hamstrings. Finally, twist

all the way back round so you are facing away from the straight leg's toes (now your foot will be upside-down with toes on the floor) and you can stretch your hip flexors. Hold each stretch for at least 60 seconds.
Glute stretch Lie on your back and bring both knees up towards your chest and place your right foot just above the left knee. Place your right hand through the hole you have created with your legs and hold the back of your left leg, resting your right elbow on the inside of your right knee. The other hand holds the back of the left leg as well. Next, pull your left leg towards you while exerting a small amount of pressure with your elbow to the inside of your right knee. You should feel a stretch in your glutes. Hold for at least 60 seconds and change legs.

HEART RATE MONITORS

Using your heart rate monitor isn't rocket science, You just need to get yourself in the right zone...

A basic heart rate (HR) monitor is a relatively cheap bit of cycling kit and training with one really couldn't be simpler.

RESTING HR

The best way to get your resting heart rate is to take it first thing in the morning every day for a week. Put your HR strap on and just lie there relaxing for a couple of minutes. Note the lowest reading you see. At the end of the week calculate your average resting heart rate and you can confidently use this figure as the basis of your training.

MAXIMUM HR

You can calculate your maximum HR by using the formula of 210 minus half your age, then subtract 5% of your body weight in pounds. Add four for a male and zero for a female. For a more accurate figure try your gym or, if you are fit and exercise regularly, take your own max HR test.

Warm up thoroughly for at least 15 minutes. On a long, steady hill start off fairly briskly and increase your effort every minute. Do this seated for at least five minutes until you can't go any faster. At this point get out of the saddle and sprint as hard as you can for 15 seconds. Stop and immediately check your HR. This is your max HR.

HR ZONES

Having established the key numbers (max heart rate and resting heart rate) you are now ready to work out your training zones. There are lots of calculators on the web and, while many use five training zones, many cycling coaches recomend six zones (including a vital recovery zone).

THE RIGHT ZONE

Make sure you discipline yourself to spend 90–100 per cent of your ride time in the right zone. This may mean getting off and walking sometimes, but stick with it. Here are some key sessions that will make you a fitter and faster cyclist.

GO SLOWER, GET FASTER

It sounds impossible but this is the basic starting point for HR training. You should start off by doing long Zone 1 and Zone 2 rides. It may be slow and boring at times but soon you'll still be riding in Zone 2 but zipping along. By going slower you'll make your body a lot more efficient.
KEY SESSION 3hrs in Zone 2. Stay in the zone and stick to it. Don't be tempted to push on the hills.

BURN FAT, SAVE TIME

By using HIIT methods (high intensity interval training) you'll burn far more fat and become a fitter and faster rider into the bargain. After a decent 15-minute warm-up you will be ready to go. Depending on your level of fitness you are going to do 4–6 all-out sprints of 30 seconds with 4–5 minutes of easy pedalling. During these all-out efforts expect to see your HR rise to 85-90% of your HR max. Give it all you have right through the 30-second burst. Do these for 6–8 weeks and marvel at the fat you've lost. However, remember if you want to lose weight you still need to concentrate on what, and how much, you consume.
KEY SESSION 15min warm-up, then 4-6 30sec sprints with 4-5min rest between.

BE AN ENDURANCE MONSTER

By doing one session of 3–4 hours in Zone 2 and another session of 2 hours in Zone 3 every week your endurance will come on in leaps and bounds. Add a few long intervals once your base is more established and you'll develop both endurance and speed.
KEY SESSION 3–4hrs in Zone 2 with 10min burst of Zone 3–4 every hour.

EASY DOES IT

Make sure you have at least one rest day per week and another day that is a really slow recovery ride done in Zone 1 or even lower.
KEY SESSION 1hr flat ride with HR below Zone 2.

TESTING, TESTING...

The Maximum Aerobic Function, or 'MAF' test, is a great indicator of how well you're responding to the training. As you get fitter and stronger, your cardiovascular system will get more efficient so that you can ride faster and fitter.
KEY SESSION Time a monthly test ride over a set distance at a set aerobic heart rate in Zone 2. Record your times so you can chart your progress over the months.

SPEED SESSIONS

Use your training time wisely. We show you how to get the most from your minutes

Just because riding a bike is an endurance activity, it doesn't mean that a training session will only have a positive effect if it lasts for hours. A 30–60 minute ride is not a waste of time as long as you focus on something specific and have a purpose...

SWEET SPOT
Your training sweet spot is the zone where you'll get your greatest return on investment. You'll find it at the lower end of the threshold level (80–90 per cent of your maximum heart rate – upper zone three and lower zone four). If training on feel and perceived exertion, you'll be concentrating on your effort and conversation will be in clipped sentences.
DO IT LIKE THIS Sweet spot training is perfect for the time poor – after warming up for 10 minutes, ride for up to 20 minutes at this intensity and you'll soon notice the benefit.

HEAD FOR THE TRAILS
If you're lucky enough to live near some decent trails, getting out for an hour is a fast and fun way to build fitness and work on your handling skills. Off-road riding is time efficient because you're straight into the zone and working hard. Try to climb and descend frequently, and include some technical challenges.
DO IT LIKE THIS Consider buying a singlespeed bike. No gears means a bike that requires the minimum of maintenance and is always ready for an impromptu ride.

RECOVERY RIDES
A genuine recovery ride is an excellent use of a spare hour. It'll speed up your revitalization from a hard ride the previous day, or give your legs a gentle reminder of what you expect from them if planning a big ride for tomorrow.
DO IT LIKE THIS Find a flat course, keep the bike in the small/middle ring and spin super easy. You should barely feel as if you're applying pressure on the below 70 per cent (Zone 2) of your maximum heart rate.

HILL REPS
Sure, riding up and down the same hill again and again isn't everybody's idea of fun, but it will make you better at riding hills.

DO IT LIKE THIS On a moderate to steep hill, warm up and then ride four to five 5-minute uphill rides, concentrating on maintaining a smooth, fast cadence, staying in the saddle and keeping at a consistent intensity.

IF YOU HAVE 30 MINS
If this is your commute twice a day it's a great addition to other training. If you have a spare 30 minutes try one of these cross-training options:

SWIMMING
A few lengths give your heart and lungs a workout, and you'll also be boosting your upper body strength.
DO IT LIKE THIS Try alternating blocks of 100m of normal swimming using fins, hand paddles, legs-only (with a float) and closed fists.

TABATA TRAINING
Dr Izumi Tabata has shown that by doing short bursts of high intensity with short recovery in between, you can increase both your aerobic and anaerobic capacity.
DO IT LIKE THIS Warm up well, and pedal for at least 10 minutes. Once warmed up, perform seven to eight 20-second sprints with 10-second recoveries in between. If you're new to this type of exercise, start with just three to five repeats and build up. Warm down for 10 minutes.

RUNNING
For maximum returns per minute of exercise running is hard to beat. For more variety, greater strength and fitness gains, and less impact on your joints, try to run off-road.
DO IT LIKE THIS Vary your pace and effort using informal interval training. When you feel good, or the road kicks up, push hard and then recover on the flat.

YOGA
If you get a sore back or neck when riding or just don't feel as supple as you once did, integrating yoga into your training schedule could be the answer.
DO IT LIKE THIS Enrol in a class or buy an instructional DVD.

SPIN TRAINING

If you're a fair-weather cyclist or feel uneasy about evening rides in the dark, train indoors. We show how you can win with spin

When personal trainer Johnny Goldberg narrowly avoided being hit by a passing car one night while out riding his bike as part of his preparations for the 3,000-mile Race Across America, he decided to take cycling indoors. Goldberg developed a programme he called spinning, designed an indoor bike based on his road bike and took it to gyms around the world.

While spinning is Goldberg's trademark – only accurately used for classes run by instructors who have attended official Johnny G Spinning instructor training – indoor cycling classes have taken off in gyms across Europe and they can offer a great winter alternative to road training.

IN A FIX

Classes take place on a fixed-wheel bike, the pedals tied to a weighted wheel, and you have a lever to alter resistance. Typically, about eight cyclists line up in a semi-circle around the instructor who will take the class through a routine. While routines and instructors vary hugely, music tends to play a big part in any session, to set the pace and speed and create the right atmosphere to motivate people.

A class can accommodate a variety of fitness levels because you work as hard as you want to. An Olympic athlete can attend the same class as a beginner and they should all be able to work at a perfect level because the instructor is in charge of leg strength and speed.

Because indoor cycling was developed to replicate outdoor cycling, it uses the same muscles, namely the quads, glutes and hamstrings, to apply downward pressure, and the hamstrings and calf to flex the knee at the bottom of the pedal stroke, to pull the foot back. Hip flexors are also used to help raise the leg so the opposite leg can push down on the pedal. At the top, the quads are used to extend the knee and push the foot forward.

By focusing on proper synchronisation of the muscles used in the entire 360-degree pedal stroke when training indoors, a cyclist can help perfect their pedal stroke outdoors.

MIND GAMES

Competitive outdoor cyclists also use indoor cycling to focus on their inner game, as it enables them to concentrate on a specific route or a particularly challenging part of a route without the distraction of traffic or other external factors. Some instructors will use visualisation as part of the session, telling you to close your eyes and go where your mind takes you, perhaps using more monotonous music to encourage the sense of escapism as you cycle.

Classes can range from endurance classes for developing the aerobic system, to strength classes to train for hill climbing, while Race Day classes aim to simulate time-trials. Other classes tend to be based on variety and

---

SPINNING SESSIONS

Indoor cycling has diversified since the original spinning concept, but most classes are based on one of four formats...

1 Pre-choreographed, where set moves are repeated to each music track. These classes tend to be more fun and choreography focused, with upper body moves used, as well as other non-traditional cycling elements.

2. Rhythm-based classes where participants are encouraged to keep to the speed of the music; music might also be used to define choreography. As with pre-choreographed sessions, these tend to include non-cycling moves too.

3 Heart rate based, where participants are encouraged to alter workload and cadence to remain in the desired heart rate training zone

for that session. These tend to be more training focused with more traditional cycling moves.

4 Visualization is mainly used by instructors to direct participants along an imaginary route, but can be more powerfully used to attain mind-body coherence – what athletes often call 'the zone' for enhanced performance, pleasure and positive mind-body health.

having fun while you train, incorporating different speeds and challenges.

Make sure you find a class geared specifically towards outdoor cyclists, as general aerobics-style classes will incorporate other exercises such as pedalling backwards and push-ups on the handlebar, which is something that's frowned upon by many indoor spinning instructors and traditionalists.

STEP IT UP

Like any fitness regime, intensity and frequency depends on your individual health, fitness, motivation and objectives. Indoor cycling allows you to spend a lot of time in the aerobic endurance zones in the winter and sessions are good for interval training as it's harder to motivate yourself to do high-intensity training alone. But remember to follow hard days with easy days – you can sit at the back and ride easy at a low heart rate when you are on a recovery day.

Increasingly, instructors are advising that participants wear heart rate monitors during sessions. Maintaining your heart rate within various training zones enables you to reach your own endurance-based or strength-based goals more easily.

TOP SPINNING TIPS

As experienced a cyclist as you might be, spinning can take some getting used to. Follow our five essential pointers for success...

1. Try several different classes and bikes, to see what suits you.

2. The instructor should explain about the fixed gear and how to set up the bike. You might wish to adjust their recommendations so that they're closer to your usual riding position. In indoor cycling there's no wind resistance so you tend to ride with a higher handlebar and also encourage a greater knee extension at the bottom of the pedal stroke than the one you might be used to.

3. Wear your cycling shorts to ride, as they'll be more comfy. Always take water to class and drink at least 1 litre per 45-minute session.

4. Work on a smooth pedal stroke, use resistance that really feels like the road outside, whether it's a flat road or a climb, and pedal at your preferred outdoor cadence (do cadence drills on a spinning bike to train the neuromuscular abilities of the legs, but remember that indoors it's so much easier to pedal faster than outdoors).

5. Train with a heart rate monitor (HRM) to ensure you have an effective workout tailored to meet your own goals.

OFF-BIKE EXERCISES

What you do off your bike can have as big an impact on your riding as what you do in the saddle. We share the best do-anywhere moves so you can emulate the elite riders...

If you think your bike needs fine-tuning, that's nothing compared to the complex machine that is the human body. Whether you are climbing, endurance riding or looking for that burst of speed in the sprint, time spent getting your body bike-ready is invaluable.

CLIMBING

The Contadors and other great climbers of this world know the difference between their mobilizers and stabilizers. The chain of movement goes from the tips of your fingers to the tips of your toes, all working in one line. Think of your body like it's a bicycle chain – your links are your muscles, which stabilize and provide strength, while your pins are your joints, which provide mobility.

The biggest area of confusion here relates to your glutes. Because most of us sit on them all day we assume they're mobilisers when they're actually stabilizers. You need to work them accordingly off the bike for real gains on it.

Imagine yourself as a table football player with an axle going through your hip so that you only move in one plane of motion with no sideways movement and no hip rocking. When you are out of the saddle or grinding up a hill, your glutes are paramount to holding the chain of movement together. Watch Alberto Contador climbing and you'll see that his axis of movement is almost perfect because he understands this and constantly works on his glute strength while off the bike and away from hills.

ONE-LEG BRIDGE CHANGEOVERS

Lying on your back with your knees at 90 degrees, feet flat on the floor and arms by your sides, lift your hips and tense your glutes. Then lift your left leg, tense your right glute and hold for two seconds. Switch legs and repeat for 30 seconds. Make your glutes work as independently as they would during cycling but without activating your back and hamstrings, so tilt your pelvis up and pull your belly button in. Do this before every ride, especially interval sessions, to fire the glutes. Up the speed by doing fast reps for a minute at a time while maintaining control and form.

LEG SQUAT WITH ROTATION

Standing on one leg, squat down and push your hips back while keeping your knees level to prevent your hips rotating. Assume a cycling position, bending forwards from the hip with a flat back and your hands out as if holding a bar. Rotate your upper body until your shoulders are almost at 90 degrees but keep the bottom half of your frame perfectly still. Hold for two seconds and do 10 reps on each side. This really hits the gluteus medius muscle on the side of your bum, which helps prevent lateral movement so your hips stay in line on that one axis when you're out of the saddle.

PRESS-UP HOLD-TO-KNEE RAISE

In a press-up position, tense your glutes and lift your right knee to your right elbow, keeping everything in the plank position. Then take your right foot back and straighten it. Just before you touch the ground, tense your right glute and change legs. Repeat 10 times on each side. This activates the gluteus maximus muscles in cycling positions. Recruiting your glutes in the saddle is amazingly hard so do this just before you get on the bike to be fired up and ready to go. By working these muscles you're also protecting your back and nervous system and preventing spasming.

SUPREME ENDURANCE

On top of all the other benefits – back protection, power, speed – a rock-hard core is your key to lasting 12 quality hours in the saddle. Your core transfers power from your body to the bike.Without stability power is wasted and you'll tire quicker and empty vital glycogen reserves sooner. The prehab and rehab exercises opposite and below are a must for any cyclist wanting to move up a gear in their riding.

DEEP CORE HOLDS/PULSES

Lying on your back, put your feet flat on the floor with your knees together and make an angle of 90 degrees. Roll your pelvis back so it's pointing towards the ceiling, pull your belly button towards your spine to activate your deep core and push your back flat against the ground so there's no arch. Hold for 10 seconds, rest briefly and repeat 10 times.

This exercise specifically strengthens the transverse abdominis (TVA) core and multifidus spine-stabilizing muscles and helps pelvic proprioception, taking the strain off your lower back and hamstrings. Don't hold your breath because this can bring in your quads and glutes when you really want to focus all your efforts on the TVAs. Do three sets of 10, keeping complete control for each movement.

PLANKS

Get into a press-up position and hold your head, shoulders and hips in a perfectly straight line while resting on your forearms. Again, activate your deep TVA core muscles by pulling your belly button towards your spine throughout. Hold for 60 seconds then rotate 90 degrees so your right hip and shoulder are pointing up and you're resting on your left forearm in a side plank position. Hold for 60 seconds and repeat on the other side.

Planks hit TVA muscles and lateral obliques to prevent thoracic rotation – and resultant loss of energy – and hip strains. Add extra pressure by throwing in side pulses. Lower your hips towards the ground and then raise them towards the ceiling while lifting your straight upper leg at the same time.

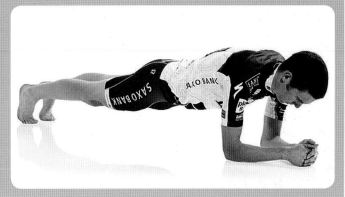

LIGHTNING ACCELERATION

You need the fast-twitch, type II muscle fibres in your glutes, quads and hamstrings to be able to turn on a short sprint. By training these muscles over a month and making specific groups expand and contract at speed you can get the edge. US researchers have found that jump squats can boost body power and acceleration by 13 per cent in just five weeks. Complete as many of these exercises as you can in 30 minutes, breaking for two minutes' recovery between each. Try to land and explode rapidly, keeping ground contact brief, while staying in complete control.

ALTERNATE LEG BOUNDS

Leap forward off your right leg as far as you can so your left leg and right arm go forward as you jump. Land on the ball of your left foot and immediately bound off it with your right leg and left arm extended. Bound up a hill to make it harder. Do 10 reps per leg in each set and do three sets, resting for 60 seconds after each.

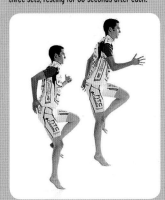

POWER SKIPPING

You remember how to skip? Now make it explosive by pushing forcefully off the ground with each hop and lifting the knee of your forward leg up to your chest. Do 16 skips per set and three sets, with a 60-second recovery rest between each.

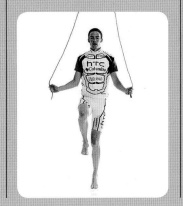

ONE-LEGGED SQUAT JUMPS

Stand on one leg and squat down until the top of your thigh is parallel with the ground, keeping your knee behind your front toe. Jump forwards and land on the same leg, squatting down to cushion the landing. Do 10 jumps in a row on one leg before turning around and repeating on the other.

DEPTH JUMPS

Step off a 50-70cm-high box or stair, landing on both feet and then jump up from both legs as high as possible. Speed off the ground is the key to this drill; react as though the ground was covered in burning ash and you had no shoes on. Repeat the exercise five to eight times.

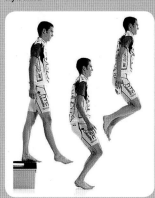

THE RULES OF CYCLING FITNESS

Set your cycling potential free by simply following a few basic guidelines...

If you're looking to win races, lose weight, beat your friends or just want to get better, faster and fitter, then the rules of fitness training will apply to you and your riding as much as they do to the top riders. Put in the effort before the race and reap the benefits when the big day arrives.

Cycling is an endurance sport, so you will need to spend more time training at an endurance intensity than anything else. Endurance workouts need to be at least 60 minutes long and ideally 120 minutes, and ridden at a strict 35–45bpm below your maximum heart rate.

These sessions will build your aerobic endurance base, making your slow-twitch muscle fibres more efficient at fat burning. The better your aerobic base, the more work you can do for the same effort, riding further and faster more easily. For races, a good aerobic base will help you keep going when the riding gets tough, get to the finishing straight in better shape, and it will also enable you to race harder for longer in the season.

LATE STARTER ENDURANCE SESSION
After a 10-minute warm-up, ride for a constant 20 minutes at 55–65% of your maximum heart rate (HR max). For maximum benefit, ride before breakfast, preferably on a turbo. Riding with already low glycogen stores will really kick-start your metabolism. These short workouts should be in addition to a weekly two- to three-hour endurance ride.

LACTATE THRESHOLD
As your lactate threshold is the point at which your muscles will start to work more anaerobically, and be overcome with fatigue, raising the level of work you can do before it kicks in is so important. In sportives this is likely to happen on long, steady climbs, whereas in races a high lactate threshold will help you stay with a break or put in a good time trial effort. To train it, you need to ride at or slightly above your lactate threshold, which is roughly 15–25bpm below your HR max.

THRESHOLD SESSION

After a good 10–15 minute warm-up, ride for 30 minutes at a constant intensity of between 81 and 85% of your HR max. A turbo trainer is ideal for this tightly controlled effort, but if you don't have one, look to perform it in the middle of a longer endurance workout on a flat road. On a more rolling road you will have to use your gearing to stay in the right zone – backing off and spinning up inclines, and applying yourself to push big gears hard on the descents.

STRENGTH

Despite cycling being a predominantly aerobic endurance sport, adding explosive strength workouts to your regular training can have spectacular results. Research has found that substituting 37 per cent of a well-trained group's endurance training with predominantly off-the-bike resistance training cut their time trial times significantly in just four weeks. Starting and finishing with a 10-minute cycling warm-up and warm-down at 75% HR max, the subjects performed sets of off-the-bike resistance exercises.

STRENGTH SESSION

With the following gym-based exercises, you need to initiate the exercise movement explosively for maximum benefit. Separate sets with short recovery periods.

1. Warm up for 10 minutes on the bike at 75% HR max
2. 2 sets of squats with 30 reps
3. 2 sets of 30 leg presses
4. 2 sets of 30 leg pulls
5. 2 sets of 30 one-leg step-ups
6. Warm down for 10 minutes on a bike at 75% HR max.
7. Repeat steps 2-6.

WARM UP AND COOL DOWN

Warming up and cooling down are both essential to get the maximum out of your training without risk of injury. A good warm-up opens up blood capillaries, activates neuromuscular systems, regulates your breathing, kick-starts your biological cooling systems and warms up muscles.

For racing or interval training, always include some brief high-intensity efforts in your warm-up – not all-out sprints so much as short bursts at a high cadence. These short, hard efforts prime the relevant neuromuscular and energy systems that will be needed in your session or ride. But this only improves performance for the following 5 or 10 minutes and the benefit can easily be wiped out if the warm-up is too strenuous. So don't go too hard!

Don't stretch! Leading research institutes have shown that pre-exercise static stretching may actually tighten your muscles, make them more prone to injury and can have a negative effect on endurance too. Save the static stretching for after your ride to increase your flexibility and improve your riding position, as well as release over-tight muscles and strengthen weak ones.

To warm up, ride steady at recovery intensity (75% HR max) for 10-15 minutes, then perform 3x10-second hard efforts at a high cadence with 3 minutes of active recovery in between.

To cool down, ride at recovery intensity (75% HR max) for at least 10 minutes and let your heart rate drop back down towards resting level. The active recovery will help your muscles flush themselves of any remaining lactic acid from your session, and help your breathing return to normal.

AEROBIC CAPACITY

Otherwise known as VO2 max, your aerobic capacity is a measure of how much oxygen your lungs can process before your muscles start working predominantly anaerobically. Everyone has a different VO2 max and to a large extent it's limited by your genetic makeup – and your age, as it typically drops by about one per cent per year beyond your 25th birthday.

An untrained person's lactate threshold is roughly 50 per cent of their true aerobic capacity, while well-

trained elites might be able to keep working up to somewhere around 90 per cent. By training at your VO2 max you can improve endurance and strength as well as push up your anaerobic threshold.

VO2 MAX SESSION

After a good 10–15 minute warm-up, ride two to three intervals of 3 minutes at the hardest possible intensity that you can sustain for each interval. Separate each interval with a 3-minute recovery period of easy pedalling. As you get fitter and find the efforts easier, increase the number of intervals gradually up to five. Finish the session with a 10-minute warm-down of easy pedalling. Don't do more than one of these sessions a week.

TESTING

Regularly measuring your performance and physiological data is a great motivator to continue your training. It's also an essential part of training efficiently. Continually check your HR max and your resting heart rate in order to increase your training load as you adapt and improve.

POWER

Power is defined as work divided by time – so an increase in cycling power requires either more force to the pedals during each pedal stroke, or more pedal strokes of the same force in a given time. The first is what you're developing with the strength session, while the second can be developed with maximum cadence jumps.

Jumps are different to sprints, in that jumps focus on acceleration based on the maximum cadence you can manage, using a smaller gear. Practising them will build your body's capacity to develop the most work over short periods of time – improving both your sprinting as well as your ability to surge and break away on road races.

POWER SESSION

After a long warm-up of about 30 minutes, do five maximum cadence jumps of 10–12 pedal strokes, with a minute of easy pedalling recovery in between. Alternate in-the-saddle efforts with out-of-the-saddle efforts and pedal as high a cadence as you can – at least 120rpm. Repeat the jump set three times, with 5 minutes of recovery-intensity soft-pedalling in between. Try to build the intensity of each jump and each set progressively.

RECOVERY

Recovery is as important for getting fit as the exercise itself, because it's only when you've completed your training session or race that the body can repair damaged muscle tissue, refuel muscle glycogen and prepare for the new level of physical exertion that you're asking of it. Recovery is important for every level and timescale of cycling fitness. From sleep, to the time off the bike at the end of the season, to pre-race tapering, to the active recovery rides after race days, to the short, soft-pedalling recovery breaks between ultra-tough intervals – all are durations of rest that are designed to help you do the maximum level of work again as soon as possible.

" Jumps improve your sprinting and your ability to surge and break away "

THE ULTIMATE HILL WORKOUT

Do you worry when the roads turn upwards? Then read on. We have the training plan to help you tackle any climb out there...

▼ Training to raise your aerobic capacity is key to successful climbing

We know that putting effort into our 'hill work' will make our lives easier in the long run, but for some reason, every time we should be doing it we are filled with dread and manage to do something else with our training session instead. But avoidance is not a healthy tactic and really there's nothing to be afraid of. You can improve your climbing in just two sessions a week and can even do some of your training on the flat.

STRENGTH FOR SHORT CLIMBS

The processes taking place inside your body differ depending on the ascent's severity. On short, sharp climbs your performance is determined by how much force you can generate rather than your aerobic capacity, so you generate a lot of painful lactic acid. This is because when sprinting up short climbs, our bodies require energy to be produced more quickly than it can be generated aerobically, so our muscles need to metabolise glucose at speed. This releases the lactic acid that creates the burning sensation. Building up the strength in your legs won't stop the burn, but it will help you to get up the short climbs more effectively.

To maximize your leg power ride three- to five-minute climbs in as big a gear as you can manage on a gradient of around seven or eight per cent. Try to keep your cadence between 40 and 50rpm for maximum effort. Once you have finished the climb, recover for a few minutes and repeat.

Don't use too big a gear or too steep an incline when starting. For a beginner, one session a week is plenty, two when you are in training for a hilly event.

" You can improve your climbing in just two sessions a week "

AEROBIC CAPACITY FOR LONG CLIMBS

As well as increasing muscle power, it is important to raise your aerobic capacity so that all aspects of your body are ready for climbing – this is especially true for longer climbs. Any incline that takes more than three minutes will be a 90 per cent aerobic effort – in order to go faster you need a higher VO2 max (the volume of oxygen your body can consume while exercising at maximum capacity). Long, steady inclines are about efficiency and riding at a higher percentage of your VO2 max. It isn't easy to increase, but all-out interval sessions of 30 seconds to a minute repeated several times should help.

Training your breathing and oxygen uptake can be done on the flat by doing five minutes hard, followed by five minutes at a recovery pace. Start by adding three intervals into your ride and build up to as many as ten.

STRONG CORE

Grinding up a hill out of the saddle requires a strong core to reduce energy-wasting body sway. But having a strong core is important for other reasons. Long mountain climbs put a lot of stress on your back and when your back gets weak or tired you can't transfer the power to your legs, so you will end up having to go much slower. By working on core muscle strength you will help your body cope with long uphill hours.

Try training sessions where you climb sitting down on the drops in a big gear. In a controlled environment you can do this until you get tired, then you can stop – so you can build up your strength by repeating this without causing injury.

DO IT AGAIN…

Hill reps work by training your body to adapt to a certain movement, allowing you to have the best power transfer. And repetition allows you to understand how your body best handles climbing. Try using different gears, different intensities and riding styles to see which climbing style works best for you.

TRAINING WITHOUT THE HILLS

You don't have to train for hills on hills – you can do some training on the flat. A hard effort for 20–30 minutes on a flat road will help you prepare for climbing and you can also do it on a turbo.

YANTO BARKER
LONG CLIMBS

Ride a climb of about five minutes sitting down and on the drops in as big a gear as you can, accentuating the aero position. This creates an acute angle on the glutes, putting extra strain on your back, which helps to strengthen core muscles and maximize power output. In a controlled environment – on a familiar hill – do this until you get tired, rest and repeat.

OVERCOME A TRAINING PLATEAU

Don't let a performance plateau get you down. Our tips will get you going again

Recover right

If you've made significant gains and now you've come to a halt, it may be that you need to give your body time to adjust to its new physiological capabilities. Stay off the bike for a week or two and let your muscles fully adapt and repair. You may initially take a small step back when you begin training again but you should soon see big gains.

Variety

Mix up the intensity of your rides so you're working on improving all aspects of your cycling. Get in a twice-weekly ride of 50 miles or so, keeping your heart rate below 80%. Incorporate interval sessions into your commute. And make sure to do at least one hill session too. By covering all bases you know you haven't got a weakness that is holding you back.

Pain barrier

Often a niggling pain might be hindering your development. Don't ignore it, get it sorted. It may be that as your riding has improved your position on the bike has changed and you need another bike fit. If you've overtrained you may need time off to heal. See a physiotherapist for a medical opinion or get a professional bike fit to get you back on track.

HANNAH BARNES
TURBO SESSIONS

Make sure you have a good 10 to 15-minute warm-up, then change up into a harder gear and do 5 minutes at a fixed tempo. Recover for 5 minutes, then do eight very hard 30-second efforts with a minute's recovery in between, replicating a short, sharp climb, followed by four 90-second efforts, to replicate a slightly longer climb. These efforts should be done in a hard gear at very high intensity. Cool down for 10-15 minutes.

GEARING

Picking the correct gearing is a matter of riding climbs and finding a rhythm that works. A lot of people will try to twiddle in a low gear, but unless their heart and lungs are incredibly fit they will find this very hard. Using a slightly higher gear and turning your legs more slowly may work better. It doesn't matter if you spin up climbs in an easy gear or grind it out in the big ring – both techniques work, so experiment with what feels right.

WEIGHT AND EATING

You weigh 60–90kg and your bike 6–9kg, so there's no question which has more potential for weight loss. A kilo off the bike will cost a fortune, losing a kilo from your body won't. Losing even a small amount of weight will make a big difference. But don't let being weight conscious stop you from fuelling correctly. You can burn at least twice as many calories an hour as you can eat when you are riding hard, so don't worry about putting on weight. Keeping hydrated and eating throughout a ride is very important. Cycling is a demanding sport and if you don't keep your energy stores topped up you will start to struggle and your performance will suffer.

LAST MINUTE...

If you have a hilly event coming up and haven't prepared much, don't despair. If you are starting from scratch, 10 weeks doing 10 hours a week including two hill sessions is enough to get a good result in a hilly event. If you've been doing some training you could bring this down to six weeks if you are consistent. People will cover the distance without much training, but the problem is pacing, especially on long climbs. You need the training not only to improve, but to understand your own boundaries.

MAGNUS BACKSTEDT
SHORT CLIMBS

When training for short, sharp climbs focus on intervals on fairly steep climbs. Pick a steep climb of about four minutes. Start with a 30-second flat-out sprint, recover on the climb and go again. Repeat this until you reach the top before recovering for four minutes and then repeat. After the second set you can leave it a bit longer to recover before doing a third and fourth set. If you do this twice a week you should notice good improvements in your ability to quickly tackle short, sharp climbs.

EXERCISE TAPERING

Reduce your training before a race and it'll improve your performance on the day. It's all explained by the science of tapering...

▶ Give yourself a mental boost by recalling times you've overcome similar challenges

A taper is a period of rest or reduced training immediately preceding a race. Paradoxically, many cyclists find the idea of cutting back harder to cope with than the gruelling training preceding it. If you do the taper right, your fitness will decrease slightly. That's a concept endurance athletes have real trouble getting their heads around.

BUT HERE'S HOW IT WORKS

Tapering is based on the assumption that training increases fitness levels and fatigue levels simultaneously. As you train harder you get fitter – which increases your performance, but you also get more tired – which decreases your performance. Tapering works because when you decrease training your fatigue level falls faster than your fitness level. So even though fitness will decrease slightly during a taper, the greater lack of fatigue means performance will be better.

Countless studies have proven this. Researchers at Ball State University, Indiana, recently found tapering brought an improvement of 4%, while a combined study at several Canadian universities found that cutting training volume by 50% for one week improved the 20km time trial performance of trained cyclists by 1min 9sec on average. Gathering all the studies together, it seems an improvement of between 1–6% is possible if you do it right.

TAPER TRAINING

But doing it right isn't easy, nor is it an exact science. Although tapering involves reducing your training load, you can do this in a number of ways: you could cut the number of kilometres you ride per day (reduce training volume); or you could cut the speed at which you ride them (reduce training intensity); or you could keep your daily rides exactly the same but simply train on fewer days (reduce training frequency).

Many studies have looked at these different methods and combinations to see which worked best. The best known was by a team at the University of Illinois, who showed that decreasing volume and maintaining intensity resulted in significant performance improvements, but maintaining volume and decreasing intensity resulted in a performance drop. Further research has refined the cut volume/maintain intensity strategy.

Researchers from the University of Lille collated all known taper studies and drew some overall conclusions. First, they found that best results were achieved following a reduction in training volume of 40–60%, depending on the individual and the ferocity of previous training. The second conclusion was that training frequency should be maintained or reduced by a maximum of 20%. So for the most part you still need to ride as often as you normally would, just for half the distance. The final – and arguably most important – conclusion is that intensity must be largely maintained to ensure fitness levels don't drop off drastically. This is an important point, but one that cyclists often take too far by actually increasing intensity rather than simply maintaining it.

Buoyed by the energizing effects of the taper, many cyclists throw in shorter, faster reps with the intention of 'sharpening up'. But research from Ball State University found this approach may turn out to be counterproductive.

"Our research shows tapering primarily benefits the type II or fast-twitch muscle fibres," says lead researcher Scott Trappe. "These fibres are broken down during very high-intensity training, so too much intensity during the taper can have a negative impact on muscle changes, which will hurt your performance."

TAPER TIMING

Another crucial aspect of the taper is timing. How long should you allow? The studies show that, on average, two weeks seems to be about the optimum length for a taper, but it depends on the length of the training block preceding it. If you've been training hard for six months prior to the race then a three-week taper is likely to be more effective.

Dr Phil Skiba of the University of Exeter has devised another strategy. Using data from hundreds of athletes, he has worked out a formula for calculating two days crucial to tapering. The first one is the day on which training will have a maximum positive effect on your race. Clearly training adaptations take a little while to fully work through so this day is often a week or two

before the race at least. The second is the day on which training starts to have a negative impact on your race performance because it's so close to race day that the fatigue outweighs the fitness gains.

"While two weeks is a good starting point, with a little trial and error, you can calculate these two days," says Skiba. "You want to reduce your training volume between them, aggressively at first and then more gradually."

This latter point is another area where cyclists often go awry. Studies show a progressive taper is superior to one that rigidly reduces training volume on a week-by-week basis. But this does not mean – as many think – that you reduce training volume slowly at first and then dramatically in the final days. In fact, the reverse is true. The best results are obtained by cutting volume in half at the beginning of the taper and then largely maintaining that until race day.

Tapers, then, are not as easy as they appear. But that isn't an excuse for not believing in them. "In my experience, while most people are very willing to put in the necessary training, they are often afraid of tapering because it feels like they're losing fitness and they're worried their performance will drop," says Trappe.

"The data simply doesn't support this. You have to trust it," he emphasized.

ADVANCED TAPERING TIPS

Pre-taper crash training

There is growing evidence that a period of extremely intense training or 'crash training' immediately preceding the taper can be very beneficial. A study at the University of Saint-Etienne in France found that 28 days of 'overload' training prior to the taper significantly increased final performance in trained cyclists. However, it also meant that for best results the taper had to be more dramatic and longer.

"Crash training is generally only a tactic for very serious cyclists, but it can be pretty effective and maybe should be used by more people," says Exeter Univeristy's Skiba. "Given that cycling is a low-impact sport, the chances of hurting yourself are low – though I'd recommend trying it for just a few days at first, in the week immediately before the taper."

Controversial carb load

Nutrition is another crucial aspect. Experts recommend maintaining a normal diet until the final week when an optional period of depletion (now out of favour with many) is followed by a carb feast to fully top up glycogen levels. However, many cyclists report that carb-loading makes them feel bloated and slow – hardly ideal preparation.

Fortunately, researchers from the University of Western Australia have an ingenious solution. They found glycogen storage is most effective immediately after high-intensity exercise, but that the bout of exercise need only be three minutes long! So they recommend that two or three days before a race, athletes should do three minutes of flat-out exercise and then consume as much carbohydrate as possible over the next 24 hours – the first 20 minutes being the most important. After this, normal diet can be resumed, so athletes don't feel bloated but tests show they'll have super-high levels of glycogen for race day.

USING STRAVA

In a short space of time, Strava has transformed the way we train. But as the app evolves from its original 'King of the Mountain' hook, we look at how we're moving with it

When Strava first appeared six years ago, it wasn't a pioneer as a ride tracking app, but that was never how the makers saw it. While cyclists could use it for that, the Strava creators' ambitions were loftier: it would be an online fitness community, a virtual hub for interaction between cyclists (and runners) all over the world.

Michael Horvath, who created Strava with his friend Mark Gainey, said they wanted to create a Facebook for athletes, and they have. It's slick, glossy, simple to use and has an appeal that reaches pro athletes and club riders.

King of the Mountain segments were, and still are, its hook, but it's the ability to share the cycling experience, to "create stories around the ride" as Strava's director of international marketing, Gareth Nettleton, puts it, that keeps the interest once the initial rush of KOM chasing has faded.

For BikeRadar.com's US editor Ben Delaney, that explains the app's appeal. Based in Boulder, Colorado, where elite and pro cyclists abound, he's long since packed in his quest to top leaderboards.

"I'm no threat to any meaningful KOM around here," he says. "I did have a downhill record until some punk named Taylor Phinney [BMC pro racer] nabbed it, but it's very much a cycling Facebook for me. I can keep tabs on where my friends are riding, who did a big ride in the mountains at the weekend or who's going hard and setting records. I dig it when people link to their Instagram accounts – I follow guys in places like Switzerland and Vietnam to get a glimpse into the riding there."

In its new UK HQ in London, Nettleton tells me Strava's evolution is a result of a growing maturity of the app and its audience. "KOMs were the thing that got people addicted early on and what we were associated with," he says, "but the network's much bigger than that now. If we were to rely on segments [timed sections with leaderboards] to grow, it wouldn't work because it doesn't appeal to the majority."

The community aspect is also evident in the experiences of people such as Juan Gomez, who used Strava's heatmap tool when he moved to Manchester from South America to find out where people were riding. The roads that glowed

bright were ones he needed to check out. "Strava has accumulated a lot of collective knowledge about routes that would be impossible to have otherwise," he says.

DRIVEN TO DISTRACTION

Not everybody takes the same view as Delaney, though, and the lure of the KOM hunt is still a major reason for using Strava. In this sense it still serves as a social community; it's just the goal that's different. For these people Strava is an online multi-player road race. It's a game that satisfies the same competitive urges as any video game, but instead of getting fat you get fit.

Whether chasing PBs, comparing yourself against Strava pro riders or going outright for a KOM, success on Strava makes you feel good. That's dopamine at work, a hormone that's released as a consequence of achievements like this.

The danger comes in chasing this rush at the expense of real, tangible objectives in races or sportives, according to ultra-endurance roadie Mike Cotty, founder of thecolcollective.com. "I like it as a motivating tool," he says, "but it's easy to fall into the trap of turning every ride into a smash-fest. I've seen riders make good progress initially by upping their intensity as they seek KOMs but if it's not structured they hit a plateau and can't understand why they aren't improving. Sometimes it takes some restraint to ensure your body gets the right adaptation from training. Factor in Strava sessions if that's what keeps you motivated, but not every day."

GOAL SETTING

Strava goals should be a means to an end, and it's important not to get too caught up chasing records. Delaney says it's easy to get fixated on chasing these 'contrived' targets – he himself has been guilty of it. A few years back he smashed into a deer "hauling ass downhill" in pursuit of a segment record, breaking a bone in his hand and totalling his bike. "I suppose that makes me an example of the worst side of Strava – focusing on a time in pursuit of an online game instead of the world around me." (The deer got up and ran away.)

Those who have grown tired of the KOM game are starting to use Strava differently. Like Delaney, London cyclist Gretchen Miller says after five years segments are so well ridden that most of us have given up hope. Instead, she uses it to track her own progress by comparing her times on segments at different points in time. It's still a motivating tool, but its motivation is derived intrinsically rather than extrinsically. "I use it as my own personal training diary," she explains. "Of course I still like to go hard on certain well-defined segments, but it never comes from a desire to be number one."

This is an example of what Nettleton talks about when he says a pillar of all Strava's in-house development is having Strava work in 'one-player mode'. "That means taking everyone else out of the equation," he says. "Are we helping to motivate and entertain you if only you can see your data? Every new feature we come up with, we put that to the test. And the answer should always be yes."

Strava is very good at getting us to ride more, and the 'gamification' of applying game thinking into non-game contexts to make them more fun and engaging – such a crucial part of Strava's DNA – is vital. Receiving emails saying so and so has taken your KOM is an incentive to get out there and take it right back.

But it's not just KOM notifications that motivate people. Each morning, all Strava users receive an email that shows what the people you follow have been up to on the bike in the previous 24 hours. It's enough to make Miller regret taking the day off. "Before Strava, there was a time when, if I was shopping, I'd be thinking that's what everyone else was doing. I almost feel guilty now when I see my friends have been out on the bike."

TIME AND PLACE

The recent death of pedestrian Jill Tarlov in New York's Central Park saw Strava make headlines for the wrong reasons. The 58-year-old was hit by cyclist Jason Marshall, a Strava user, banged her head on the pavement, and later died. Marshall hasn't been charged and it's unclear whether the speed he was travelling at played a role in her death, but it did reignite the debate over where Strava is appropriate.

"The very worst... cyclists... are the ones using the parks to launch their personal hour record attempts," wrote cycling blogger and advocate Eben Weiss, aka Bike Snob NYC, in the wake of Tarlov's death. "I'm loath to implicate Strava in any of this. Yes, I have a strong dislike for [it] ... But it did not invent the sort of selfish, moronic weenie-ism that compels cyclists to speed through the city's most heavily used green spaces in the middle of the day... To blame Strava at all is to take responsibility from the riders."

Weiss makes some good points, in the sense that it's up to us as cyclists to figure out where putting our heads down and aiming for segments is appropriate. Categorized climbs: absolutely. Bike paths, parks, descents: absolutely not. Yes, Strava can be like a video game, but unlike video games we can't lose sight of the fact that this is real life.

Nettleton says Strava encourages responsible use as much as possible. "If someone wants to race through red lights there's nothing we can do," he says. "But we've tried to introduce things like allowing users to flag dangerous segments, so there's not even a temptation."

GEEKING OUT

On a cheerier note, the app has not only inspired cyclists to ride but also cycling-mad computer whizzes like Ben Lowe to build extensions to it. In 2012 he created VeloViewer, an app that syncs with your Strava account to produce a geekier interpretation of your riding. If Strava is the mainstream pop juggernaut of social fitness apps then VeloViewer is the edgier alternative act.

Lowe built it originally to view Strava on his Windows phone when it was still limited to the iPhone, but moved it on to plug what he believed were holes in Strava's functionality. At last count it had 76,000 users, with 2.3 million page views in the last three months. As he continues to build and refine the app, these are figures that are only going up.

But not only is Strava helping getting us in better condition, it could be about to do the same for our roads. As part of what it calls Project Metro, Strava is selling the anonymized raw data accumulated through our rides to cities in the hope that it will improve cycling infrastructure.

London, Portland, Glasgow, Brisbane and Leeds are just some who have paid Strava to date. These metropolitans will drill into it and see what's happening in terms of cycling activity on given roads, which junctions are used more and which are being avoided.

How Strava continues to evolve remains to be seen, but one near certainty is that it's here to stay. What could have been a quirky flash in the pan has evolved into an integral part of cycling's fabric. Uploads have come from virtually every country on the planet, and the 100,000 new users joining each week are contributing to the three million activities uploaded per week. Strava always keeps schtum when it comes to detailed user numbers, but it continues to expand its reach, making it the social fitness app of our times.

What Nettleton will reveal is that they are trying to make Strava more forward-looking. "In a sense at the moment it's looking backwards, what you have done, but we want a more rounded take on people's athletic lives, to enable them to get to the start of a race or sportive in the best condition. Whatever we come up with, it's always with the sole aim of motivating and entertaining."

CRASH AND LEARN

Ride a bike and chances are, at some point, you'll crash. But by looking at how the pros deal with disaster it's possible to reduce the after-effects, both physically and mentally...

Cyclists suffer arguably more injuries than most other athletes, but the damage is not limited to the pros. Crashing is experienced by all road cyclists at some point, but we can learn from how the pros deal with their pain.

SCHOOL OF KNOCKS

Abrasions are one of the most common crash-induced injuries for cyclists, typically on the knees, elbows, hips and hands. "If it is a very serious abrasion, surprisingly it is less painful than a superficial abrasion," says Dr Richard Freeman, Team Sky's medical chief. Superficial abrasions – 'road rash' – can be incredibly painful because they affect the sensory nerves.

Superficial abrasions need to be cleaned up with iodine and a scrubbing brush. Cleaning debris out of wounds is easier on clean-shaven legs – one of the reasons pro cyclists shave their legs. You should use a hydrocolloid dressing, which will drop off once you've healed, or a non-adhesive gauze pad held in place with micropore tape and a tubular bandage. Dr Freeman advises using Adaptic Touch, a non-adhering silicone dressing that allows fluid to pass through to the secondary dressing, reducing the chances of maceration (when damp skin turns white and soft). "Usually within 10–14 days the wound is looking pretty good. The skin grows over and the nerves are less irritated."

Deeper abrasions have more risk of getting infected and damaged tissue often has to be cut away. "These need to be packed like a medical wound with various iodine-based antiseptic dressings and allowed to heal from the inside out," says Dr Freeman. "It takes more energy so the patient feels weaker and can't usually ride at their pre-crash level for several weeks."

Another common injury sustained by road cyclists is a broken collarbone, caused by falling on the shoulder at speed. This is easy to diagnose and treat, although amateur cyclists will tend to have to endure a longer rehabilitation period than a pro cyclist. Most hospitals will tend to treat this with a figure of eight bandage, and it will heal very slowly over about six weeks. In contrast, elite cyclists will tend to have a metal plate inserted into the dislocated shoulder, under anaesthetic, and can be back on the bike within five days doing turbo work.

Falling on an outstretched arm is also common, when fear and instinct combine to try to prevent your head smashing on tarmac. This can result in a broken scaphoid bone – a carpal bone in the wrist, at the base of the thumb. According to Dr Freeman, this injury is notoriously difficult to diagnose and is often overlooked. "If missed, they don't heal properly, and then a bit of bone dies and that is a nightmare. It makes for an unstable and painful thumb, and even surgery can't salvage the joint then." If correctly diagnosed, a broken scaphoid is treated by immobilizing the lower arm in a rigid cast for six weeks.

LEARNING CURVE

While physical injuries can mostly be healed over time, mental knocks can be harder to overcome. Pain, after all, is there for a reason – to protect us from further damage.

When cyclists crash, all the sensory details of the incident are stored in the brain, including what we saw, heard, smelt and felt. So, when back on the bike, the nerves are there for good reasons – to prevent us from crashing like before.

Learning from our mistakes – or misfortunes – can help us to overcome the fear and get back on the bike. Try writing down exactly what happened to cause a crash and what, if anything, you can do to prevent a recurrence. Reinforce the fact that you are safe and can still ride competently by getting out on the bike and doing progressively more taxing experiments. For example, if you crashed going

TREAT THOSE CUTS AND GRAZES

Had a spill? Here's how to treat your missing skin!

Minor road rash
The removal of the epidermis (the skin's outer layer) is unlikely to bleed but it will still sting. More serious abrasions are likely to bleed and be painful. In both cases clean the wound to remove dirt and debris, then rinse with water.

Deep clean
Once you've cleaned the wound apply an antiseptic to prevent infection, and cover with a sterile dressing that should be changed regularly. Sportique's Road Rash Balm (sportiquebodycare.com) is designed for cyclists. Keep the wound clean as it heals to prevent infection. And, of course, if it's really nasty and deep see a doctor.

Arm protectors
If you're prone to crashing and losing skin from your arms then you could try preventative measures. Stantovelo's arm warmers contain protective foam rubber pads on the lower forearm to the elbow which, says designer and cyclist Guy Stanton, is the part of the arm that takes the brunt of road rash incidents.

downhill following someone's wheel, then go out and ride with a buddy and get comfortable riding behind them on the flat, then start repeating downhills with your companion, gradually increasing speed and downhill gradients until you regain your performance – and your confidence.

But you should also accept that your nerves and anxiety are there for a reason. Learn to ride within your ability despite the feeling of nerves and they will gradually melt away as you see that you can still ride and stay upright.

Following these principles can enable you to overcome nerves, sometimes in just a couple of hours, but if you avoid facing your fears it can be an interminable process.

CRASH COURSE

Crashing hurts, but make like The Fall Guy and you can minimize the pain, says pro stuntman and mountain biker Rob Jarman

Over the bars
Try to get your hands up in the air and ready. Extend your leading arm towards the ground to start absorbing the impact, bow your head and tuck your chin into your chest, while protecting your head with your other arm. As your leading arm hits the road, let your momentum roll you over the same shoulder, a bit like a lopsided forward roll. Keep your head tucked in and you'll end up on your back. Hopefully your feet will have clipped out of the pedals at some stage – but either way, be prepared to fend off your own flying bike, which could be falling right on top of you!

Sack of spuds
As well as being painfully embarrassing, a low-speed tumble like those caused by failure to disengage pedals can be surprisingly painful. The reason slow crashes can sometimes hurt the most is that you don't have any momentum in your body to roll or spin out of it – instead, you hit the floor square on and your elbow and hip take all the impact. To avoid this, lean away from the floor, keeping your body upright until the last moment. Push your bike down so that the bars and inside pedal take the sting out of the fall, and then roll over your shoulder and onto your back as your body hits the road.

Slide rules
Legend has it that at 60mph a road will burn through an inch of flesh per second of sliding. Okay, you won't be going that fast, but even at 18mph you'll get yourself some decent road rash. As the bike goes down, you should try to rotate your upper body to face the direction your bike is sliding in. If you have time, take your lowest hand off the bar and drop your shoulder so that the back of it can take most of your impact with the road. If you're going really fast, put your feet out in front of you and push them down into the road surface to use as a makeshift brake.

PURE MADNESS

For professional cyclists, the adrenaline and desire to compete – and win – is often enough to block out the pain when a crash first occurs, driving them straight back on the bike to continue riding.

Team Sky's Michael Barry is no stranger to crashing. When he was an amateur, he finished one race in France despite having a fractured femur. "I crashed on a wet descent, then rode the 10km to the finish. When I got to the team car I felt nauseous from the pain." He also crashed in the 2002 Vuelta a España, and was hit by a motorbike. "I had to ride roughly 50km and two mountain passes with broken ribs and open wounds on every limb and my torso. When I finished I collapsed.

"In bike racing there are no time-outs so we push through the pain to regain contact with the peloton, to finish and to hopefully continue for another day. On some level the crashes always stick with me as they have made me more cautious. But I think the easiest way to overcome fears is to simply keep riding."

When Team Sky's Geraint Thomas was training in 2005, the rider in front of him clipped some metal debris. It flicked up into Thomas's front wheel, stopping him dead and causing him to land on his handlebar. He needed an emergency operation to remove his spleen.

"It was definitely scary, especially when the doctor told me if my spleen kept bleeding I would die," says Thomas. Thomas's post-crash anxiety was overcome by his desire to return to competition, just six weeks later. "Initially I was a little nervous as I could still feel my stomach muscles were sore. But once I was racing I never really thought about it – I just wanted to race."

Thomas also crashed in 2009, when he broke his pelvis and fractured his nose after crashing into a safety barrier in the time trial stage of the Tirreno–Adriatico in Italy. He was unable to compete for six weeks.

"Crashing has calmed me down a bit and I learnt when and where to take risks in a race. And they have helped me appreciate just being able to race my bike, which I love," he reflects.

CRASH TEST

What to do if you and a car collide...

Self-defence
Cyclists are vulnerable in collisions with vehicles, particularly left-turning HGVs. Cycle intelligently and safely.

Avert danger
When toppled from your bicycle, your priority is to avert further danger to yourself. If you're unable to move out of harm's way, shout, wave or whistle to attract assistance.

Witnesses
Acquire independent witnesses immediately. If you are injured, ask a passer-by to collect contact details.

Beware tactics
It's a legal requirement to supply details after a collision. Note the numberplate, make, model and colour of vehicles.

Emergency assistance
Always call the police, indicating you have been the victim of a 'running down'. This call will be logged and can be very useful evidence subsequently.

Evidence
Photographs and sketch diagrams are vital. If you have a camera on you, take as many shots as you can of the scenario, numberplates, drivers and passers-by. Sign, date and put a time on your account.

Injuries
Insist on a full hospital check-up and seek medical attention for any subsequent twinges. Get photographs of bruises and lacerations. Maintain a record of all expenses, such as taxis.

Property damage
Do not forget potential compensation for your mangled bike and clothing. Get good photographs of the damage and keep all receipts for any repairs.

Police liaison
Get the number of the attending police officer and their duty station, the police reference number, and ask for a copy of their Police Collision Investigation report and their sketch diagrams and photographs. Follow up with polite but persistent inquiries about the prosecution process against a guilty driver.

Specialist solicitor
With membership of a cycling organization, you will find lawyers who are sympathetic and knowledgeable.

REINVENT YOUR RIDING

By adapting our training, riding habits and diet, we can reshape our abilities as cyclists

Take 2g of red krill oil supplements per day, on top of a fish-rich diet. The omega-3 fatty acids help to reduce muscle inflammation and breakdown.

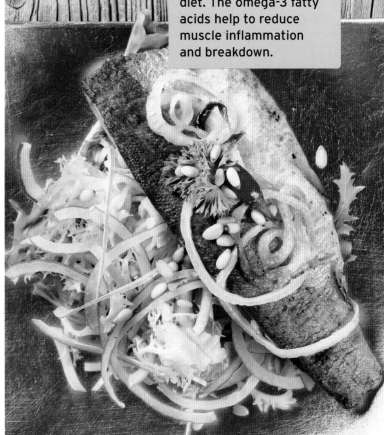

The room for manoeuvre in changing what kind of cyclist we are is huge. Genetics dictate to a certain extent, but through training and developing our skills, we can turn what might once have been limitations into strengths.

1. USE AGE TO YOUR ADVANTAGE

Reinvention can come about simply through the passing of time, and the progression of young road racer to older time triallist is a well-beaten path. BikeRadar.com editor Jeff Jones is a good example.

Jones, 43, had road raced in his native Australia and in Belgium for 20 years before he started taking 'testing' seriously when he moved to the UK in 2006.

"I was always a terrible sprinter (I once finished third in a two-man sprint) but I knew I had fitness and staying power," says Jones. "I knew I had to be good at something."

Time trialling proved to be his niche as he approached middle age. He hired a coach, Ric Stern, who helped turn him into one of the best in the UK – and the world: in 2011 he rode 305 miles to break the world 12-hour time trial record.

Such a transition is not unusual - cyclists lose their 'top end' or explosive power with age but are able to sustain higher threshold powers, essential for good time trialling.

2. REFINE YOUR NUTRITION

British Cycling and Team Sky nutritionist Nigel Mitchell has played a crucial role in helping riders like Sir Bradley Wiggins and Geraint Thomas transition from the track to road and vice versa. In moving from short endurance efforts on the track – like the team pursuit – to longer endurance efforts on the road, Mitchell says his riders will lengthen the volume and decrease the intensity of training, with diet playing a crucial role in this adaptation.

"If we starve the body a little of energy, that will help enhance that change from power to endurance. But we must be careful – if we push too hard we can damage and burn away the muscle, so we look to increase protein intake and restrict carbs a little to protect them."

For all types of training, a supplement Mitchell recommends to reduce the stress on the muscles brought about by hard training is fish oil. "We need to stress the muscles as that's the stimulus for adaptation," he says, "but if we have too much stress it can mean the protein synthesis isn't what we're looking for. Fish oils help to dial down muscle inflammation from training and aid recovery."

3. MANIPULATE YOUR MUSCLE FIBRES

Just how radically can we reinvent our cycling? We know training will make us go faster for longer, but how far can we go in reshaping our abilities? Can, for example, a cyclist genetically predisposed to sprinting turn himself into an endurance rider?

Muscle fibres are one of the first places we should look. They can be broken down into two types: slow-twitch (type one) for endurance, and fast-twitch (type two) for sprinting. On average across the general population our muscles are made up of 50 per cent of each, but elite track sprinters can have as much as 80 per cent fast-twitch fibres, and climbers up to 80 per cent slow.

While it is virtually impossible to change fibre types from one to another, muscle physiology will adapt over a long period of time to specific training. If you're a sprinter training for endurance, your muscles will adapt in the type one direction. You wouldn't necessarily see a change in myosin type – the protein involved in contraction – but you might see a change in aerobic potential.

Aside from the top competitive levels of cycling, where a track or road sprinter could never adapt far enough to compete with the best endurance cyclists in the world, it seems the scope is there for the typical cyclist regarding such a transformation.

4.BECOME A CLIMBING KING

Matteo Carrara began his career as a powerful sprinter type, weighing 77kg, but through training and diet worked to improve his climbing by reducing his weight to as low as 61kg. Despite this, the former pro turned coach (cadenceperformance.com) says he was never a natural climber and had to work on other areas of performance, such as technique, to climb with the best.

"You'll see guys like Alberto Contador dancing out of the saddle but he's an exception. I needed to learn to pedal from the saddle. The best way for me to succeed at something I wasn't naturally suited to was to stay seated, keep my body still, and be as efficient as possible."

5. IMPROVE YOUR BIKE SKILLS

For roadies looking to enhance their skills, they can do worse than heading off road. Madison Genesis pro Tom Stewart, who's 24, grew up mountain biking and only entered his first 4th cat road race at 20. He still rides off-road in the winter and believes it sets him up for the road. "The nature of the efforts on climbs and technical sections gives a rider a strong engine and a lot of 'grunt'. Your cadence can be low and you're rarely just sat spinning away, so that makes you strong. It also, of course, helps you with bike handling skills. I think that goes both ways, too. I think a good rider can jump on a mountain bike and be pleasantly surprised by their capabilities."

6. WORK ON YOUR TECHNIQUE

Aerobic fitness is often seen as the major barrier to progression in cycling, but there's a huge skill factor, too. "Descents are a problem for a lot of people," says Matteo Carrara, who was a gifted practitioner of tearing downhill throughout his professional career.

"If you don't have the mountains to practise on I'd recommend racing criteriums to improve your technique. You'll build the confidence to take corners faster and faster, and you will learn where to brake and where not to brake. If you learn the corner, you learn the downhill."

7. EXPAND YOUR AMBITION

By his own admission Andrew Burpitt's cycling could at best be described as haphazard in early 2013. Although the then 31-year-old City banker had completed an Ironman and a few marathons, he hadn't seriously prepared for any of them. This, he decided, had to change. He signed up for La Marmotte. One of the most challenging sportives in Europe, it encompasses 5,180m of climbing, including Tour de France climbs such as the Col du Telegraphe, Col du Galibier and the legendary Alpe d'Huez. Andrew vowed to train properly, watch his diet and "chuck some money" at it.

He hired Matteo Carrara as his coach and with four months to prepare, set about reinventing his body from an initial 91kg and 280w threshold power (3.07w/kg) to 74kg and 355w threshold (4.79w/kg) on the start line. He adopted the blood type diet that Carrara had used in his career successfully, which means eating specifically for whichever one of the four blood types you are: O group should eat a high-protein diet, A should be free of red meat and closer to vegetarian, B can thrive on dairy, and AB a mix between types A and B. (The diet has been criticized by the nutrition community for the lack of evidence in supporting its claimed benefits.)

"I always thought I had the potential for cycling. I'd go for rides with friends who were decent riders and ostensibly supposed to be a much higher standard than me, and hold my own. I'd also gone for army selection years ago where I was told my lung capacity was absolutely massive. The time had come, really, to get serious because I didn't have many years left to reach my full potential.

"One of the biggest things Matteo brought to the table was my bike fitting. It was tweaked over a number of months and while it was very aggressive it was also super-comfortable. I was very efficient. If you looked at me from behind you wouldn't see any flex in my hips and as such, zero wasted energy."

In finishing 140th in the Marmotte in 6hr 30mins, Burpitt's efforts show just what is possible if you put your mind to something. But even he admits that his training regime wasn't sustainable in the long-term, having to juggle it with a young family and a stressful job. A crash while racing two days after the Marmotte put him out of action for a month and killed his momentum for even longer, but having recently got back on the bike he's targeting the world amateur championships. He's returned in a better condition than his first reinvention and intends to use his base to train smarter, fine-tuning over a longer period with less radical weight loss to make his second reinvention more evolution than revolution.

TRY THIS...

Try something you haven't done before. You might find that the sort of cycling that suits your physiology is simply something you haven't given a go yet. Our physiological limits are there to be pushed in all of us.

Andrew Burpitt explains his reinvention

Month 1 - March
- Starting point: Weight 91kg, threshold 280w
- Objective: Weight loss, bike fitting
- Rides: Alternated between power workouts and low-intensity/high-cadence longer rides
- Diet: Breakfast – 70g porridge with jam; snack – apple; lunch – salad and 70g rice; dinner – 120g chicken/fish, 70g rice/pasta, some vegetables
- Power sessions: All in zone 3 (lactate threshold) with 45rpm cadence. Typically 6x4mins with small rest in between, building up to 12x4mins by the end of the month. During this month my watts were determined by my heart rate

Month 2 - April
- Starting point: Weight 82kg, threshold 315w
- Objective: Continue diet, build on power and recovery
- Rides: Alternated between longer power sessions and recovery rides
- Power sessions: All now watt-based. I started the month doing a typical time ladder session: 4, 5, 6, 5, 4mins power at 290w and ended it at 310w. During these sets my HR would move into zone 4. Recovery rides would consist of sessions in zone 2-3 with average cadence of 90-95rpm, making sure there were no hard efforts

Month 3 - May
- Starting point: Weight 79kg, threshold 330w
- Objective: Build on threshold, and concentrating on maintaining power for longer
- Rides: Started to incorporate a criterium on a Tuesday night, which worked as a high-intensity session
- Power sessions: Typical sessions started as 2x10mins at 300w, moving up to 3x15mins @ 310w. Also began to incorporate watt ladders: 3mins @ 300w, 2mins @ 340w, 3mins @ 300w, 2mins @ 350w, 3mins @ 300w, 2mins @ 360w

Month 4 - June
- Starting point: Weight 76kg, threshold 345w
- Objective: Increase threshold and ability to maintain it; recce the Marmotte course
- Rides: Majority at easy, high cadence with efforts on climbs
- Power sessions: Longer, with longer intervals at higher wattage, typically 10mins @ 320w, 5mins @ 340w, 10mins @ 300w, 5mins @ 350w, 10mins @ 300w, 5mins @ 360w

MAINTENANCE

Keep your bike in tip-top condition and you will be rewarded on the road with a smooth and efficient ride. Don't be daunted by the skills needed to maintain, clean and tune a machine, just follow a few simple guidelines and your bike will soon be performing - and looking - like new. And, you'll even be able to perform those unavoidable emergency repairs on the road

CLEANING YOUR BIKE

Want a smoother-running bike in 16 easy steps?
Just follow this straightforward walkthrough guide

1 SCRUB CHAIN
The chain is the most important part of the transmission. The first step to cleaning it is to use hot water. Wearing rubber gloves will enable you to use hotter, more effective water. Add regular washing-up liquid to your bucket of water and allow it to foam up. With the chain in the biggest gear, apply the mixture vigorously using a stiff bristle scrubbing brush. You'll see a bright, shining chain emerge.

2 DEGREASE CHAIN
With the chain free from dirt, apply a biodegradable degreaser to the chain and allow it to soak into all the links. This will remove any debris and sticky residues you can't see and make for a free-running chain. Rotate the cranks backwards a few times to get the degreaser right into the links. Allow to drip-dry, or wash off with clean water.

3 WIPE CHAIN
Use a soft rag to wipe the chain completely clean – you'll be surprised what still comes off a clean-looking chain. You're trying to massage the links, moving them through as wide a range of movement as possible – this helps expose the sections of link normally hidden from view.

4 LUBRICATION
Apply lube only when the chain is clean. We prefer to lube a chain as little as possible, with as light a lube as we can get away with. Use a dripper bottle, because it's easier to apply accurately and with minimum wastage. Coat the whole chain, spinning the cranks to force the lube into the links. That's where lube is most useful, not coating the outside plates as many believe. Wipe excess lube away with a rag.

5 SCRAPE OUT REAR MECH
There's no point having a free-running chain if the jockey wheels of your rear mech are bunged up. Use an old spoke or the blade of a thin, flat-bladed screwdriver to carefully hook out any old grass and oily gunge that's trapped between the jockey wheels and the mech arm side plates.

6 SCRUB JOCKEY WHEELS
With the serious grime gone, use a little degreaser and an old toothbrush to scrub the jockey wheels (not forgetting the insides of the mech arm). It's possible to unscrew the jockey wheels from the mech arm, but it's advisable not to unless you've got a thread lock to use when reinstalling the pivot bolts. Sadly, we've seen too many rides ended by bottom jockey wheels falling out.

7 LUBE JOCKEY WHEELS
Re-lube the jockey wheels. They really only need the very lightest touch of lube, as they'll pick up enough from the chain through use. Remember these little wheels attract a lot of dirt and, with lube being sticky, it doesn't pay to make matters worse by overdoing it. Wipe the excess away with a rag. They should look dry.

8 UNCLIP CABLES
Set the rear gears into the largest rear sprocket and then, without letting the rear wheel spin, shift into the smallest rear sprocket. This will free up a bunch of inner cable and allow you to pop the outers from the slotted cable stops on the frame. With the cables now fully unclipped from the frame you can inspect, clean, re-lube and reinstall everything.

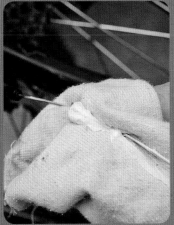

9 WIPE CABLES
Slide the outers to expose previously covered sections of inner cable. Give the entire inner cable a wipe over with a section of rag soaked in degreaser. If you come across any sections that are rusty, replace with a new inner cable. Most dry cables can be reinvigorated with a little light grease.

10 LUBE CABLES
The best way to apply grease evenly to a cable is to first apply the grease to a clean (lint-free) rag. Holding the rag in one hand with the greased section between thumb and forefinger, gently pinch the section of inner cable in the rag and draw it through. The idea is to allow the grease to get into the fine strands of the cable without creating any blobs of grease.

11 SCRUB FRONT MECH
Front mechs always suffer from neglect. They're hard to access and are often jammed full of mud and have pivots drier than a cracker biscuit. The first thing you can do to get your front mech swinging happily again is to apply steaming soapy water and give it a good clean. Use a small toothbrush to get right into the parallelogram and underneath the band.

12 WIPE THE FRONT MECH
Give the mech a good going over with the rag. Use a thin strip of rag to thread through the body of the front mech – this allows you to floss the body. Don't overlook the inside of the front mech cage, as these get pretty grubby from rubbing the chain all day. A couple of minutes and you should have a gleaming front mech.

105

13 LUBE THE FRONT MECH
Use the lube dropper bottle to apply drops of lube to all the pivots on the front mech. These take a lot of load and can use all the help you can give them to remain mobile. Shift the mech into the smallest chainring and then work the parallelogram with your fingers to get the lube worked in.

14 DE-GUNK REAR SPROCKETS
The rear sprockets are the final port of call on this bicycle maintenance mystery tour. They're full of technology to help faster shifts, but also full of grease, mud and grass. Pick the worst lumps out with an old spoke or the blade of a thin, flat screwdriver. You'll be surprised what hides in those tight spaces, even on expensive, open alloy carrier versions.

15 SCRUB REAR SPROCKETS
Get the hot, soapy water on them and get scrubbing with a brush. Really stubborn grot can be shifted with a dose of degreaser and another hit with the scrubbing brush. Getting to the backs of the sprockets can be tricky, but it's really worth persevering, as the cleaner you make it, the less easy it is for new mud to stick.

16 WIPE REAR SPROCKETS
Give the sprockets some flossing with your strip of rag. This helps dry the sprockets and also buffs away any outstanding marks. The cleaner you can keep your sprockets, the faster they'll shift and the longer they'll last. Dirt acts like a grinding paste when in contact with any part of your transmission, so get rid of it.

TOP TIPS

▶ You can get away with just cleaning the important bits, but a full wash-down should be part of your regular post-ride plans. Take the wheels off the bike and wash everything, beginning with the underside of the saddle and working downwards.

▶ Add a drop of lube to your brake lever pivots – they dry out too. Ditto the shifters. For SRAM X9/X0 gears, simply unscrew the top caps and drop a few drops on the spring and cable nipple. With Shimano, undo the plastic grub screw and put a few drops inside before replacing the grub screw.

▶ If you love your bike, show it off by taking a soft duster and some nice polish and giving the paintwork a good buffing it'll never forget. Apart from making the bike look as shiny as new, it will also make it harder for dirt to stick to the frame the next time you're out riding.

REPAIRING A PUNCTURE

Keep the air in your tyres with this guide to fixing punctures

106

TOP TIPS

Two small holes in a tube placed fairly close together indicate a pinch puncture. This is caused by the tube getting trapped between the tyre and the rim. Tyres not inflated hard enough are a frequent cause of this. Check that the tyre's sidewall is not cut.

A hole on the inner side of the tube indicates a puncture caused by a spoke head. Check inside of the rim to ensure the tape covers the spoke holes and no spoke end protrudes above the inner surface of the rim. If it does it will need filing down.

1 FINDING THE PUNCTURE
Starting at the valve, check all the way around the tread to find the cause of the puncture. Remove any glass or grit you spot. Even if you find one possible cause, continue checking the tyre until you get back to the valve. Do the same when checking the tube.

2 REMOVING THE TUBE
Let the air out and remove the valve – retaining the ring if fitted. Push the valve up into the tyre. On the side of the wheel opposite the valve, slip a tyre lever under the tyre's bead and a further tyre lever about 5cm away. Pull the nearer tyre lever towards you, lifting the tyre's bead over the edge of the rim. Continue until the one bead of the tyre is completely free of the rim. Pull the tube out. Remove the tyre completely from the rim – with most tyres this can be done by hand unless exceptionally tight.

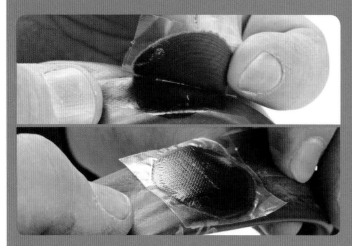

5 PATCHING THE TUBE
Apply a second thin layer similarly. Once again, allow to dry – the rubber cement will change from shiny to matt. Inflate the tube slightly – this will help to highlight the position of the hole. Firmly press the patch into place after removing the backing foil. If there's a thin cellophane backing on the patch, it can be left on. Dust the repair with chalk, talcum powder or road dust to prevent it sticking to the tyre casing.

6 CHECKING THE CASING
Before refitting the tube, double-check the tyre casing from inside for the cause of your puncture. On one occasion after riding a canal towpath with hedge clippings, I found over half a dozen thorns! Placing the tube over the tyre will help you to discover the position of the puncture. Run your fingertips carefully around the inside of the tyre to feel for the cause of the puncture and remove.

PUNCTURE REPAIR KIT ESSENTIALS

Essential items should include some patches, rubber solution, tyre levers, a piece of fine emery paper, a small, adjustable spanner if using wheels with hex nuts, an Allen key if using Allen-bolt-fitting wheels, and a reliable pump. A keyring LED is also useful if you're riding in the dark with a dynamo. For Presta valve tubes, a Schrader converter can be useful, as you can then use a car pump to inflate your tyres. And a spare tube. Pump aside, all this equipment should pack in an underseat bag.

Bands and beads

Kevlar-banded tyres will resist punctures better than those without a puncture-resistant band. But don't confuse them with Kevlar-beaded tyres, which can easily be folded.

Weekly check-up

Check your tyres for cuts in the tread, swelling in the sidewall, or serious wear. Tyres with cuts or swelling must be replaced. Remove any grit or glass embedded in the tread. Check your tyre pressures. Tyres inflated to the correct tyre pressure will have fewer punctures and a longer life. The recommended pressures are normally marked on the sidewall of the tyre.

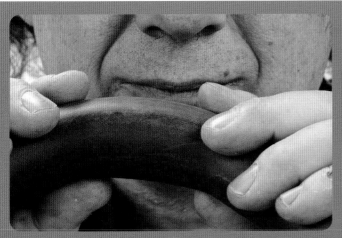

3 INFLATING THE TUBE
Inflate the tube and listen for air escaping. Passing the surface of the tube over the lips is a useful trick. If the hole still can't be found, re-inflate the tube and pass it through a bowl of water until you spot escaping bubbles. Then dry the tube before proceeding to the next step.

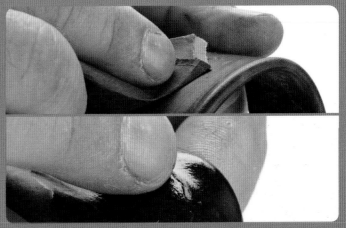

4 PREPARING THE TUBE
Select the correct size of patch – use a bigger rather than a smaller patch if in doubt. Roughen the surface of the tube around the hole with emery paper. Ensure that any moulding marks are flattened completely. Apply one drop of tyre cement and spread it thinly with your finger over a 2cm circle around the hole. Allow to dry.

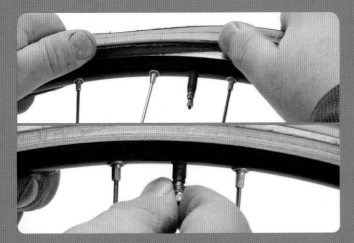

7 REFITTING THE TYRE
After repairing the tube and checking the tyre for sharp debris, refit one bead to the rim. Slightly inflate the tube and refit it to the rim, putting the valve through its hole first. Starting at the opposite side of the rim to the valve, use your thumbs to lift the tyre's bead over the rim. Work around the rim until there's just one small section of tyre left. Push the valve up into the tyre and then, using your thumbs, ease the remaining section of the tyre's bead over the edge of the rim.

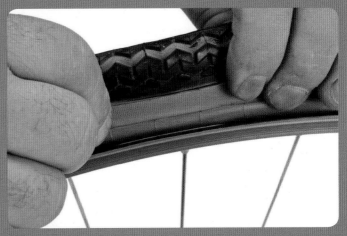

8 MAKING FINAL CHECKS
Check that the tube isn't trapped between the rim and the tyre bead. Inflate to about 1.4 Bar. Check that the moulding mark around the tyre follows the rim evenly all the way around. If not, deflate a little and ease any high spots down and pull low spots up. Inflate to the recommended pressure and check once again that the tyre's bead is still seated evenly and that the tyre isn't lifting off the rim at any point. Finally, check that the tread is running reasonably straight by spinning the wheel.

INDEX YOUR GEARS

Mechanics make it look simple, but getting your gears running sweetly can be a fiddly and frustrating job...

1. BEFORE YOU START

Gears work best when the chain and cassette are clean and not worn. Check the cables run smoothly from the shifters to the derailleurs, then clean and lubricate them. Ensure the derailleur hanger isn't bent or damaged. It's easier to adjust gears if the bike is off the ground.

2. SETTING THE LIMITS

Limit screws stop the chain from falling off the gears, and are usually found on the mechs marked as H and L. Put the bike into its highest gear (biggest ring at the front, smallest at the back), slacken the cable by loosening the cable retention bolt and screw in the barrel adjuster clockwise. Screw the 'H' stop in or out until the chain runs smoothly and the jockey wheel is lined up with the smallest sprocket.

3. INDEXING THE REAR GEARS

Tighten up the cable retention bolt and shift into the next gear. Turn the barrel adjuster anti-clockwise until the gear shifts and runs smoothly. This should automatically index all the gears, so now carefully shift into the lowest (smallest ring on the front, biggest at the back) gear to set the 'L' stop. Using the same method as before, adjust it to stop the chain falling off and align the jockey wheel and sprocket.

4. INDEXING THE FRONT MECH

Still in the lowest gear, slacken the cable and screw in the barrel adjuster. Use the 'L' stop to move the mech so it is close to but not rubbing on the chain. Tighten the cable retention bolt. In the highest gear on the back, shift onto the biggest chainring and maintain tension on the cable by keeping pressure on the lever. Adjust the 'H' screw to stop the chain falling off and avoid chain rub.

5. IF IN DOUBT...

If done incorrectly it can be expensive and dangerous for you and other road users. I would always recommend taking your bike to your local bike shop if you are not confident in doing the work yourself. Many shops offer a viewing area so you can watch the mechanics working on your bike, and they should always be happy to offer advice and tips.

INSTANT UPGRADE

Strengthening your willpower will make you happier according to a study from the University of Chicago. If you are able to say no to that slice of cake and keep up your self-control you are likely to be happier and more satisfied with your life and able to make better decisions. It'll make getting that next KOM easier too...

FIT A NEW WHEEL SPOKE
A broken spoke is always a possibility on rough
roads, so how do you get your wheel back on track?

GET HOME FIX
Firstly you are going to need to get home. A broken spoke will rarely pop out completely, so
you'll need to secure the two ends for the rest of the ride. Either twist the broken spoke around
a neighbouring spoke or, if you have some to hand, you could secure it with tape.

OUT WITH THE OLD
Once home, you'll need to remove both ends of the broken spoke. Take the tyre off the rim,
remove the inner tube, lift the rim tape and remove the spoke nipple from the eyelet. At the other
end, extract the remaining spoke from the hub – you might need to remove the cassette for a
drive-side rear wheel spoke.

IN WITH THE NEW
Pass the spoke through the hub first, then have a look at the pattern of the rest of your spokes
and match it as you thread the new one – with a 'three-cross' wheel it will need to go outside the
first two spokes and inside the last that it crosses. To reinsert the spoke nipple, screw it onto a
spare spoke, pull it into the rim eyelet, then hold it in place with a screwdriver as you remove
the spare spoke. Thread in your new spoke, and refit the tube and tyre. Adjust the tension with a
spoke key to match the others.

ADJUST YOUR BRAKES
Proper adjustment will help you stop quicker
for longer – especially handy in winter

WHY
As your brake pads wear down, which can happen at an alarming rate on wet and mucky
roads, you need to adjust your brake callipers to keep the rubber close to your rims for
effective braking.

WHEN
Keep an eye on your pads and adjust them to bring them closer to the rims when you notice the
distance increasing. Where you want them set depends somewhat on feel, but if they are over
5-6mm from the rims you really should bring them in. You don't want to pull your levers all the
way in before you start slowing down!

HOW
In the first instance, at the end of your brake cable where it attaches to the calliper is a barrel
adjuster, which can be used to tighten the inner cable. Turn it anti-clockwise to bring the pads
closer to the rim, and clockwise to move them out when you fit new pads. If you need to, you can
also release the cable clamp on the calliper with an Allen key, pull the cable through as much as
you need, then retighten into place.

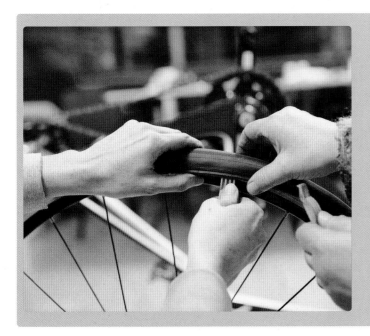

MINIMIZE YOUR RISK OF PUNCTURES
Regular blowouts could be a thing of the past...

UNDER PRESSURE
If you store your bike in a garage or shed where the temperature varies, the tyre pressure will
change and you could lose some air. Under-inflated tyres leave tubes with some slack in them
that can cause pinch punctures as they are pressed against the tyre wall. Ideally, check your tyre
pressure before every ride, or at least once a week.

CONDITIONING
Check that your tyres are in good condition. An ageing tyre will show signs of cracking,
discolouration, wearing away of the tread and thinning on the rolling surface. All of this
means that the tyre will be more fragile, making it increasingly likely to puncture.

SLIMY
If you suffer regular punctures get a tougher tyre. Specialized Roubaix Armadillo Elite, Schwalbe
Durano Plus and Continental Gatorskins are good all-weather tough tyres. Alternatively try Slime
Lite Smart tubes. These are pre-filled with a slime sealant and at around 114g they only weigh 4g
more than the average standard road tube. These will seal a hole up to 3mm in diameter with little
loss in pressure.

FIX A BROKEN CHAIN

A snapped chain doesn't need to mean a phone call or a long walk home, though it might mean dirty hands

WHAT YOU'LL NEED
A chain tool: portable ones are easy to pick up, and some multi-tools come with a chain tool. Slip one in your saddle bag and leave it there... you never know when you might need it. It's also worth carrying a spare quick link if your chain fastens with one, or a spare whole link if it doesn't.

GETTING STARTED
Fit your chain around the smallest chainring and the smallest sprocket so that it has as much slack in it as possible. Position the break at the bottom of the chain beneath the chainstay.

USING THE TOOL
If your chain tool has two sets of pegs for the chain, you will want to use the set furthest away from the punch with the chain against the back of the tool. Screw in the punch to drive out the 'male' rivet from the broken link, which should give you a chain with 'female' rivet holes at both ends. Fit the quick link by threading one rivet through each set of holes and tension the chain by stamping on the pedal with the brakes on.

IF I DON'T HAVE A QUICK LINK CHAIN?
Follow the initial steps, but don't drive the rivet all the way out. Instead, drive it until it sits just in the outer link. Now take the chain out of the tool and flex it to pull the chain apart. Now fix the other end of the chain into place over the small bit of rivet still visible on the inside of the link.

INSTANT UPGRADE

Variety is the spice of life, so make sure you mix things up when it comes to riding your bike to ensure you keep yourself motivated. Ride different routes, incorporate different sessions into your rides, and even get out and ride with different people. You'll be a better rider for it.

Now put the chain back in the tool and screw the punch to drive the rivet back into place until it projects as far from each side of the link as the others.

READY TO GO?
It's worth giving your new link a few waggles to ensure the pressure of the tool hasn't created a stiff link – otherwise yes. You might find your chain won't quite go big ring to big sprocket, but it should work otherwise. If you're on a singlespeed or hub gears, you'll need to attach that spare link rather than shorten the chain. Now just wipe your hands and get pedalling!

FIT VALVE EXTENDERS
Deep-section wheels are great, but anything with a rim over 60mm will require valve extenders...

OUT OF BODY
First of all you will need to remove the inner tube's current valve core from the body. Your extenders will come with a small tool that fits over the end of the valve, and grips it at the flattened areas. Give the valve head a twist and the valve core will then unscrew from the body.

TRANSPLANT
Take that core and screw it into the wide end of your valve extender. The narrow end of the extender will now screw into the hollow body of the tube's original valve. The extender is fitted with a small rubber washer, to help stop air escaping at the point where the two pieces join. This can wear with time, though, so...

TAPE IT
Plumbers' Teflon tape can be your friend in this situation. Wrap a couple of layers of tape around the thread on your extender before inserting it as it helps to improve the seal. Screw this into your valve body, and use the small tool again to grip the flat section on your extender and tighten it up.

QUICK FIX TIPS

Tools required
Allen keys, pedal spanner, resin mallet, fine sandpaper, WD40, grease, copper slip.

Hidden danger
Inspect under the light and accessory clamps on seatposts, handlebars and stems for cracks.

Treat your bosses
Remove bottle cage boss screws, grease generously, and reinstall; repeat process twice over winter.

PERFORM A MID-WINTER BIKE MOT

The rain and snow of the winter months can take their toll on your precious bike. So this is the ideal time to snuggle down with your steed and a few tools and ensure you avoid a mid-winter's nightmare with these seven easy steps

1 LUBE BEFORE INSERTION
Don't let the seatpost corrode: clean the seat-tube with a shot of WD40 and a cloth pushed down with a screwdriver. Grease steel and aluminium in any combination. Use copper grease for titanium with another metal. For carbon with any other material, use assembly paste. Apply twice over winter.

2 GOOD DRAINAGE
With the seatpost out, it's a good time to drain any water that might have got in the frame. Remove the wheels and tilt the bike forward, tipping any water in the stays to the bottom bracket area. Flip it upside-down, allow to drain and repeat until dry. Spray the inside of metal frames with WD40.

3 ENCORE UP FRONT
Ahead stems on metal steerers should be greased as well. On quill stems, as found on classic, retro or fixie bikes, unscrew the top bolt until it protrudes just a little. Tap with a resin mallet or block of wood to dislodge. Twist the bar free and grease as in step 1. Reassemble and tighten firmly.

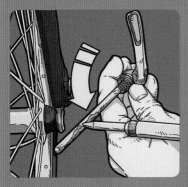

4 AXLE ATTACK
Leaving skewers in the hubs for years can lead to them becoming welded into the axle by corrosion, impairing correct clamping function. If this has happened, use another skewer to tap through with a mallet. Clean with light sandpaper, grease generously, oil the cam mechanism and reinsert.

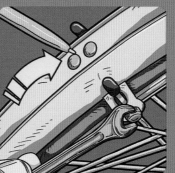

5 GUARD YOURSELF
Inspect all mudguard struts, attachment brackets, fasteners at frame eyelets and the mudguard itself, especially where it's riveted to a bracket. Check front rivets in particular. At any sign of corroded or crumbling rivets, dislodged struts, or rotted mudguard material, repair or replace immediately.

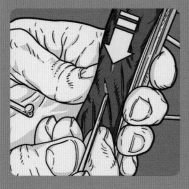

6 GET PICKY
Little bits of glass and sharp rock cling to your tyre's tread, where they will happily sit, working their way through to the inner tube with every revolution. Closely inspect the entire tread surface, picking out any bits with a scribe or sharpened spoke. Use a drop of super glue to close small cuts in the surface.

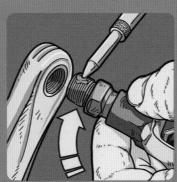

7 RIGHTY TIGHTY
Pedal threads that are welded stuck due to corrosion are a nightmare, especially when you're packing your bike for that winter training camp. Periodically remove the pedals (at least twice over winter), and clean the crank threads and pedal threads with a brush and a squirt of WD40, then grease generously.

PREPARE YOUR BIKE FOR AN EVENT

How to make sure your bike is ready for that century ride or a much-anticipated sportive...

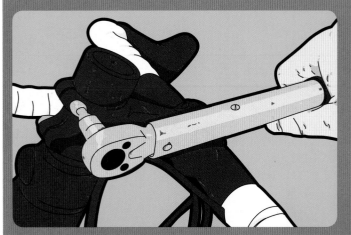

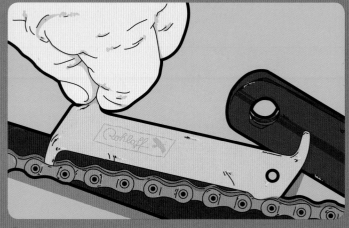

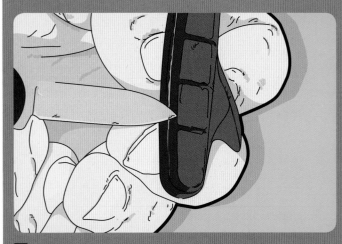

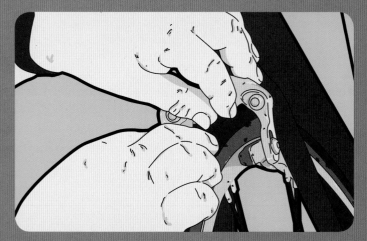

1 NUTS AND BOLTS
Use a torque wrench to check bolt tightness. Overtightening bolts could potentially cause catastrophic component failure. Check components for damage – inspect carbon steerers just above the crown; carbon handlebars either side of the clamp area; and seatposts where the clamp is bonded to the post and just above the frame. Check cranks around the pedal eye and axle end.

2 CHAIN CHECK
Check the chain for wear – a Park Chain Checker or Rohloff Caliber is easiest but a steel rule is fine. If the pin to pin distance over 24 links is more than 308mm replace the chain; replacing it reduces the chance of having to replace the cassette (if the chain is worn the cassette will probably need replacing). Clean the chain using a chain cleaner and use a quality lube on the inside of the chain links.

5 BRAKES
Check brake blocks for wear – if they have lost more than a quarter of their depth, replace them. Check the blocks are mounted firmly and that they do not rub the tyre. Remove any embedded grit. Check that the nuts fixing the brake to the frame are tight and that the brakes are centred. Check brake cables for fraying – if frayed, replace the inner cable.

6 WHEELS
Check rim wear indicators. If there are no indicators look out for a concave braking surface or measure rim wall width – replacing any rim below 1mm thick. Check for loose spokes and uneven tension, remembering that drive-side spokes will be tighter. Tighten brakes so that the blocks almost touch the rim – the rim should be true sideways to within 2mm with no dips or high spots.

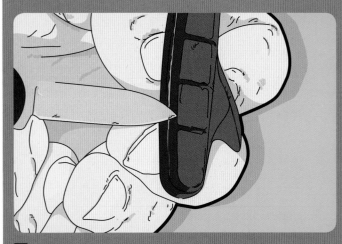

CLEAN THEN LUBE

Making sure your chain is properly lubricated is an essential part of any pre-sportive bike check, but you should never apply fresh chain lube to a dirty chain. We recommend using a chain cleaning machine with biodegradable chain cleaner to remove old layers of chain lube before any race or sportive. This allows the fresh chain lube to work more effectively for maximum performance!

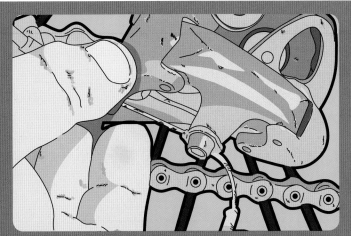

3 CABLES
Check inner cables for signs of fraying at the shifters, stops and derailleurs. Check outers for cracking or sharp kinks. Replace kinked outer cables – the section to the rear mech is particularly vulnerable. If the inner cable is just frayed at the derailleur end, trim and fit a new cable end. If the cables are more than about two years old they should be replaced in their entirety.

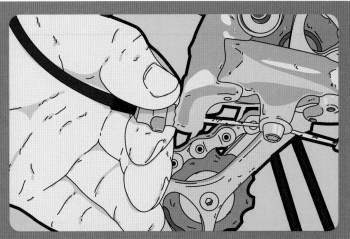

4 GEARS
Adjust gear indexing to avoid mis-shifts and a noisy drivechain. Fine tune your shifting by turning the derailleur's barrel adjuster. Shift through the cassette – if shifting to easier gears isn't smooth wind the barrel out. Wind the barrel in to make dropping into harder gears easier. Use quarter turns until perfect. Up front, ensure the stop screws prevent overshifting that will drop the chain.

7 TYRES
Inspect for splits, cuts or cracks, removing embedded flints or glass. Replace a split or severely worn tyre. Check that clinchers are at the correct pressure. With tubeless tyres, regularly check that the valve core is snug and check pressure. Inflate tubulars to their normal pressure and check that they are still stuck to the rim – it should be impossible to push them off the rim when inflated.

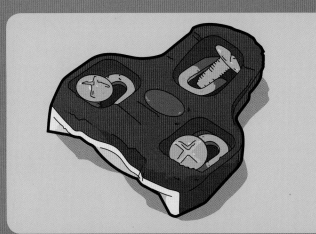

8 PEDALS
Regularly check pedals for wear at the front and rear ridges. With Look pedals the 'wear holes' should be clear to see; if not, replace the cleats. Metal cleats are harder to check and should be examined extra carefully. Every few months unscrew the pedals and check the spindles have a smooth feel. Refit using anti-seize grease and firmly tighten – though don't overtighten – to about 30mm.

ACHES, PAINS AND RECOVERY

Bending forward, arms braced and legs spinning for hours on end might make for a thrilling ride, but your body won't always enjoy it - especially when you eventually dismount. Here's how to prevent those nagging pains, deal with the aches that inevitably arise and use your recovery time to make sure you are fit and ready to ride next time

CYCLE SURGERY

After a season in the saddle even the pros will have a few aches and pains. Here's our head-to-toe breakdown of how to cure the bane of many a cyclist

SORE NECK

Problem

Apart from aggressive 4x4 drivers, the next biggest pain in the neck for cyclists is... well, neck pain. Over long distances the neck can become sore as you try to keep your body in an aerodynamic position while still scanning the road ahead. With your hands on the drops the top of your spine becomes almost horizontal, so bending the neck to look ahead is quite an unnatural position. Much like looking at the top of a skyscraper from the street for a prolonged period, it will ache sooner or later.

Cause

Although spending a lot of time on the drops can be a little uncomfortable, the neck should be able to cope. Poor bike set-up can make this problem worse than it needs to be, according to sports physio Ian Brocklesby. "If your bar is too low or wide, or your top-tube is too long, you'll put your back and neck under strain," says Ian.

Solution

"The best way to avoid neck pain is to ensure that your bike is set up properly," says Ian. "Get a professional bike fit to be certain you're set up right. But if pain persists consult a doctor in case it's a sign of something else, such as degeneration or arthritis. There are other preventative and soothing techniques. You can ease pain by applying warmth to the neck with hot packs or a hot water bottle, or massage the trapezius and muscles at the side of the neck. Massage helps relieve trigger points, the areas of occasionally severe tenderness, as well as removing by-products of chemical build-up resulting from exercise."

HANDS

Problem

On long rides, many cyclists can suffer from a tingling sensation in the hands. This condition commonly affects the little and ring fingers, but can affect the whole hand.

Cause

This problem can arise when you've kept your hands in the same position for extended periods of time. It's not just caused by the pressure from your weight, but also the transmission of road buzz and vibration through the bars.

Solution

Address your riding position to take pressure off your hands. Often the solution is to shorten your reach so more of your weight will be borne by the saddle. The problem can be lessened by wearing gloves with gel padding, and there are many good padded bar tapes.

LOWER BACK

Problem

Watching cyclists bent double for hours during a ride, it's little wonder that the lower back represents a common cause of discomfort.

Cause

Again, focus on your bike set-up. Put your heel on the pedal at the six o'clock position and sit on the saddle. Your leg should be almost straight. Pelvic position is paramount. Tight quads tilt the pelvis forward, while tight hamstrings tilt it back. In both cases, your lower back takes the strain when the burden should be borne by the bigger muscles in your core.

Solution

Pushing bigger gears can fatigue the glutes and hamstrings, and can lead to some sharp pain. You need to strengthen your core away from the bike, and focus on stretching to maintain pelvic position even when you're dog-tired. Ignore the gluteus medius at your peril. Try the Leg Squat on page 76.

HIPS

Problem

Despite not producing much power themselves, the hips are the catalysts allowing the legs beneath them to propel you in piston-like fashion into the hills. One of the most important muscles keeping the hips working the way that they're supposed to is the psoas. This undervalued component of your hip flexors tightens when you're on the bike or in other bent-over positions.

Cause

People in sedentary desk jobs often find this tightening tilts their pelvis, causing their back to arch so they can't tense their glutes – the most important muscles in any cyclist's armoury. Get your psoas in good condition and your cycling should reap immediate benefits. A weak, tight psoas can mean that you'll end up with knee issues, because other secondary hip flexors take over and cause pain.

Solution

Kneeling on your right knee with your left leg in front of you, knee at 90 degrees and foot flat on the floor, tilt your pelvis forwards and upwards until you feel the stretch. Hold for 5–10 seconds, rest and repeat 10 times on each side. If you're at a loose end at work, stand up and tuck one leg back on your chair so your back knee is at 90 degrees and the other is below your hip. Tilt your pelvis forwards and upwards. At least 90 per cent of cyclists don't stretch their psoas, which means they rely too much on their hamstrings, so they fatigue quickly.

" At least 90 per cent of cyclists don't stretch their psoas, which means they rely too much on their hamstrings, so they fatigue quickly. "

KNEES

Problem

Many cyclists are troubled with knee pain at one point. Every turn of the pedals flexes and extends the knee joint, and in just one 80-mile ride that can amount to more than 25,000 repetitive movements.

Cause

Knee problems rarely stem from the knees themselves. The problems usually stem from above – the glutes, quads, or hamstrings, or from below – the feet.

Solution

Try using lower gears and a higher cadence, which will still keep your fitness levels up without piling on the pressure. If the pain subsides, then gently start upping the levels again, but remember not to increase your training by more than 10–15% per week.

FEET

Problem

Feet are a common worry; some people suffer from an ache across the arch of their foot or a burning sensation in the ball, while others may lose feeling altogether.

Cause

95% of the time the issue comes from either shoes or pedals. Your comfortable casual shoe size will usually coincide with your best cycling shoe size, but as a rule of thumb you should leave approximately 1–2cm between your foremost toe and the end of the shoe.

Solution

When trying on shoes it's better to go later in the day, when your feet are slightly more swollen and bigger. There are lots of different closure systems available nowadays. Ideally, the uppermost of the straps should be ratchet-closed to allow micro-adjustment of tension.

STRETCHING TRUTH

When to stretch
After a ride – or as a standalone session after warming up – use static stretching to help restore muscles to their resting length, or as a way to lengthen shortened muscles.

How long?
To allow time for the stretch response to take place, which occurs once the muscle relaxes and stops trying to protect itself, aim for at least 20 seconds.

How many?
The American College of Sports Medicine advises two to four times for each stretch.

How often?
ACSM advises flexibility training two or three times per week.

STRETCHING YOURSELF

The human body isn't designed to be hunched over a bike for hours, so how do you keep yourself supple and stretchy?

Cyclists may be renowned for their supreme cardiovascular fitness, phenomenal power output and colossal thighs – but when it comes to flexibility, most of us are decidedly lacking. This isn't surprising when you pause to consider what riding a bike entails.

Performing a repetitive action through a limited range of motion means that the legs are neither fully extended nor fully flexed. Joints are never taken through their full range of motion. To compound the problem, cycling is one of the few activities in which muscles contract only concentrically (while shortening) and not eccentrically (while lengthening) so over time this can result in 'adaptive shortening', the process by which muscle fibres physically shorten.

HOT TOPIC

But does it matter? It depends who you ask. Scientists still hotly debate the topic of whether stretching is beneficial for athletes, detrimental, or makes no difference either way. Riding a bike is not something that we evolved to do. It's not a natural movement like running or walking, and is therefore more likely to cause muscular imbalances and postural changes.

As an example, the forward-leaning, crouched position adopted by roadies and track cyclists tends to make the hip flexors tighten and shorten, causing an anterior pelvic tilt (a source of lower back pain and more

" Riding a bike is not something we evolved to do like running, so is more likely to cause muscular imbalances."

importantly, a protruding belly!) and an excessively arched lower back. If muscles get tight, they pull on bones and put things out of alignment, increasing the risk of pain, discomfort and injury.

But poor flexibility, and its consequences, don't just give you bad posture and hike up your injury risk – your cycling performance is at stake, too. You need a good range of motion in the hips and lower back to achieve an aerodynamic time trial position. Without it, your power output will be reduced because you won't be able to get maximal force from the gluteal muscles. Also, if you have a stiff lower back, you'll typically overreach with the arms, putting too much weight on the hands and causing tightness across the upper back and neck.

REVERSE THE POSTURE

While you may not need to be able to wrap your feet around your shoulders or bend over backwards to ride your bike, you do need to maintain – or, more likely, regain – a 'normal' range of motion in the joints to ride comfortably and efficiently, and to be able to adapt your riding position where necessary. You also need to consider the joints and muscles that cycling doesn't use, otherwise flexibility will diminish.

The areas that are tight in cyclists are pretty universal; stiff quads, hip flexors, hamstrings and lower backs and tight, 'closed' shoulders and chest muscles are top of the list.

To redress the balance we need to reverse the cycle posture. For example, stretches that extend the lower back are a great antidote to the flexed, forward-leaning position on the bike. Yoga has been suggested as a favourable complement as it is a way of elongating the muscles, but also it enhances your body awareness, so you notice what feels tight or stiff – and know what to do to alleviate it.

CALF STRETCH INTO A WALL

Stand facing a wall with toes pointing forward. Place your hands flat against the wall at shoulder height. Bring one leg behind you then place the foot flat on the floor (making sure your toes are still pointed straight forward). Slowly lean forward over your front leg, but keep your back knee straight and your heel flat on the floor. You should feel this stretch in the big muscle of your calf (gastrocnemius). You can deepen it by bending your front knee.

CAMEL POSE

This yoga pose opens the groin, thighs and back, and stretches the chest, the shoulders and neck. Sit in a kneeling position with your feet against a wall. Slowly bring the thighs and torso upright. Inhale and gradually move your back into an arc on the exhale until the back of your head makes contact with the wall behind. If you can't reach your heels, place a pile of thick books on either side of your shins and reach those. Take at least five breaths.

EXPANDED LEG POSE

Begin with your feet wide apart (the wider, the easier it will be). Placing your hands on your hips, inhale deeply and then bend forward on the exhale, bringing the torso only as far down as you can while maintaining a long spine. If your hamstrings are really tight, the knees can be bent, releasing back tension. Place your hands on a pile of books in front of you. Work towards eventually placing your hands in between your feet.

QUAD STRETCH

Start on all fours with the soles of your feet against a wall. Take your right foot off the floor and place it against the wall with your toes pointing up the wall. Slide your knee down towards the floor, making sure that the shin and knee are in contact with the wall at all times. Put your left foot flat on the floor in front of you. Take at least five breaths, then gradually take your hands off the floor and on an inhale, place your hands lightly on your left knee.

DOWNWARD FACING DOG

This relaxes the entire spinal column, opens the hips and stretches the back of the legs. Begin on all fours with your hands in front of the shoulders and toes tucked forwards. Breathe out, lift your knees from the floor, straighten your legs and raise your bottom, working to press your heels to the floor. Push through the shoulders so the bottom is pushed back and the stretch can be felt through the back and hamstrings. Hold the position.

SEATED GLUTE STRETCH AND HIP OPENER

Sit on a chair, with the sole of the right foot on the floor in line with the right knee. Place your left ankle on and just beyond the right knee. Keeping the spine as long as possible, inhale then fold at the hips on the exhale, bringing your torso over your left shin. Take at least five breaths. As you relax into the stretch you may eventually be able to place both forearms on the legs.

REVOLVED BELLY POSE

This stretch releases tension in the spinal column, hips and shoulders and relieves discomfort in the lumbar spine. Lie on your back with your knees bent, bring them into your chest. Inhale and, with the next exhalation, roll your knees to the right side and rest them on a pillow. Stretch both arms out on the floor to open the space between the shoulder blades then slowly straighten the legs. Aim to touch your hand with your toes.

SUPPORTED BOUND ANGLE POSE

This stretch releases tension in the diaphragm, chest and shoulders, the groin and hips. It can be held for as long as you like. Sit on the floor directly in front of the end of a bolster (or a few folded blankets), and bring the soles of your feet together so that your legs form a diamond shape. Reclining on your elbows, lie back onto the bolster and stay like that for 5-10 minutes. Breathe deeply and relax.

CORE STRENGTH

'Develop those core muscles' is a common gym mantra. But for cyclists it is 100% crucial

You're out for a long ride and an hour or so in you're feeling super strong. But, as time goes on, a niggling tightness starts to develop in your lower back. Tightness changes to pain and soon you're wiggling in the saddle, performing odd pelvic thrusts at your headset and even stopping intermittently to stretch. Does this sound familiar? Assuming you've had your bike set-up checked, the problem lies within you and your core.

Any core conditioning needs to be relevant to your chosen activity. When you cycle your legs are the pistons that drive you and will get steadily stronger the more you ride. However,

as you power along your butt, lower back and abdominal musculature are also working hard, especially as you climb. The position you're holding puts additional strain on your core. Even if you're riding on the tops you'll be rounding your spine to some degree and putting strain through your back. Go down on the drops or onto aerobars and the strain increases. So, although core strength is an issue, core flexibility is equally important. To compound things, when you're cycling in a fixed position, your core can become lazy.

Here's how you can banish back pain from your riding using a simple sequence of exercises...

PELVIC TILTS

Lying on the floor with knees bent, push your lower back into the floor. This should have the effect of flattening and engaging your abdominal muscles. Tilt the pelvis forward, allowing a small hollow to develop between the floor and your lower back. Try to keep the movement small, controlled and limited to the bottom section of your back. Hold the forward tilt for a few seconds and then return to the start position by rocking the pelvis back and pushing your lower back into the floor. Once you're comfortable with this movement you can perform tilts while on the bike – this is a great way to help back tension on long rides. Perform 10 reps in a slow and controlled manner.

ROLL-UPS

From the same start position as the pelvic tilts push the lower back into the floor. Carry the movement on by slowly pushing your hips towards the ceiling and, in doing so, peeling your spine away from the floor. Hold in the 'up' position for a count of five. As you lower, do so in a controlled manner, imagining placing each vertebra down individually and lengthening the spine. Perform 10 reps in a slow and controlled manner.

CAT

On all fours, engage your abdominals obtaining that 'flattened' feeling. Arch your back up towards the ceiling trying to imagine a rope attached to your belly button pulling you up. Hold the arched position for a count of two. Bow down by hollowing your back, imagining the rope is now pulling you down. Hold the bowed position for a count of two and return to the start position. Perform 10 reps in a slow and controlled manner.

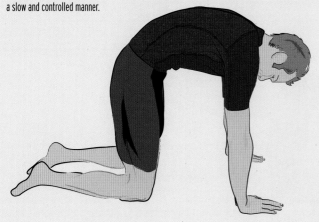

CRUNCHES

Lying on your back with your knees bent and feet on the floor, lightly support your head with your fingertips. Push your lower back into the floor and try to maintain that feeling throughout the movement. Crunch up by lifting the shoulders off the floor. Keep head up and neck relaxed, try to imagine an apple under your chin. Do not come up any higher than 30 degrees and keep tension in your abdominals. Come up to a count of three, hold for a count of two at the top and then lower, keeping control for a second count of three. Perform 10-15 reps in a slow and controlled manner.

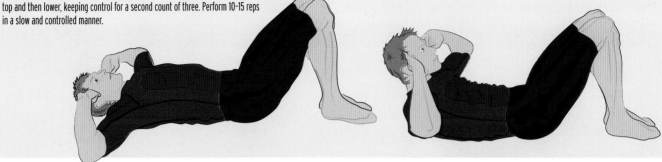

BACK EXTENSIONS

Lying face down, look up and hold your fingertips against your temples. Slowly arch up, lifting your chest and upper abdomen off the floor. Pause in the 'up' position before returning slowly to the start position to work your back. Perform 10-15 reps in a slow and controlled manner.

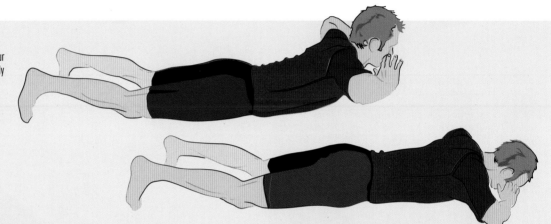

PLANK

Adopt a press-up position but, rather than supporting your weight on your hands, rest on your forearms and elbows. Engage your abdominals and try to hold a position where there is a straight line from the top of your head to your heels. Avoid sagging in the middle or 'jack-knifing' your bum upwards. Maintain strict form and hold the static position. Hold for 30-60 seconds.

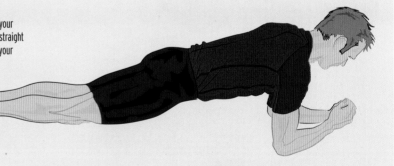

SUPERMAN

Start on all fours and concentrate on keeping your abdominals engaged and your back flat. Once you're stable and happy with your position lift your right hand up and forward and extend your left leg up and behind you. Pause in the 'up' position, return slowly to the starting position and repeat, using the opposite arm and leg. Alternate for 20 reps in a slow and controlled manner.

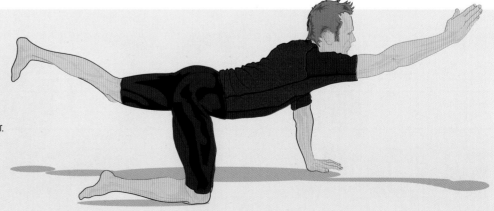

SIDE PLANK

Lying on your side, stack your feet on top of each other and support your weight on the forearm and elbow of one arm. As with the regular plank, you're aiming for a straight line from shoulder to foot. Avoid rotating towards the ground by extending your other arm up towards the ceiling. Hold for 15-30 seconds on each side.

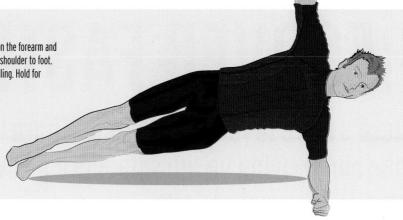

CHILD POSE

A very relaxing pose, a great stretch for flexion of the lower back. Kneel down and sit back on your heels. Keeping your backside in contact with your heels, curl forwards bringing your forehead onto the floor. If you struggle to keep your bum down place a cushion between it and your heels. Relax into the pose, breathing deeply. Either stretch your arms out in front of you or simply allow to rest by your side. Hold for 30-60 seconds.

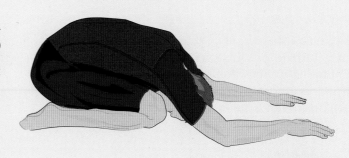

LOW COBRA POSE

Another yoga pose, like child pose, this time working on lower back extension. Start in the same way as a back extension but place your elbows and forearms on the floor to support your torso. Imagine yourself as the Sphinx. Once again, breathe deeply and relax into the stretch. Hold for 30-60 seconds.

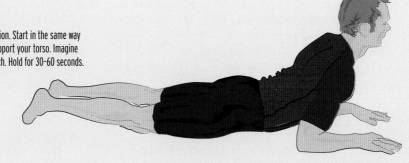

CORE ISSUES

Through the winter try to do this routine on most days, but in the spring and summer you can drop down to two or three times per week. It'll only take 10-15 minutes and, in most cases, will sort out any pesky back issues on the bike. If you really can't find time for the whole routine then prioritiZe the pelvic tilts, cat, plank, child pose and low cobra pose. If you're really serious about sorting out core strength issues you could also enrol in a yoga or pilates course. Another option is to get out on your mountain bike. Off-road riding is a superb conditioner for all cycling-related fitness including core strength. Having to balance and adapt to rough trails will make you a better and stronger rider.

Simple exercises to do at home

If you've got these core exercises nailed and feel like enlarging your repertoire a bit, then there are plenty of resistance routines you can do to increase your strength on the bike.

Using a Swiss ball and dumbbells, there are lots of workouts you can try, all of which will improve your metabolism, increase your bone density, muscle mass and overall fitness. Some cyclists avoid resistance training believing extra muscle bulk will make them heavier and therefore slower on climbs but, unless you embark on an Arnie-style body-building regime, you'll only improve your strength, making you faster.

If you've got the space then working out at home is a great option. You don't have to venture out on cold evenings and there's no gym membership fee to pay. However, to push yourself on beyond the basics you will need to invest in some equipment.

Resistance training equipment essentials

▶ **Swiss ball:** You can get a Swiss ball – also called an exercise ball, stability ball and gym ball – from most sports shops. Follow the manufacturer's instructions to get the right size for your height.

RECOVER FASTER

There's more to recovering from a hard training session than simply lying on the sofa. Here's how to make the most of your rest periods

Let's be honest. Many of us regard anything other than actually turning the pedals as a waste of time, as far as improving cycling fitness is concerned. But proper rest and recovery are just as much a part of the process of getting stronger, faster and fitter as riding. "The importance of rest should never be underestimated," says Tour de France winner Sir Bradley Wiggins. It's during rest that your body gets stronger.

This is well documented by research – studies have shown that not allowing enough recovery time can lead to incomplete glycogen replenishment, increased levels of cortisol (a stress hormone) and decreased levels of human growth hormone (HGH) – factors that combine to make your performance suffer and leave you feeling sluggish and weak.

TAKE A BREAK

Rather than riding hard continually until you feel knackered then having to take a few days off, it's best to have planned rest days, like the pros. Work, social and other life commitments might dictate when you can't train, so make those your rest days and build your training programme around that.

But how much rest do you need? This is very individual and it depends on all kinds of things – from what other demands you have on your time and how fit you are, to your age and your goals. Since his return to pro cycling in 2003 at the age of 42, Malcolm Elliott has said that he sometimes needs two consecutive rest days to be able to perform at his peak. There are no set rules about how much rest you should take, but there are general principles, such as following hard training days with easy days or rest, and adopting a three weeks hard, one week easy approach to training. If you structure your training with built-in periods of rest and recovery, you'll have to take fewer ones due to illness, fatigue or injury.

But before you dive onto the sofa, bear in mind that recovery doesn't just involve doing nothing. While rest is essential to your recovery strategy, it isn't the only factor. In fact, a study from the University of Victoria in Canada found three different 'active' recovery practices (low-intensity exercise, massage and ice) helped recovery between bouts of high-intensity cycling more than passive rest.

Equally, rest doesn't always mean, er, rest. While Wiggins takes one full day of rest per week, for example, he also incorporates 'recovery rides' into his schedule - a 'rest day' could mean a two-hour easy ride on flat roads. However, proceed with caution; an easy session can so easily become a competitive ride against friends or the clock. Push yourself too hard and you've wasted your rest day. Let's take a closer look at some of the other strategies worth using to get you back in the saddle feeling fit and fresh...

RAID THE FRIDGE

"As far as nutrition is concerned, the two most important issues for recovery are timing and quality," says Karen Reid, registered sports and exercise nutritionist, dietician and creator of the website performancefood.co.uk. Wiggins agrees. "Hydration and nutrition during a hard ride are essential to keep going, but it's what I take onboard afterwards that allows my muscles to adapt and grow stronger," he says. "Fast recovery after every session is crucial, so I have to make sure I'm ready and raring to go for the next one, which is often on the same day. I use recovery shakes, which are ready-mixed and contain the perfect balance of carbs and protein."

Reid breaks the recovery process down into three phases: rehydration, replenishment and repair. "In dietary terms, that means you need fluid and electrolytes, the right amount of easily absorbed carbohydrate and a good quality source of protein," she explains. "You have to get these steps in the right order, because if the cells are dehydrated, you can't transport nutrients to them – nor can you synthesize glycogen, as each gram is stored with 4g of water. Proper rehydration has to come first."

But what's the best option? Well, a sports drink will provide fluid, electrolytes and some carbohydrate, so it's a good all-rounder. But if you've been guzzling sports drink on the bike all day, you may find that the last thing you want is something else sugary, in which case, water, along with a salty snack, is a good alternative. "There isn't sufficient salt in the commercial sports drinks, so I get my athletes to eat something like pretzels or Snack a Jacks," says Karen Reid. "This stimulates thirst, as well as replacing electrolytes."

Step two is replenishment, primarily of depleted glycogen (carbohydrate) stores. "A sandwich with a savoury filling, or a milkshake along with a piece of fruit, helps to provide carbohydrate calories and some antioxidants to help deal with the oxidative stress placed on the body." Aim to consume 1g of carbohydrate per kg of body weight, along with 10–20g of protein – and do it as soon as possible.

While the window of opportunity that exists in the 20–30 minutes after training is the optimal time to refuel, Reid says there isn't so much urgency if you aren't going to be doing another session that day or the following morning – though you should still eat within a couple of hours of finishing training.

Repair is the final stage of the nutrition strategy. This refers both to the immune system and muscle tissue. "It's very common to do a tough session and then come down with a nasty bug a couple of days after, as the immune system is suppressed," says Reid.

Research shows that taking protein along with your carbohydrates post-exercise can help attenuate this, as well as stimulating muscle repair. "I find that oily fish is really good for damping down inflammation and muscle soreness," says Reid.

Your armoury against infection should also include plenty of fresh fruit and vegetables. "There's much more supportive evidence for food-derived compounds than for vitamin and mineral supplements, in terms of maintaining good health."

As important as nutrition is to recovery, then, it doesn't necessarily mean having a cupboard full of expensive recovery products. "The ultimate goal is to ensure that you go to bed with everything in equilibrium, because this is when the body repairs itself."

HAVE A RUBDOWN

The jury is still out on how – as well as if – massage really works. It's a difficult subject to study objectively because the effects can be both physical and mental, and who's to say that one is less important than the other? A study from Canada, for example, assessed the effects of massage on markers of physiological damage and found no benefit – but the massage was still perceived as 'beneficial' by the participants who took part in the study.

If you're getting a massage and stretching as well as using compression tights, for example, you know you're preparing well for your event, and that's a psychological boost. If you schedule it in regularly, the other advantage is that the therapist will be able to spot the early warning signs of impending injury, such as areas of tension or adhesions – and then work to help you avert the problem.

A post-event massage is the best time for a rubdown, but avoid anything too vigorous in the hours following a very tough race or training session, when muscle damage is still occurring. It's best to wait two or three days, when you can benefit from a deeper, more remedial treatment. And if you don't have a therapist or a willing volunteer, you can always massage your legs yourself – working towards the heart.

WEAR TIGHTS

While runners and triathletes have embraced compression garments with enthusiasm, it's less common to see cyclists donning them. Studies, including one published in the *Journal of Sports Science and Medicine*, have shown that they can help accelerate recovery by allowing faster cell repair. But not all compression clothing ranges are created equal. According to research in the *Canadian Journal of Sport Science*, the pressure exerted by a compression garment must be graduated or graded, in order to mimic the haemodynamic (blood flow) effect of exercise and to increase venous return. In other words, the compression should be greatest at the bottom and exert less pressure further up.

GET A GOOD NIGHT'S SLEEP

It stands to reason that you need to get your zzzzs in if you're going to perform at your optimum. Do athletes need more sleep? According to a study from Wheaton College in the US, they do. The researchers found that sleep deprivation amounting to 30–36 hours could reduce cardiovascular performance by an alarming 11 per cent.

Thirty-plus hours might sound like a lot of deprivation, but if you consistently get six hours per night when you should sleep for eight, you'll accumulate a deficit of this amount in little over a fortnight. As well as compromising the immune system, which could force you to lose valuable training time through illness, insufficient sleep means reduced levels of anabolic (muscle-building) hormones, impaired concentration and even mood shifts.

If you can't get the requisite eight hours or so at night, try to fit in a daytime nap. Ideally, right after a hard training session. It will aid recovery as well as give you more energy for the remainder of the day.

Incorporate some or all of these recovery strategies into your personal programme, and not only will you stop falling asleep at dinner parties and coming down with colds, you'll also be powering up those hills with ease... We wish you a speedy recovery next time you take a well-deserved break.

" A recovery ride can so easily become a competitive ride against friends or the clock."

SMALL MUSCLES BUT BIG RESULTS

These often overlooked muscles are key to keeping you injury-free and achieving your body's full fitness potential. Here's how to make them work for you...

While watching your big guns blaze might be what propels most people gym-wards, spare a thought for the little guys of the muscle world. They're the ones that really hold the secret to your cycling success – without these smaller supporting muscles, the likes of your quads, glutes and core can't perform anywhere near their peak, and you might even be heading for debilitating injury.

Working the muscles deep inside your core, hips and shoulders can increase overall strength gains by up to a third, prevent injury and directly improve performance in the saddle. These five hard-to-pronounce muscles might never earn top billing, but focus on them for one month to rejuvenate your ride and ignite new growth.

VASTUS MEDIALIS OBLIQUE (VMO)

WHERE IT IS
It's the bulge you see on the inside of time triallists' thighs, just above the knee.

WHAT IT DOES
The VMO stabilizes your knee and provides extra sprinting power. Regular cycling and most gym exercises over-develop the outer quad muscles, pulling the kneecap laterally and leading to patellar tracking disorder, or what's known as 'runner's knee'. It occurs when the muscles on the outside of the leg are much bigger than those on the inside, so pull the kneecap across, making it rub against other tissue. University of Sheffield scientists found that working your VMOs increases short burst acceleration by up to 20 per cent.

HOW TO WORK IT
Do stability ball VMO squats. Place the ball in the small of your back, against a wall. Next, put a football between your thighs, just above the knees. Perform a slow squat, getting lower until the tops of your thighs are parallel with the floor. Pause and return. Do three sets of 15–20 repetitions. This works the quads, hamstrings, core and glutes for improved overall strength and stability. Alternatively, do leg extensions with your toes pointed outwards, which targets the VMOs.

"Working the muscles deep inside your core, hips and shoulders can increase overall strength gains by up to a third, prevent injury and directly improve performance in the saddle."

TRANSVERSUS ABDOMINIS (TVA)

Where it is
This band of muscle runs from your side to the front of your abdomen. It's set behind the six-pack.

What it does
The TVA corsets your stomach. It's your single biggest core muscle; the ab muscle you need for a washboard stomach. But the benefits extend beyond the aesthetic. Sports scientists at the University of Scranton in America found that working your TVA reduces lower-back injury rates by almost 20 per cent, and can increase cycling efficiency by stabilizing the pelvis by up to 10 per cent.

How to work it
In a press-up position, rest on your elbows, with your back flat, and pull your belly button towards your spine. Hold for 20 seconds, then lift your left leg and right hand and maintain for a further 20 seconds. Repeat with the opposite arm and leg. Do three sets with minimal rest times between them.

INFRASPINATUS

Where it is
The infraspinatus is the most important member of the rotator cuff group of muscles, attaching the shoulder blade to the upper arm.

What it does
Thank this crunch cameo player for creating support around your body's most unstable joint, something you'll be grateful for when, not if, you crash or need to transfer power in climbs. The shoulder has the greatest range of movement of any joint yet is held together by this tiny rotator cuff muscle. Researchers at Loughborough University found that cyclists who added a simple five-minute rotator cuff element to their workout three times a week for a fortnight reduced their chances of dislocation – the most common upper body trauma in cyclists – by over a third. Strengthening your shoulders also provides stability and posture, taking strain off the neck over uneven ground.

How to work it
Do horizontal cable pulls. Stand side-on to a cable machine with a 2.5–5kg weight attached. Hold the handle at waist height with your closer hand. Keeping your body perfectly still, extend your arm horizontally away from the weight stack as far as possible in a controlled movement. Pause and return slowly. Do 10 reps, then turn around so your other arm is closest to the stack and repeat the exercise. You're focusing on the internal and external rotation of the internal unit, which requires a small load. Anything heavier and you'll risk injury. That will just leave you wincing while you squeeze your top on in the changing room.

PSOAS

Where it is

Connecting your hips, lower back and tops of thighs.

What it does

This undervalued component of your hip flexors tightens when you're on the bike. 90 per cent of cyclists don't stretch their psoas, which means they rely too much on their hamstrings, so they fatigue quickly. Lie on your back and pull one knee to your chest. Keep your other leg straight. If the psoas is a normal length, the straight leg will rest on the floor. If the straight leg sits above the floor, your psoas is stiff or shortened.

How to work it

Kneeling on your right knee with your left leg in front of you, knee at 90 degrees and foot flat on the floor, tilt your pelvis forwards and upwards until you feel the stretch. Hold this position for 5–10 seconds, rest and repeat 10 times on each side.

GLUTEUS MEDIUS (GM)

Where it is

On the upper and outer side of your bum, just below your hips.

What it does

The GM stabilizes your thigh bone to ensure there is minimal rotation. It keeps all your force moving in one plane so the cycling movement becomes more efficient and you avoid long-term hip injury. When it starts working it switches off over-active, fatigued muscles such as the hip flexors. This controls the lateral movement of your hips, and when you're putting force on the pedals, they're pushing back. If there's any lateral movement you'll lose the reverse-T shape between your spine and pelvis, decrease power and increase risk of lower back injury. The muscles in your back will go into spasm to protect that T position, but they'll soon give up if they are overworked. The iliotibial bands will work too hard. Instead of pushing into the pedals they'll tighten and have to stabilize your leg to prevent knee injury, which in the long run can actually cause knee injury.

How to work it

Mini band walks. Loop a piece of elastic around your ankles, then do small side steps for 15 metres in both directions. Repeat three times. Make sure all movement is generated at the hips and glide rather than see-saw. Alternatively, lie on your side doing leg raises, using the band. Do three sets of 10 every other day, focusing on keeping control and a stable position.

JOINT PAIN

Pain from over-use can develop in various areas of the knee. We look at specific conditions and offer tips to treat them

Cycling over-use injuries that lead to knee pain stem from three broad categories: changes in the intensity of your training (cycling-specific causes); changes in your equipment (bike-specific causes) and your intrinsic anatomical and biomechanical makeup (rider-specific causes). Here we look at the areas of the knee where pain might be felt and the specific conditions that can lead to this. All of them will have contributory factors from these three problem domains – the key is to identify which of them is most relevant to you and make a change for the better.

This information is limited to some of the more common over-use injuries, so if you've sustained an acute injury or experience sudden pain, or if your symptoms don't improve with this very general advice, please seek appropriate medical help.

ANTERIOR KNEE PAIN
Pain experienced at the front of the knee – on and around the kneecap (patella) – is the most common presentation of cycling over-use injuries, in part due to the anatomy of this area. The large quadriceps muscles attach to the shin bone via the patella, so the forces of pedalling are transmitted across the patellofemoral joint (PFJ) whenever we bend our knees, essentially squashing it back against the thigh bone. Although more common in explosive sports, the part of the tendon attaching the patella to the bony prominence below the kneecap can become inflamed (patellar tendonitis). If this area is persistently sore to the touch you should seek medical help. It should respond to using ice, anti-inflammatories and physiotherapy treatment, with or without strapping.

However, if you're reading this and you have anterior knee pain from riding your bike, chances are you've got what's known as patellar compression syndrome. The scourge of riders and runners alike, it can floor you, causing pain when off the bike and ride-stopping agony when on it.

During the push phase of pedalling, we seldom complete the last 35 degrees of knee extension; a movement which is largely under the control of the vastus medialis oblique muscle (VMO). This means that over a long period of time, and often in spite of outward appearances, the muscles down the outside of the thigh become stronger and tighter than these less-used medial muscles. The patella is pulled subtly off-kilter and forces through the PFJ increase, causing diffuse pain anywhere around the kneecap. The soft tissues around the lateral aspect of the patella slowly shorten over time and make strengthening exercises of the VMO muscle alone largely ineffectual.

The key to treating such a condition is to loosen off the lateral structures before attempting to redress the balance and concentrating on building medial muscle bulk. It's also worth pointing out that cycling isn't the only time that we bend our knees and stress the PFJ. Crouching down to pick something up and tackling stairs are more obvious activities, but sitting at a desk with feet underneath the chair for prolonged periods of time will produce the same effect. So, if you're troubled with anterior knee pain of this type, try to keep your leg out straight whenever you have the choice.

Bike-specific problems to be aware of as potentially contributing to anterior knee pain are a saddle that's too low or too far forwards; pushing big gears and over-long cranks.

The next phase of rehabilitating patellar compression syndrome – after a week or so of regular stretching and self-massage – is to work on building up the VMO muscle, to balance out the stabilizing forces on the patella. It's a slow process and can feel pointless initially, but persist with loosening the lateral side then strengthening the medial side, and in a couple of weeks you'll feel a difference.

There isn't much point in taping up the patella, because the forces generated when you're out on your bike are too great and the taping just won't hold. Particularly resistant cases can be tackled by a sports physiotherapist, who can work specifically on mobilizing the tight lateral tissues that are around the patella.

POSTERIOR KNEE PAIN
Pain found behind the knee is far less common a complaint, and much more straightforward to understand. It's almost always due to over-extending the knee. Bike-specific problems to look out for are a saddle that's too high or too far back, although these are just as likely to cause pain further up the hamstrings.

If you suffer from persistent pain behind your knee then you should be looked at medically to exclude a Baker's Cyst. They are a harmless bulging of synovial fluid into the space behind the knee. Your doctor can discuss treatment options with you.

STRENGTHEN THE THIGH'S MEDIAL MUSCLES

The following exercises are all designed to strengthen the vastus medialis oblique muscle – the main force pulling the patella medially. As such they focus on the 'missing' 35 degrees of knee extension neglected when pedalling. Work through them progressively.

▶ **Static quads**
A so -alled 'open chain' exercise (because the foot end of the leg is not fixed) to start with. Sitting on the floor with your legs out straight, push your knee down into the ground by contracting the VMO muscle steadily. Hold for 20 seconds and then repeat.

▶ **Straight leg raise**
Sit on a chair with your problem leg out straight. Hook your foot through the handle of a heavy bag and lift slowly, with your knee locked straight. Hold your leg out level for as long as possible and repeat. Throughout the exercise, keep your foot pointing outwards at a 45-degree angle.

▶ **Dips**
Stand on one leg. Repeatedly dip down just a few inches to flex your knee to around 35 degrees and then straighten again. Repeat many times. Keep your knee in line with the second toe and don't let it point inwards as you dip. You can add some resistance by holding equal weights in each hand. Even better is to do this exercise on a slight downward slope (for instance, with the heel of your foot raised slightly) – you will feel an even greater burn in the VMO as you exercise it.

INSIDE THE PATELLOFEMORAL JOINT

Femur
The body's biggest bone, the hip is at one end and the knee at the other.
Patella
The kneecap is a floating bone that sits in the tendon coming from the quads.
Tibia
The shin bone. Thigh muscles attach it to lever the knee joint.
Tendon of the quadriceps
The large muscle running down the front of the thigh.
Patellofemoral joint
The space behind the kneecap that can cause knee pain.
Patella ligament
How the quads eventually attach to the shin bone.

MEDIAL & LATERAL KNEE PAIN

Pain at the sides of the knees is fairly common and the culprits here are almost always the feet, or more specifically, pedal cleats. To this end, such pain is often noticed during or after the first ever ride with cleats, or with a new pair of shoes or replacement cleats.

The structures causing the pain are most often the collateral ligaments, which sit on the outsides of the knee joint, stopping them from bending the wrong way. Badly placed cleats will either affect the Q angle (how far apart your feet are positioned) or cause excessive rotation of the knee joint, stressing one or other of the collaterals.

If this is your problem area, check your cleats regularly for excessive wear, always make sure you draw around cleats with a felt tip pen to mark their position before replacing them and experiment with different cleat types until you find one that has the right amount of float for you (too much or too little can both cause problems).

Another painful condition that is very closely related to patellar compression syndrome is 'iliotibial band syndrome'. The iliotibial band (ITB) is a thick fibrous strap of tissue that runs all the way down the lateral thigh, from the pelvis to just below the knee. It's the structure that has a habit of tightening up over time and pulling the patella off centre if your VMO muscles aren't strong enough to counteract.

Although this is most commonly seen in runners, it's an unpleasant condition that is thought to be exacerbated by weakness of the gluteus medius muscle – another

essential core muscle that gets neglected by cycling – and also by wearing cleats that point your toes too far inwards.

In the acute phase of the injury the mainstay of its treatment is the same as for any inflammatory condition – that is rest, ice and regular anti-inflammatory medications such as ibuprofen and aspirin, if tolerated. Rehabilitation after this is very similar to that described for patellar compression syndrome, but with a focus on building up the gluteus medius muscle instead of (or as well as) the VMO. Near-religious stretching, especially of the iliotibial band, should precede strengthening exercises.

A return to normal activities should be phased in gradually, being guided by (a lack of) pain. Incredibly resistant cases can be operated on, but it's rarely required if you follow the regime set out here.

THE GOLDEN RULE

While all this information may give you some basic strategies for getting yourself out of trouble when you are plagued by knee pain, the old adage rings true: stay out of trouble in the first place! Many problems with the knee can be avoided by not making sudden increases in your training regime or drastic changes in how your bike is set up – it takes at least six weeks for your body to adapt to positional change. Look after your legs and they will look after you: stretch all the big muscle groups after each ride and treat them to the occasional massage too.

Lastly, don't neglect your core muscle strength – smaller core muscles can relieve much bigger limb muscles of surprisingly large loads.

KNEE STABILZERS

Vastus muscles and rectus femoris
Medical names for the separate parts of the quadriceps (front of thigh) muscles.

Iliotibial band (ITB)
A thick, fibrous strap of tissue running down the outside of the thigh. Can get tight, pulling strongly on the kneecap.

Lateral retinaculum
Short, tough ligaments tethering the kneecap to the ITB. Can shorten over time, compounding the problems of a tight ITB.

Medial retinaculum
Similar to lateral retinaculum but less fibrous, exerting less of a pull on the kneecap.

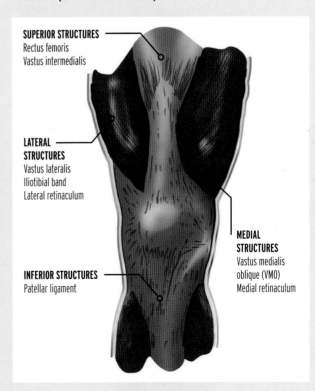

SUPERIOR STRUCTURES
Rectus femoris
Vastus intermedialis

LATERAL STRUCTURES
Vastus lateralis
Iliotibial band
Lateral retinaculum

MEDIAL STRUCTURES
Vastus medialis oblique (VMO)
Medial retinaculum

INFERIOR STRUCTURES
Patellar ligament

STOP THE HURT

As well as the usual neck, back and knee complaints, cyclists can suffer other ailments, which can be just as painful and performance-restricting...

SADDLE SORENESS
What is it?
We weren't made to perch on hard saddles, with moisture, friction and pressure playing havoc with the skin of the perineum. Chafing is common, often caused by cycling in wet clothing, and it can be relieved by applying an emollient or taking a short break from the saddle.

When friction becomes severe, ulceration may occur, and a saddle sore may start as folliculitis - inflammation of a hair follicle, looking a bit like an acne spot - and could develop into a boil or abscess. Such lesions might need to be incised and drained by a medic. For severe cases of so-called 'biker's nodule' or 'third testicle', surgical removal could be on the cards.

What can you do?
Make sure the saddle and handlebar are at the correct height and position - a professional bike fit is well worth investing in. Get out of damp clothing immediately after cycling, ensure that your chamois is dry and clean to start with and use a chamois cream. If you already have the problem, time off the bike, warm baths, and cortisone or antibacterial or antifungal creams should help resolve matters.

HOT FOOT
What is it?
Burning, numb or painful feet - posh name plantar neuropathy - is a common complaint and it's what you get when nerves are compressed by pressure generated between a fixed-cleat pedal and a tight cycling shoe.

In Morton's neuroma, another pressure-related condition, fibrous material collects around a nerve running between the long bones in the foot, typically between the third and fourth metatarsals (your big toe is the first). Despite its name, Morton's neuroma is not cancerous, and can be diagnosed using ultrasound or an MRI scan, where it appears as a solid mass of at least 5mm diameter.

What can you do?
Try positioning your cleat a bit further back, wear shoes with a wider toe box, loosen shoe straps, or use a wider pedal. Manual therapy is an option, but in difficult cases of Morton's neuroma, cortisone injections or a 'sclerosing alcohol' injection directly into the fibrous tissue may be needed. Cutting or removing part of the nerve may also be considered, but such procedures don't always work.

PERINEAL VASCULOPATH
What is it?
When you're sitting upright on a seat, the two bony bits in your backside that you actually sit on are called ischial tuberosities. However, when you adopt the racing position, your pelvis tilts forward, transferring weight to the soft perineum, which houses a rich collection of blood vessels and nerves. The risk of perineal compression problems is highest for heavier cyclists and during time trialling and indoor riding on rollers.

Lack of oxygen to the penis may ultimately lead to erectile dysfunction (ED), and one report found ED rates of 24 per cent among amateur cyclists riding more than 400km per week.

Nerve compression may result in genital numbness, with rates varying from 10 per cent among amateur cyclists during an eight-day, 500-mile event, to 91 per cent in a study of 17 cycling policemen.

What can you do?
A rider's position, bike fit, and riding technique play the greatest roles in prevention and treatment of perineal compression.

Although the symptoms of perineal compression are transient for most cyclists, the long-term implications are unknown at present.

CYCLIST'S PALSY/CARPAL TUNNEL SYNDROME

What is it?

'Cyclist's palsy' – ulnar neuropathy in medical parlance – is caused by prolonged compression of the ulnar nerve, which controls sensation in your ring and little fingers. The condition commonly occurs through riding with handlebars too low or too far forward, or during riding without changing grip, cycling downhill or over rough ground, cycling with poorly padded gloves or handlebars, or applying the so-called 'death grip' out of fear.

In one study of 25 cyclists participating in a 600km event, 23 reported experiencing hand numbness, and in another study of 89 cyclists on an 80-day tour covering 4,500 miles, 36 per cent experienced hand numbness. Depending on the branch of the ulnar nerve affected, the hand may become 'clawed'.

Less common than cyclist's palsy is carpal tunnel syndrome, where the median nerve is compressed at the wrist, by gripping the top of the handlebar, for example.

What can you do?

Treatment options include rest, changing hand position regularly, ensuring hands and handlebar are well padded, using clip-on aerobars, and raising the bar or shortening the reach. You might also try stretching exercises and/or a course of anti-inflammatory treatment. If in doubt, seek medical attention.

ILIOTIBIAL BAND SYNDROME

What is it?

One study found that 85 per cent of 518 amateur cyclists experienced an over-use injury; and another study which followed 108 pro cyclists over one season found that over-use injuries occurred in 58.3 per cent.

Among cyclists, the site most prone to over-use injury is the knee, accounting for 62 per cent of injuries among pros. The commonest cause of pain at the side of the knee is iliotibial band syndrome (ITBS). The iliotibial band (ITB) is the thick piece of tissue that runs from the pelvis to the side of the knee. Although some have argued that ITBS arises from compression of fat underneath the ITB, others contend that the syndrome encompasses a range of possible mechanisms.

What can you do?

Possible causes of ITBS include a steep rise in training mileage and intensity, worn cleats, riding in windy conditions, time trialling, and pushing big gears. Treatment options include foam-rolling, stretching, massage, and various bike-fit treatments such as cleat adjustment, and leg-length evaluation.

❝ Among cyclists, the site most prone to over-use injury is the knee, accounting for 62 per cent of injuries among pros. ❞

FOOT CRAMPS

What is it?

Foot cramps are painful and if they happen frequently can be enough to keep you off your bike. They involve the intrinsic muscles in the foot, which normally help to provide stability to the metatarsal arch during walking. Dehydration and shoes that don't fit properly are avoidable causes of an attack.

Another theory is the nerves that coordinate the contraction and stretching of the muscles get out of kilter when repeatedly performing an activity the foot was not designed for – the muscles are used in a different way when pedalling than when walking.

What can you do?

Theoretically, foot cramps should lessen the more riding you do. During an attack, it's often possible to ride through the pain, but if not, the best thing to do is dismount and stretch the foot. To do this, gently pull your toes upward, taking your shoe off if necessary. It may be possible to prevent the cramps by regularly stretching the calf and foot when off the bike – see **http://bit.ly/ RzJLps** for some recommended exercises.

> **"** *The risk of perineal compression is highest for heavier cyclists.* **"**

STITCH

What is it?

Exercise-induced Transient Abdominal Pain (ETAP) – or stitch – is a problem well known to runners, but a study done in Australia in 2000 showed that 32 per cent of cyclists had suffered the painful condition during rides. ETAP typically produces a sharp pain just below the ribcage and occasionally at the tip of the shoulder blade. One study found that over half of athletes suffering from ETAP found it had a negative effect on their performance.

The most widely held belief is that ETAP is caused by a lack of oxygen getting to the diaphragm, as blood is diverted to exercising muscles. Other explanations include muscle cramps in the chest wall and abdominal muscles, stretching to the ligaments that attach the abdominal organs to the diaphragm, irritation of the lining of the abdominal cavity and referred pain from the thoracic spine joints. The final theory may be more relevant to cycling because it's thought to be associated with the sort of over-flexion of the spine needed to bend over the handlebar.

What can you do?

Regular stretching of the upper spine and lateral abdominal muscles may help, combined with working on your core strength. Avoid hypertonic fluids such as fruit juice and time your pre-race meal to make sure it's well digested before you ride. If you do get a stitch then slow, deep breathing or bending forward seem to be the most effective strategies to get rid of it.

HYDRATION

Hydrating right is not just vital for your health, it's also important for performance. Here's how to get it right

There are a lot of myths about hydration, and about how and what you need to drink in order to stay fully hydrated. Hydration status is best thought of as the level of water in your body. This can be estimated using equipment that measures the electrical conduction (or bio-impedance) of a small current. You can even get bathroom scales that use this technology for under 80 euros.

But probably the simplest hydration indicator is urine colour. Clear and copious is the goal! However, vitamin supplemented bars, gels and antioxidant supplements can cause dark urine, so be warned. Vitamins B and C can turn urine yellow at even small doses but this does not necessarily mean you're dehydrated.

IF YOU'RE THIRSTY, DRINK

One of the major fallacies about fluid consumption is that you can teach yourself to survive without water. This probably stems from sports where fluid was restricted in order to minimize body weight, such as boxing and bodybuilding. Many old-school riders and coaches used to advocate this as a way to make riders harder and learn to survive without liquids. While it will make sessions harder and the rider (hopefully) mentally stronger, this is, quite simply, dangerous.

Fail to sweat effectively and your core temperature can start to rise, leading to complications such as heat stroke. So if you're thirsty, drink.

As a general rule, the larger the rider and the faster the speed, the greater the sweat rate, but in fit or larger individuals it is likely to exceed one litre per hour.

YOU NEED TO DRINK, EVEN WHEN IT'S COLD

In the summer good hydration is particularly important because of the heat and faster riding speeds, meaning more and quicker heat build-up, but thinking about your hydration is not just confined to the hot months: physical exertion will lead to sweating, regardless of the ambient temperature.

Drinking to offset the loss of fluid and help cool your body's core is vital. Yes, you can survive an hour without drinking but several hours' sweating, gaining internal heat, with blood that is getting thicker and less effective, is a recipe for disaster. It's important for riders of all levels and abilities to see fluid replacement as part of riding and to learn how much they need to offset thirst and maintain energy levels.

CAN'T DRINK? MAKE UP FOR IT AFTERWARDS

There will always be times when you can't drink as much as you'd like and have to deviate from your normal drinking plan – whether because of the terrain, speed of riding or you've simply run out of liquids. You're likely to lose between one and two kilograms in average UK temperatures in a 25-mile time trial – but you'll be able to complete it, just as marathon runners can run for more than two hours over a similar distance without drink.

Instead of worrying that you might be dehydrated, attend to your fluid replacement as soon as you can after the event. Your immediate post-ride hydration should constitute 150 per cent of the missed fluid intake. If you usually drink 600ml in an hour, then you'll need to take in 900ml of a sports drink with electrolytes after riding. These are best absorbed after being chilled in the fridge.

YOU CAN IMPROVE ON NATURE

Water. What could be better than pure, natural water? One of the biggest myths about fluid intake is that you can't beat water for hydration – it's not true, you most certainly can. Sports drinks work better at maintaining hydration during rides and rehydrating you after, as the added electrolytes – sodium chloride, potassium, magnesium, and calcium – help your body maintain its optimum hydration status. Research shows that you absorb 35 per cent more water, and rehydrate better, when consuming a 4:1 ratio carbohydrate and protein drink than if you drink just water alone.

If recovery-type drinks are too rich or expensive for you, down a bottle of your favourite fluid replacement drink as soon as you get off your bike – you'll still absorb three-quarters of what you drink.

CHEMISTRY OF THIRST

We all know to replace electrolytes when riding in the heat, and all good sports drinks will contain them. But what exactly are they?

Electrolytes regulate thirst and enable your muscles and nerves to function. They're present in our body tissues, muscles and blood and conduct electricity in the body, passing chemical messages and regulating the body's fluid levels. The balance of these salts and minerals needs to be just right to help our muscles work at their peak and optimize our riding performance.

KEEPING IT LEVEL

Electrolytes are positively and negatively charged salts and minerals that allow messages to be passed from the brain to the muscles. Without them, our muscles will cramp, become weak, and lose power. However, too high a concentration will make you feel sick, dizzy and can lead to coma or even death in extreme circumstances. In the body, electrolytes take the form of sodium, potassium, calcium and bicarbonate, but in our sweat we lose more sodium, so it's the most important one to replace on a ride.

SODIUM COUNTS

Usual blood levels for sodium are around 3,300mg per litre. The Institute of Medicine (IOM) recommends that adults should consume 1,500mg sodium each day to replace the amount lost. For endurance athletes this figure increases – but to varying degrees. For example, in an average athlete, the sodium concentration of one litre of sweat can range from 800 to 3,600mg, but an unfit person's sweat can contain up to 4,500mg of sodium.

SODIUM LOSS AT A GLANCE

- Clothes: those that don't breathe cause you to sweat
- If you eat more salt: you'll sweat more sodium
- Genetics: heavy sweaters run in the family
- Athleticism: the sweat of a very athletic person is likely to contain fewer electrolytes
- Temperature: hotter weather will up your sweat rate, but you can sweat in any temperature

FACT!

Salt is 40 per cent sodium and the upper level of daily consumption of salt is just one teaspoon

FACT!

You absorb 35% more water when drinking a 4:1 ratio carbohydrate and protein drink than if you drink just water.

ALTERNATIVES TO WATER

Water is not the only form of hydration available, so we look at the options...

Every cell in your body relies on a constant supply of water to carry out a range of functions. But you don't have to stick with plain water. Here are a few alternatives...

TEA
Tea contains over 700 chemicals, including vitamins (C, E and K), caffeine and polysaccharides, and is associated with the cell-mediated immune function of the human body and beneficial intestinal microflora. Caffeine levels are generally lower than in an equivalent measure of coffee, and it's less diuretic (reduces the amount of water in the body), so it's more hydrating.

COFFEE
Coffee contains 80–125mg of caffeine per 30ml cup. It also contains 8 per cent of your daily niacin needs, and 1 per cent of daily potassium needs. However, it's diuretic so it can dehydrate you.

SPORTS DRINK
These drinks replace fluid and electrolytes lost through sweat and provide energy lost through muscle use. They also contain sodium, which takes water directly into the blood when it's absorbed.

GREEN TEA
Green tea is packed with antioxidants – in particular catechins, which help people who exercise to lose weight. A Japanese study found that drinking green tea could help boost endurance by up to 24 per cent.

ORANGE JUICE
Potassium-rich orange juice helps aid recovery as the potassium lost from your muscles during exercise needs to be replaced to stop muscle cramping and cardiovascular irregularities. Also the electrolytes in orange juice replace those lost through sweating, its carbohydrate helps restore muscle glycogen, and vitamin C helps keep cells healthy.

CHERRY JUICE
Not only is it full of antioxidants, but according to research in the US, long-distance runners who drank the juice twice a day for seven days before a big run had significantly less muscle pain than those who drank any other fruit juice.

MILKY DRINKS
A warming drink such as hot chocolate or malted milk is sweet enough to boost sugar levels and give you a sense of wellbeing, warm enough to help you feel sleepy and lacking in stimulants such as caffeine.

145

COFFEE BREAKDOWN
Coffee and cake is a cycling tradition. But which coffee and when?
Caffeine by itself can promote fat metabolism and retain muscle glycogen, so a black coffee before a fasted ride in the morning may increase the amount of fat you burn. However, an over-reliance on caffeine can compromise your sleep quality. Instead, save the caffeine hit for when you need it.

But which coffee type is best and when? Evan Lawrence, competitive cyclist and owner of US coffee shop 53x11 Coffee, suggests a double espresso for a pre-ride energy shot. "This gives the boost of caffeine but misses out the milk, which can have a negative effect on your stomach." During a ride, Lawrence would again go light on milk. "An Americano with sugar and a dash of milk is best." This heightens energy without the risk of gastric discomfort from too much heavy liquid. After a ride, Lawrence would change tactics and choose milk for recovery. "Go for a latte or a coffee mocha with full fat milk for extra calories. You'll be getting some essential protein, calcium and fat, which are all needed for recovery."

FOOD AND NUTRITION

Every cyclist is fuelled by the food and drink they consume. If you are taking the trouble to tune your body and bike, it only makes sense to ensure you eat and drink to keep yourself as fit as possible. This chapter sets out how you can plan your breakfast, snacks, meals, hydration and on-bike food to ensure you perform at your best

EAT YOURSELF FIT

There's more to riding than hours of training – the right nutrition is key to getting the best from yourself. Here's how to eat yourself faster...

▶ A combination of the right training and diet will help up your power-to-weight ratio

You've bought the kit and are putting in the hours. But are you also looking at what you're putting inside your body? To get fitter, recover faster, become leaner and suffer less injury and illness, what you eat before, during and after a ride is crucial.

BUILDING MUSCLE

Muscle is protein – so you need to eat protein to gain muscle and get stronger. "Animal protein contains all the amino acids we need to synthesize muscle cells for growth and repair," says physiologist Dr Neil Walsh. "Which is why if you're protein deficient you may feel weak, struggle to add muscle or be so sore after exercise."

As a cyclist, you want to carry more muscle than fat. But you also want to be light. So should you be necking protein shakes and raw eggs? "That might work for bodybuilders, but there's no evidence endurance athletes have an increased requirement for protein," says Walsh. "So long as you have a diet that meets your energy needs, made up of carbohydrate, protein and some fat, you have all you need." A normal, sedentary person needs 1.2g protein per kilo of body weight a day. "But if you're upping your food intake to match your energy requirements, you'll get this amount naturally."

GETTING LEAN

There are no great secrets to losing fat. Walsh says you simply have to make sensible food choices and create an energy deficit by taking in less than you're expending. He cautions against training hard while seriously restricting your diet though. "If you want to become a better cyclist,

❝ *Water is okay, but try adding diluted fruit juice or an isotonic sports drink. And for extra edge? Caffeine.* ❞

you can't ride empty. Not only do you risk nutrient deficiencies, your ability to train will suffer too. To work out your calorie requirements, wear a heart rate monitor when you train and note average calories burned," he suggests. "Add this to the recommended daily intake for a sedentary person of your gender."

The current Department of Health guidelines are 2,550 calories for men and 1,940 for women. Walsh advises eating a healthy, balanced diet that includes lots of fruit and vegetables, wholegrains, lean protein, low-fat dairy, and essential fatty acid such as omega-6 and omega-3 from oily fish and seeds – in other words, foods with high nutrient values and low calorie densities. Ensure variety – your meat shouldn't always be steak, your grains not always wheat. Also avoid processed foods, fast food and ready meals, high-fat and high-sugar foods and alcohol.

RACING HARD

"Your ability to race fast depends on your energy and endurance," says Dr Asker Jeukendrup, cyclist and professor of exercise metabolism. He points out that in longer races, the right food can mean finishing or not.

Your body needs fuel, so you need to increase carbohydrate stores leading up to a race. "Two to three days is fine," says Jeukendrup, "and carb loading doesn't mean eat as much as possible. It's only the carbs you increase."

You'll need 7g carbs per kilo of bodyweight (525g for a 75kg man, for example). And while nutritionists recommend unrefined carbohydrates (brown rice, wholewheat pasta, wholegrain bread) at all other times, pre-race is a time when white is alright.

"You don't want to challenge your digestion, so avoid fibre – wholegrains or leafy veg – the day before and the morning of a race," Jeukendrup advises. "Instead, opt for refined carbs with a high glycaemic index (GI), that are absorbed quickly. There's no one pre-race food. Some people like pasta, then porridge for breakfast. Others don't sleep if they go to bed full, and are too nervous to eat in the morning. That's where carb sports drinks come in handy.

"Your morning goal is 100g carbs," continues Jeukendrup. "Then, if the race is an hour long, aim for

30g during. If it's two hours, have 60g per hour. Check the label of your sports drink or carb gel. If the race is longer, you'll need 90g an hour, but get this from a specialized glucose and fructose mix – if you try to consume 90g from a normal glucose product, you'll get digestive problems, as you can't absorb more than 60g an hour from glucose alone." Some people prefer real food, and can stomach a banana, flapjack, jelly beans or sandwich during a race. "This tactic tends to be harder in the second half of longer races. It's thought that there's more blood in the muscles and less in the gut, making digestion difficult," says Dr Jeukendrup.

Your other energy essential? Hydration. "Limit water loss to two per cent of your bodyweight. Any more and performance suffers. A five per cent loss means a 30 per cent performance drop," he says. "Drink 1 litre of fluid an hour to replace 1kg in weight," he says. Water is okay, but try adding diluted fruit juice or an isotonic sports drink. And for extra edge? "Caffeine is proven to increase speed and endurance, so have a coffee an hour before racing, or choose a carb gel with added caffeine."

GOOD RECOVERY

"Post workout, your glycogen stores are depleted, your muscles have micro tears that need rebuilding and chemical build-up that needs removing," says nutritionist Becky Stevenson. "If you fail to recover you won't have enough fuel to train as well next time and you'll suffer muscle soreness. This culminates in heavy legs, disrupted sleep, raised levels of stress hormones and suppressed immunity."

Recovery means refuelling with carbs, protein, fluid and salts. "Carbs raise your blood sugar level so insulin is released. This opens up your muscles to let nutrients in. Carbs replenish glycogen stores in your muscles and proteins repair them. Just protein won't maximize your hormone environment; just carbs and you're not protecting the muscle you've gained," she explains.

"Research demonstrates a higher rate of glycogen storage in the two hours following exercise, so eating during this window will maximize the process," Stevenson says. "This is fine if you're not going to be training again for a few days. But any sooner and you should aim to refuel within 20 minutes."

Your ideal recovery snack is high carb, with a little protein. "Aim for 1–1.2g carbs per kilo of bodyweight. If you weigh 75kg that's 90g – about three thick slices of bread. The ideal amount of protein is 10–20g. You'd get this from a low-fat milkshake drink or two to three mini cheeses," says Stevenson. And don't forget rehydration. Stevenson is a fan of isotonic drinks: "We know the body retains more fluid if electrolytes are consumed. Water alone dilutes body salts, sending a message to your kidneys to excrete fluid to restore the balance. An isotonic drink maintains the correct salt balance, so it won't send this message."

FIGHTING ILLNESS

"When you exercise, you put your body under oxidative stress. Free radicals exist naturally in the body, but as you exercise and take in more oxygen, you increase free radical production – and the potential damage that does to cells," says Stevenson.

Long-term, this leads to chronic disease. Short-term, it means increased muscle soreness, fatigue and propensity to illness. The solution is to eat more antioxidants, which scavenge free radicals in the body, and you'll find loads in fruit and vegetables.

And finally, Dr Neil Walsh has carried out extensive research on how athletes can prevent illness. His findings? Eat enough.

"Athletes who don't match calorie intake to their energy needs have lower immune function. Training hard while losing weight is a recipe for illness," he says.

As well as eating enough, you need to eat your greens – and reds and yellows and purples. The Government guidelines of five-a-day should be a bare minimum. "Cyclists who are training hard need more like 10 a day, weighted towards vegetables in a rainbow of colours for maximum nutrients," says Stevenson.

FOODS FOR GOOD RECOVERY

Your body needs to repair after training or you and your performance will suffer. So give your recovery a boost with these tasty treats...

BEANS ON TOAST
Choose low-sugar beans and wholegrain toast (unless you're training again within 24 hours, in which case have white). Add cheese for calcium.

SMOOTHIES
Make a smoothie with low-fat milk, a banana or berries, and oats to provide a tasty and nutritious mix of protein and carbohydrates.

CEREAL
Try a generous portion of cereal with skimmed milk. And shun sugary options in favour of fortified flakes, so that you get the added vitamins and minerals.

RECOVERY DRINKS
Recovery drinks are an easy choice if you're racing or riding far from home, as the manufacturers have done the nutrient maths for you.

FOODS FOR FIGHTING ILLNESS

You need to fight the stress your body is under during exercise. Here are some of the best foods to boost your immune system and keep illness at bay...

FRUIT AND VEG
For antioxidants as well as fibre and a host of vitamins and minerals, eat fruit and veg. Aim for 10 portions a day in a rainbow of colours.

MACKEREL
Oily fish contains the omega-3 essential fats that no serious cyclist should be riding without. Aim for two to three portions a week.

BERRIES
A good source of immune-boosting vitamin C are berries – up your intake of these, as well as citrus and kiwi fruit, in times of rampant cold or flu outbreaks.

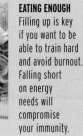

EATING ENOUGH
Filling up is key if you want to be able to train hard and avoid burnout. Falling short on energy needs will compromise your immunity.

CHOOSE THE BEST BIKING BREAKFAST

What are the best options for fuelling your morning ride?

Oatmeal
Porridge oats are one of the best sources of slow-release energy, and can help reduce the risk of heart disease through reducing LDL (bad) cholesterol. Mix with cow's milk, which has more muscle-building protein than soya, honey and a few almonds – among the lowest-calorie nuts.

Turkey
For some of us breakfast simply isn't breakfast without a large helping of cured pig. But for a healthy meaty start to the day, try turkey instead – 100g of turkey sausage has about 196kcal, 100g of pork about 339kcal, and turkey sausages contain about one and a half times as much protein as do their porky cousins. Grill a couple and put between two slices of wholegrain bread.

Cereal
Breakfast cereals have a bad reputation. In a sugar-frosted market swimming in chocolatey milk, this is no surprise. But there are excellent choices out there, among the best of which are Weetabix and Shredded Wheat. Both are good sources of slow-release carbohydrates, to keep you fuller for longer, and both are great smothered in milk for a hit of muscle-building protein. Add blueberries for sweetness.

Yoghurt
Fruit yoghurt is a staple breakfast but many ready-made ones are full of sugar, guaranteeing a mid-morning energy slump, which can only be fixed by chocolate or cake. This is even more the case with many fat-free options, which are pumped full of sugar to make them taste bearable. Buy greek yoghurt instead, which has twice the protein of many regular yoghurts, and add blueberries and honey for a long, slow release of energy.

Eggs
Substitute foods are usually pretty grim: protein cupcakes and flour-free 'bread' tend to be as bad as they sound. However, banana pancakes made from just banana, egg and a dash of baking powder are really quite nice. Mash a ripe banana until smooth, beat in two eggs, add less than half a teaspoon of baking powder and fry blobs around 5–10cm wide in olive oil for about a minute each. Delicious and packed with energy, protein and potassium, Eggs don't have to be fried, poached or scrambled!

CYCLIST'S FUEL

As a cyclist it's important you fuel properly. There are three key nutritional elements to help you train stronger and recover faster

Now that you're putting your body through more rigorous exercise, good nutrition is more important than ever. What you eat before and after hard exercise is crucial to maximize your performance and recovery and stay healthy. Despite what you might think, getting the right balance of vitamins and minerals in your diet doesn't require a PhD or a supply of laboratory grade supplements...

Carbohydrates, proteins and fats are the key building blocks to any athlete's diet and should make up the majority of your meals. If you understand the role each element plays in your diet, you can then make your own personalized nutrition plan to help you replenish your body with the minerals and vitamins it needs.

PROTEIN
What is it?
Protein is the main structural component of muscle tissue so is vital for growth and repair. Proteins are made up of various sequences of amino acids, nine of which are essential and must come from your diet. The rest are non-essential and can be synthesized by the body.

Why you need it
Protein is needed to build tissues, cell membranes and muscle cells. Without it, the body would literally waste away. It's especially important for athletes as it helps the body to grow and repair. It also provides a source of energy as an alternative to carbohydrate during exercise and is the primary fuel for cells of the immune system.

How much you should eat
About 12–20 per cent of your daily food intake should be from lean protein sources such as turkey, chicken, oily fish or nuts. Low-fat meat is an ideal source as it contains all nine amino acids. For vegetarians, pulses and grains are good sources, while soya and hemp contain all nine essential amino acids that are found in meat.

For a cyclist trying to maintain their current muscle mass, the daily protein intake should work out at around 1–1.5g per kg of bodyweight. So if you weigh 76kg (12 stone) you should eat around 76–114g of protein a day.

When you need it
Ideally, protein will be a component of every meal to help control blood glucose levels and support muscle development. After exercise you should try to consume protein within 45 minutes to help muscle recovery and maximize glycogen storage.

Get it here
Eggs, chicken, fish, black beans, tofu, chickpeas.

CARBOHYDRATE
What is it?
Carbohydrate is an organic compound made of carbon, hydrogen and oxygen. It provides the body with its primary energy source, essential for physical activity. Carbohydrate appears in three forms: monosaccharides and disaccharide, which are sweet, and polysaccharides, which have little or no sweetness. Sweet carbs are generally referred to as sugars while non-sweet carbs are labelled starches.

Why you need it
Carbohydrate is stored in the form of glycogen in the muscles and liver. You need to ensure you have an adequate supply for exercise and to replenish your muscles afterwards. Insulin released as a product of carbohydrate processing helps to prevent muscle breakdown after hard exercise, instead promoting muscle synthesis and replenishing glycogen.

How much you should eat

About 40–60 per cent of your daily calorie intake should come from carbohydrate – more when you're training hard - and there are approximately four calories per gram of carbohydrate. Carbs are all ranked on the glycemic index (GI). Ones that are broken down quickly by your body, causing a rapid increase in blood glucose, have a high GI rating. Low or medium GI foods take longer to break down, making you feel fuller for longer.

When you need it

Carbohydrate should be a part of every meal, especially if you're in training. Try to eat low to medium GI carbs such as brown rice, sweet potato, wholemeal bread, couscous and green veg, before exercise (more than three hours) to stock the muscles with plenty of slow-release fuel (glycogen). Keep high GI carbs to the times when your body will readily use them, such as shortly before, during or directly after a cycle of more than an hour, otherwise they'll be stored as fat. Post-exercise, eating carbohydrates within 45 minutes of finishing will encourage muscle repair, which can be improved further by adding protein.

Get it here

Bread, bananas, rice, pasta, potato, yoghurt.

FAT

What is it?

Fat is another essential part of our diet consisting of hydrogen, carbon and oxygen, just like carbohydrates. The difference is that they have double the calorific content of carbs or protein. Fat can be divided into three groups: saturated, monounsaturated and polyunsaturated.

Why you need it

Although fat gets a bad reputation certain types are essential in the body's diet. Monounsaturated and polyunsaturated contain fatty acids which are used to dissolve vitamins A, D, E and K, so without some of these fats in our diet we would be lacking these key nutrients. Unsaturated fats also help slow the passage of food through the gut, allowing it to be properly digested.

How much you should eat

It is recommended that our daily intake of fat should be around 70g for women and 95g for men. These amounts should not exceed 20g/30g of saturated fats. Unsaturated – or good fats – are found in natural oils, nuts and oily fish. Saturated – or bad – fats might raise the level of cholesterol in the blood, which increases the risk of heart disease. These fats occur in meat and dairy products and are often in processed foods such as cakes and biscuits.

When you need it

Fat slows the passage of food through the body and decreases the rate at which the body absorbs carbohydrates. So you should avoid eating fats shortly before or during exercise. Otherwise small amounts of unsaturated fats should make up part of your daily diet.

Get it here

Steamed fish, avocado, nuts and olive oil.

153

INSTANT WIN

After a long ride, try to eat carbohydrates and protein within 45 minutes to top up your glycogen stores and promote muscle recovery. A handful of fruit and nuts is ideal or sit straight down to a meal such as spaghetti bolognese.

SUPERFOODS

These so-called 'superfoods' are nutrient powerhouses packing large doses of antioxidants, polyphenols, vitamins and minerals - and they're available at your local supermarket...

ONE CUP OF STEAMED BROCCOLI
CALORIES 54
FAT 1G
CARBOHYDRATE 6G
PROTEIN 4G

BROCCOLI
Staying lean
Why: The trick to staying lean is to make your body think it is fuller than it actually is. Always drink a lot of water and eat bulking foods that are high in fibre so they fill you up. A particularly good bulking food is broccoli, as not only is it fibrous, it is also packed full of antioxidants, so it's very good for your body in general.

Antioxidants are nutrients and enzymes believed to counteract the damaging effect of oxidation that occurs when you take in too much oxygen, for example when exercising. Although there is some evidence that contradicts this, experts agree that antioxidants are good for the body.

How and when
Broccoli is a low glycaemic index (GI) carb meaning it has slow-releasing energy, making it good for an early evening meal – particularly on a rest day when you don't need to replenish burned fuel.

Go easy
If you eat a lot of it, the fibre in the broccoli can give you stomach discomfort and wind. Rather than eating a whole plateful it's best to keep it in its typical role as an accompaniment to meat or fish or in a pasta dish.

BLUEBERRIES
Immune system
Why: Antioxidants fight the free radicals thought to harm us, and are a result of us taking in so much oxygen when we exercise. Any fruit or vegetable that is colourful is high in antioxidants that will boost your immune system. Blueberries in particular are fantastic. You need a food with vitamin C, zinc and antioxidants, and blueberries have all of these.

One antioxidant they're high in is quercetin, which contains naturally occurring antihistamine and anti-inflammatory qualities. Some studies have shown that the quercetin in them may also have a vasodilator response, helping get blood to the muscles that need them. So it is beneficial for cyclists in many ways.

How and when
Blueberries are brilliant in smoothies, making them a great option for breakfast.

Go easy
Eating a lot of blueberries has the potential to cause stomach irritation. Also, get blueberry juice stains on your clothes and you'll never get them out.

100G OF RAW BLUEBERRIES
CALORIES 57
FAT 0G
CARBOHYDRATE 14G
PROTEIN 1G

100ML OF BEET IT!
CALORIES 36
FAT 0G
CARBOHYDRATE 9G
PROTEIN 1G

156

BEETROOT JUICE
Sprinting
Why: Beets are naturally high in nitrates and nitric oxide, which opens up the blood vessels, improving your gross mechanical efficiency. In layman's terms you can do more work on fewer calories. The optimal period for the benefits of beets on exercise is for activities of 3–27 minutes, so it is particularly good for sprinting.

How and when
Ideally take a shot of 'beet it' (www.beet-it.com), which contains 5ml of nitrate (the same as three beets), 1–3hrs before training every day as this is how long it takes to get into the system. Likewise, take it on event day 1–3hrs before you ride. To make it yourself, clean, peel and chop three beetroots before blending them with a quarter of a cup of water, and then strain the juice through a cheesecloth.

Go easy
If you've ever had kidney stones you should avoid beets – and in fact any food that is high in oxalate such as spinach, berries and nuts – as this can combine with calcium in your body to create more stones. Also, be warned that they can turn your urine pink.

STEAK
Vo2 max
Why: When you exercise, your blood becomes thicker due to the lack of fluid, so your body kills off some of your red blood cells to dilute your blood and make it easier to transport again. The trouble is, you need red blood cells to move oxygen around the body. Steak contains a lot of iron that helps produce new red blood cells, boosting oxygen delivery and aerobic capacity and your VO2 max.

Many athletes opt for taking iron in supplement form instead of getting it from natural sources. But beware, this won't digest in the same way and it is easy to overdose, which can lead to bloating and constipation, Steak, however, is also an excellent protein for the body, helping your muscles to recover.

How and when
Choose sirloin steak rather than rump or tenderloin, as it tends to be leaner. Drink a glass of orange juice with it as the vitamin C will help to aid iron absorption.

Go easy
Red meat can be quite fatty so be sure to go for a lean cut, and don't have it too often in order to avoid piling on the pounds.

ONE 3OZ GRILLED SIRLOIN STEAK
CALORIES 211
FAT 13G
CARBOHYDRATE 1G
PROTEIN 22G

ONE CAN OF SARDINES IN WATER
CALORIES 130
FAT 7G
CARBOHYDRATE 0G
PROTEIN 17G

SARDINES
Avoiding injury
Why: When we think of preventing muscle injury we tend to overlook one of the biggest muscles of all – our gastro-intestinal tract. Prolonged exercise can injure the gut lining. This is due to hyperthermia, where the body gets too hot and we dehydrate, losing red blood cells that act as a barrier to infections.

Introduce sardines to your diet and the omega-3 oil will act as a natural anti-inflammatory. They also contain essential sodium.

Try to get your calorie intake from immune-boosting foods with plenty of protein, antioxidants and important minerals like iron calcium and zinc. Sardines are great for all these, providing around 20% of your daily iron needs, 60% of your calcium needs and 8% of your zinc needs per can.

How and when
Sardines on toast is a healthy and nutritious lunch. Choose wholegrain bread for slow-releasing energy.

Go easy
Eat them at your desk and the smell won't please your colleagues.

SWEET POTATO
Energy
Why: It has a low GI, making it great for sustained energy, and loads of other qualities that make it an excellent choice for cyclists.

Compared to a standard potato they have a much higher nutritional density and are loaded with vitamin A, C, iron and calcium and brimming with beta-carotene, vitamin C, magnesium, potassium and fibre. They're naturally sweet, have a high water content, so they're easy to digest, and aren't as inflammatory as other energy-rich carbohydrates.

How and when
Sweet potatoes can simply be used as an alternative to normal potatoes. They are perfect to add to soups, curries and risottos to boost your energy levels and your immune system. Wrapped up in foil they can even be used as a snack when you're out riding.

Go easy
Although sweet potatoes have a number of advantages over potatoes (slower-releasing energy, more potassium and fibre), they do have less protein, so you don't want to swap them in every meal.

MEDIUM POTATO BAKED IN SKIN
CALORIES 103
FAT 0G
CARBOHYDRATE 24G
PROTEIN 2G

ONE MEDIUM CHICKEN BREAST, SKINLESS
CALORIES 142
FAT 3G
CARBOHYDRATE 0G
PROTEIN 26G

CHICKEN
Strength
Why: "Strength refers to muscle density, and you need protein for this. Although there are vegetable sources, the best and probably easiest is meat," says Dr Allen Lim. "In the 2010 Tour de France, when I was the director of science and training for Team RadioShack, at the end of 17 of the 21 stages the whole team wanted chicken fried rice." Lean chicken is a great source of protein that contains creatine and beta-alanine. These are amino acids that help to create strong muscles.

How and when
A Thai chicken curry with rice is an ideal meal. The short grain rice is rapidly absorbed into the bloodstream to help muscles recover quickly, the spices act as an anti-inflammatory, the sodium from the sauce and minerals in coconut milk replenish lost electrolytes, and you get lean protein from the chicken.

Go easy
Don't gorge yourself. A chicken breast contains around 26g protein, and in reality your body can only absorb around 30g in one meal. Any more is not digested so will just be wasted.

TEA OR COFFEE
Alertness
Why: Caffeine is the one single variable that almost all professional cyclists agree on. At the big races you'll see them all taking caffeine in one form or another. This is because caffeine is a stimulant that has been shown in several studies to boost alertness and performance. Users have been proven to react faster in cognitive tests and numerous research papers have been published on caffeine's positive impact on an individual's sprinting and endurance capabilities.

   A lot of energy gels contain caffeine, but in its most commonly used form you can get caffeine from coffee and the UK's favourite beverage, tea.

How and when
It takes caffeine about an hour to get into the system, so have a coffee 60 minutes before you start your ride and at regular intervals throughout to keep you topped up. Aim for around 6mg per kg of bodyweight (a regular cup of coffee contains between 115 and 175mg).

Go easy
Although caffeine's benefits have been proven, some people are more sensitive to its effects than others.

A MUG OF BLACK FILTER COFFEE
CALORIES 2
FAT 0G
CARBOHYDRATE 0G
PROTEIN 0.5G

BOWL OF PORRIDGE
CALORIES 291
FAT 9G
CARBOHYDRATE 38
PROTEIN 8G

OATS
Endurance
Why: Oats have a low GI and release energy into the bloodstream gradually. They also contain protein, fibre and minerals including calcium and iron, B vitamins and vitamin E. Some studies have shown that vitamin E can boost stamina and endurance. As well as this oats fill you up, aid concentration and help you to maintain a healthy digestive system.

How and when
Start the day with the ultimate endurance breakfast – a bowl of hot porridge drizzled with honey or syrup. Add a chopped banana or a handful of blueberries. There are other ways of eating oats, of course – granola with milk or yoghurt is an alternative breakfast, you can add oats to pancake and cake mixtures, or make your own flapjacks and oatcakes make for a great on-ride snack.

Go easy
Be wary of getting your oats in pre-packaged cereal form as it'll often contain sky-high levels of salt and sugar. Also 'quick-cook' packaged oats provide less sustenance so try to use the less refined, jumbo varieties when you can.

EGGS
Recovery
Why? Eggs are a nutritionally dense protein food. They contain all the essential amino acids and loads of vitamins to help build and maintain muscles. They are an excellent source of protein for recovery. In a large egg, you can get 8–10g protein. They also contain vitamin B12. Without enough B12 in your diet, the body will struggle to repair muscle damage and ligament injury.

How and when
The first 15 minutes after exercise is when your body is most receptive and recovers at a faster rate than normal. After you come in from a long ride, take three large eggs and whip up an omelette or scrambled eggs on toast (quick-releasing energy to replenish your glycogen stores) – it only take a few minutes to prepare this 30g protein hit to get your muscles recovering as fast as possible.

Go easy
You should store eggs in the fridge and cook them thoroughly as they can contain salmonella, which can cause sickness in some people unless the eggs are dealt with properly.

THREE LARGE EGGS SCRAMBLED
CALORIES 300
FAT 22G
CARBOHYDRATE 4G
PROTEIN 24G

NUTRITIONAL FACT OR FICTION?

Cycling has its traditional fuelling practices and dietary conventions. But are they based on scientific fact or just myth?

BONKING

Bonking is one of the worst experiences to have while out cycling. You feel so low on energy that you just feel like you aren't going anywhere and just want to stop riding. It's often described as like "pedalling squares".

What has actually happened is you haven't fuelled with enough carbohydrate during your ride and you've used up most of the stored carbohydrate (glycogen) within your body.

If you don't take in enough carbohydrate as you ride, your blood sugar level drops – your brain detects this and slows you down. You generally only have enough stored glycogen to last you for around 90 minutes of exercise, although this depends on how hard you ride and how well stocked up your glycogen stores were before you set off. This is why carb loading is recommended before a very long endurance event and why you should always at least have a good carbohydrate-based breakfast before you set off.

FASTED RIDES

Fasted rides were once the staple of many pro riders' training schedule, but while fasted training can help to train your body to use fat as fuel rather than just carbs, there's no strong evidence to suggest it helps performance. In fact, if you do most of your rides fasted it can hinder performance, as you're not training the carb pathways which you need to perform at the highest intensity. Done repeatedly, it can even depress your immune system, making you more prone to coughs and colds.

If you are going to train fasted, only do it once or twice a week and keep the sessions to no more than two hours long. Make sure you recover properly afterwards with some carbohydrate and protein together.

DRINKING ONLY WATER

For low-intensity rides in cool conditions, you can probably get away with using only water in your bottles if your ride is only 1–2 hours long. But even if you're doing a short ride, while you don't need any additional carbs, electrolytes are still key in maintaining hydration. Your body retains fluid better in the body if your drink contains sodium, and most electrolyte sports drinks contain 30mg of sodium per 500ml serving.

POST-RIDE BEER

As tempting as a beer on the way home might be, it won't help your cycling performance or your recovery, as alcohol dehydrates you and can further deplete your glycogen stores. To recover optimally, try to avoid the alcohol for at least 3–4 hours post-ride, and preferably the night before your ride too!

BACK-POCKET BANANAS

While bananas are high in carbohydrate, the sugar in them isn't released to the body to use very quickly. Bananas are mainly made of fructose, and fructose is a

low GI sugar, which means it's released slowly and takes some time to become available to the working muscles. Fructose has to be processed by the liver before it can be used to produce energy, and this process can take up to 90 minutes, making anything fructose-based not very well suited to situations where you need to be producing a large amount of energy quickly.

FLAPJACKS

Flapjacks are a tasty option for your back pocket but they can be very high in fat, with around 15g in a typical 75g bar. Fat is digested slowly and delays how quickly foods and fluids empty from your stomach, making you feel full and bloated when you up your effort level.

JAM SANDWICHES

Enduringly popular among cyclists, jam sandwiches aren't the worst choice you could make when you're looking for some fast and slow release carbohydrates. However, they're far from the most practical, as you'd need at least one per hour during your ride to take in the recommended amount of carbohydrate. This is where energy gels and bars become useful as they allow you to carry lots of energy in minimal back-pocket space.

FIZZY DRINKS

You'll see many Grand Tour riders being frantically thrust cans of Coke and other fizzy drinks at the end of a stage, or even taking a small can from their musette mid-way through. While the sugar and caffeine can give you a rapid energy hit, the simple sugars in it can play havoc with your guts afterwards.

Simple sugars need more water with them in order to be absorbed than longer chain carbohydrates do (such as maltodextrin, the carbohydrate choice of many sports drinks), meaning that they may actually dehydrate you further. Simple sugars also feed the bacteria in the colon, which can lead to more gas and bloating. If you need a caffeine and energy hit, try a maltodextrin-based energy gel with some added caffeine.

SO WHAT'S THE CORRECT WAY TO FUEL ON YOUR BIKE?

Hydration and energy are your main priorities during your ride. Carbohydrate-electrolyte drinks are the optimal way to deliver fluid to the body, and will be a source of energy too.

Additional sources of carbs that can be taken during rides include energy gels and bars. Sports nutrition products are formulated to give you exactly what you need, quickly, without anything else added that may slow down the absorption of the nutrients and risk causing gastrointestinal distress, both of which can affect your performance.

If you prefer to use regular foods during rides, always try to target high GI carbohydrates to release energy quickly. Any additional protein will lower the GI of the food, so try to keep this to a minimum.

Fat is digested slowly and will sit heavily in your gut, so try to avoid this during rides as much as possible.

Whether you choose sports nutrition or regular food, always aim for 60g of carbohydrate per hour and drink at least 500ml of fluid.

" The pros might get fizzy pop after a long day in the saddle but it's not recommended."

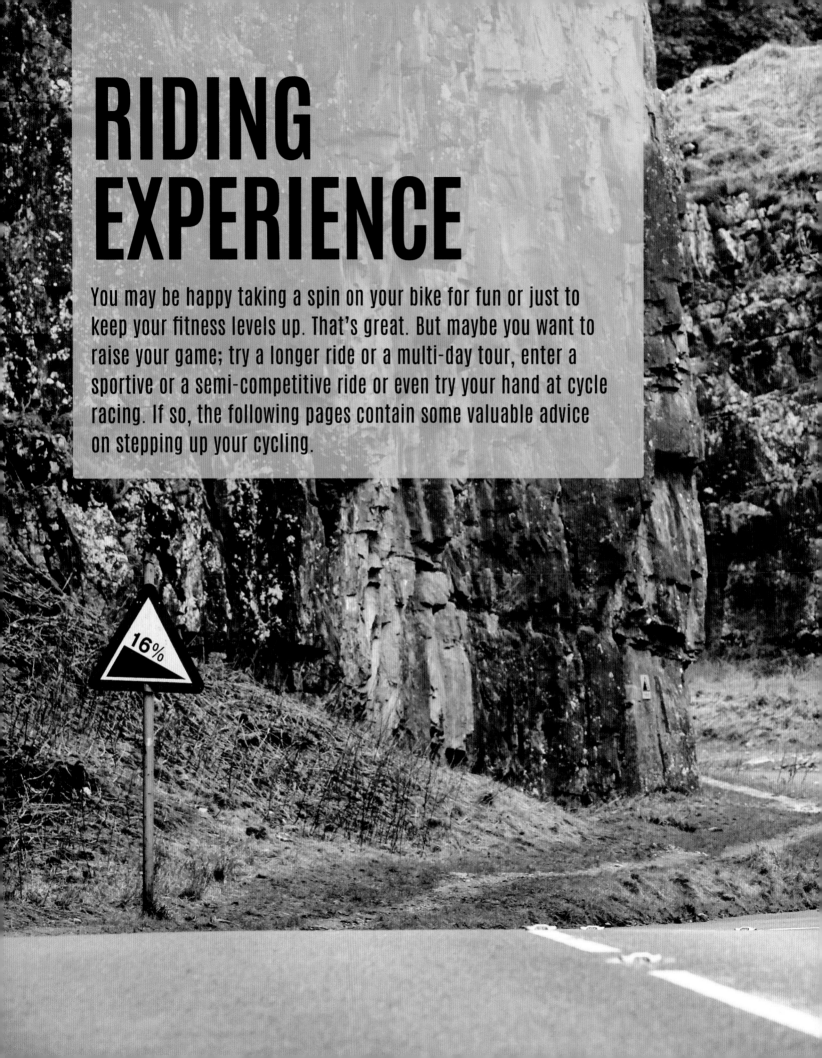

RIDING EXPERIENCE

You may be happy taking a spin on your bike for fun or just to keep your fitness levels up. That's great. But maybe you want to raise your game; try a longer ride or a multi-day tour, enter a sportive or a semi-competitive ride or even try your hand at cycle racing. If so, the following pages contain some valuable advice on stepping up your cycling.

COMMUTER WORKOUT

Commuting is a fantastic training opportunity for the time-poor cyclist. Here's how to make the most of your trip to work

The past few years have seen a dramatic increase in the popularity of cycling events, particularly charity challenges and sportives. 'Ordinary' cyclists are becoming more inclined to challenge themselves beyond cycling to work once or twice a week by throwing in the odd weekend ride. With most sportives clocking in at over 100 miles and 3,000 metres of tough climbing, many cyclists look to their commutes to improve their riding skills and boost their weekly mileage. The good news is that with a few simple drills and a bit of organization, it's perfectly possible to get more out of something that's often viewed as 'dead time' in a cyclist's week.

SHORT COMMUTES

By their nature, short commutes include a large proportion of town or city riding, so it's dangerous to attempt to increase your performance while threading your way through the oblivious rush-hour traffic. While there may not seem to be that much you can do in such a short space of time, you can still work on high pedalling cadences.

The high-cadence work helps increase your comfortable 'cruising' cadence. There's no magic number here, but it's possible to increase cruising cadence by about 10 per cent in a year, although there's obviously an upper limit.

When it comes to starting from a red light, especially on a relatively short commute of three to four miles, the most effective thing a rider can do is to start in a big gear and accelerate against a lot of resistance for 15–20 seconds. You should then shift into a smaller gear and bring the cadence up to 90+ rpm. You can do this on repeated lights and get a great acceleration workout that builds a lot of cycling power and improves muscle fibre recruitment.

The logical step for short-commute cyclists looking to get more from it is to extend their riding time. Trying to instantly add 30 minutes to a ride when you're in a mad flap trying to get out the door in the morning probably doesn't seem appealing. The best approach is to increase your ride time in five-minute increments so you gradually get used to allocating the extra time.

Assuming that a cyclist travels to work at the commuting average of around 12mph, cycling for an extra 15 minutes will add a useful three miles to a journey – which amounts to 30 miles over the course of a week. If time really is too much of an issue in the morning then only adding time to the ride home is a good compromise.

Lots of cyclists find when they move house or job, their commuting distance goes through the roof and they're no longer able to ride into work as they aren't up to the increase in mileage. However you can build up to your target distance over a period of time. Drive some of the journey and cycle the rest, increasing your cycling distance each week. Or try cycling to the next train station each week. Eventually you will be able to cycle the whole journey and increase your fitness in leaps and bounds.

GET ORGANIZED

Organization is the key to commuting long distances consistently. A change of clothes is essential and if you hope to commute more than a couple of days a week it may pay to drive in or get the train to work one day a week to take in one or two weeks' worth of clothes. On the same day, you can take the dirty set home to wash ready for next time.

You'll also need to be organized with food. All that exercise means you'll need to increase your daily calorie intake to ensure you have enough fuel for your rides. It's difficult to make good food choices when you're at the mercy of the work canteen or local convenience shop, so stock up with healthy snacks and plenty of fruit to help you avoid eating chocolate bars because that's all you could find.

For general fitness, commuting often is great, but for devoted cyclists who are working towards specific performance goals, commuting can complicate their training and make it difficult to get really high-quality performance during training workouts.

You always have to balance training and recovery, and if a cyclist is doing structured training rides throughout the week and then adding a 14- to 20-mile commute on top of that, there's often too little time for recovery during the week. When using longer commutes for training – in place of rides dedicated to training – just commute three or four times a week.

COMMUTING AS TRAINING

It's important for cyclists to distinguish between a commute and a training ride. Part of the problem is they look at the ride as a commute instead of as a training session and hence fail to fuel and hydrate adequately for a high-quality effort. The other problem is the rides occur at the beginning of the day and after a full day of work. Many athletes aren't properly fuelled for a high-quality workout during their commutes. You have to remember that commuting is a twice-a-day proposition, and that means a lot less time to replenish carbohydrate stores – especially if you're riding at a high intensity in order to turn a commute into a training session.

It is, however, possible to strike a balance between commuting and intensive training. You can achieve a nice compromise by commuting more during times of the year when you're not training as much or as hard, and commuting fewer times a week during times when you really need to focus on highly effective training sessions.

Personal trainers will tell you most people enjoy exercise, it's just getting started that's the problem. But when you organize your exercise around commuting by bike, you get rid of the 'shall I?/shan't I?' sticking point. Once you're out there, you never regret it.

THE FITNESS GUIDE TO COMMUTING

Mix things up on your regular commute to maximize your fitness

Acceleration
Use enforced stops at junctions as opportunities to practise your acceleration. Get the power on as fast as you can for 10 seconds and flick up through the gears swiftly before settling down to a sustainable pace.

Extend your route
You've got your kit on and you're out there anyway, so why not add some extra endurance training by simply increasing the length of your ride? Turn one standard evening commute into your week's big training ride and you'll have more time to play with over the weekend.

Vary the intensity
Road traffic will influence how hard you can ride, but you can also vary the intensity. Aim for most of your rides to be 60–80% of your maximum effort, but a weekly 90% blast, where conditions allow, will help boost your top-end speed.

Find a new route
Riding the same roads day after day can become uninspiring. Get out a map and find a new route, ideally with less traffic – there are always options.

High-resistance pedalling
Use higher gears than normal so that your cadence is ultra-low to stimulate the development of your leg strength. This will affect your ability to accelerate from a standing start, so be sensible about where you try it.

Fartlek training
Also called 'speedplay' – an interval session where the intensity and the duration of each interval is random – this is ideal for commuting where junctions and other road users influence how fast you can ride the various sections. So, sprint to the next set of lights, then keep it steady until the mini-roundabout, stay in the saddle up the hill past the golf course… and so on.

High cadence
Concentrate on spinning your legs fast – about 10 per cent quicker than normal. Resist the urge to shift to a higher gear and instead rely on crank rpm to increase your speed. Getting used to a higher cadence could improve your endurance and acceleration, so focus on it at least one ride a week.

Skills practice
Practise trackstanding at lights and junctions – it's a handy skill to have. Plus, get it right and you'll look super-cool – and that's vital! Can you get all the way home without dabbing your foot?

Safety first
We're not suggesting that you treat traffic like a playground. Concentrating on your own safety, as well as that of other road users, must always take precedence over developing your fitness.

HOW TO HILL CLIMB LIKE A PRO

The specialist climber is one of the toughest roles in cycling. To be King of the Mountains you'll need to be well prepared, in peak fitness and mentally strong. Here is how to get from the bottom of a hill to the top as quickly as possible...

STEP 1. TRAIN YOUR POWER

To build the explosive speed that separates graceful grimpeurs from the straining masses you'll need to strengthen your climbing muscles and build your capacity to exercise well above your sustainable pace...

Just one session per week after a rest day will work wonders for your hill climbing strength. You'll really benefit from a good 30- to 45-minute warm-down on flat roads after this, so even though your legs are screaming don't just wobble home.

▶ Aim to arrive, warmed up and ready to climb, at the base of a quiet 5-10 per cent hill that will take more than three minutes to climb.

▶ Shift into the big ring and select the third smallest sprocket and as you reach the first ramp of the climb accelerate as fast as possible and maintain your 100 per cent effort for 30 seconds without shifting.

▶ Stay in the same gear and sit down to continue climbing as fast as you can until you are unable to push your cadence above 60rpm any longer.

▶ As soon as you've ground almost to a standstill, shift into an easy gear, breathe deeply and keep pedalling. You have six minutes to regain your composure, recover and get ready to hit the hill once more.

▶ These efforts are tough, but keep attacking every one until you can't maintain 60rpm past one minute; don't reduce the gearing and don't 'pace yourself' on the sprint starts.

▶ You know you're working at the right level if you can only manage three to six full-on efforts of at most three minutes each. If you're outside this range, your gradient, gearing and/or commitment need some adjustment.

▶ After a 30- to 45-minute warm-down ride make sure you ride easy for two days, at least, until the rigours of this session have soaked in.

STEP 2. UP YOUR CADENCE

To complement the firepower that your big gear session will develop you'll need to raise the cadence you can efficiently ride at when climbing. Power = force x speed, so finding an efficient and rapid pedalling technique is vital...

- As part of a medium-length endurance ride head out to the hill you'll race on, or one that is as similar as possible to the gradients you'll face. Just before you hit the hill, shift into the easiest gear you have and start to raise your cadence.
- Aim to ride the climb with the highest cadence possible. Every climber has a different style that feels easiest and most efficient, so use these efforts to experiment with your technique and body position.
- Focus on remaining relaxed in the upper body, breathing deeply and finding the technique that helps you pedal faster with the least effort.
- Ride your target hill six times in succession with a short recovery period equal to the length of your climbing effort between each climb.
- For the first, third and fifth repeat stay seated and then complement that with riding the second, fourth and final effort standing on the pedals.

" You know you're working at the right level if you can only manage three to six full-on efforts of at most three minutes each."

- Once you've completed your efforts head off to finish your endurance ride and begin recovery for the next session.

STEP 3. LOSE WEIGHT

Power to weight is the most important aspect of climbing any kind of hill, from short sprint hills to long mountain passes. This is the ratio of a rider's power measured in watts divided by the combined weight of their body and bicycle.

The easiest way to improve this is to lower the weight of the bike with lightweight parts and removal of unnecessary items. It's also worth noting that rotational weight counts more than any other part so light wheels – in particular reduced rim weight – will help massively.

You can also try to improve your power with a sensible diet to shed any unwanted pounds. Beware, however, that riders tend to start losing power once they reach a certain weight, which won't improve your power-to-weight ratio.

STEP 4. PACE YOUR RACE

This is where most people tend to go wrong in a longer hill climb – they've done all the training, lost weight and bought the lightest bike possible but still set off like a bat out of hell for a climb of seven-plus minutes. Longer climbs are too long to rely on anaerobic efforts and fast twitch muscle fibres and require more of a controlled effort.

STEP 5. GIVE YOUR ALL

It's not easy to wring every ounce of energy out of yourself when your body is screaming at you to ease off. You have to judge where to put maximum effort in, but if you're giving everything your body will be in agony before the finish line. Knowing you have more to give, and digging it out of yourself, is crucial.

STEP 6. DO YOUR HOMEWORK

Three key tips to riding one hill really well are that you need to go into it fresh, you need to get your gearing right and you need to know how to judge your effort. The final two points depend entirely on the hill, so you need to get to know it before you race on it. At the very least recce the climb the morning of the race, but ideally check it out much earlier and practise on it if at all possible.

All these aspects improve with experience though, so the chances are that if you think about climbing a specific hill faster, then you probably will.

STEP 7. MEASURE YOUR EFFORT

At some point you're going to have to go eyeballs out, and for short, power climbs it's vital to look at the hill and judge where to use the effort. Don't just focus on powering up the early bit. The steep top section will seem to go on forever – and you will really pay for the speed you had at the bottom.

STEP 8. MIX IT UP

Depending on the rider's style and the gradient people ride either standing or seated. Standing allows you to accelerate harder but uses more energy with upper-body work and is also less aerodynamic.

Try to stay seated unless the gradient ramps up so steeply that standing is necessary to keep the pace up – often anything over eight per cent. Seated hill climbing allows you to get into a rhythm and save the standing muscles for when they're really needed on steeper gradients.

Mixing standing and seated climbing can help with pacing on the climb – it is faster spending more energy going harder and more into the red on steeper sections that would normally drag the average speed down. This means you can then grab some rest on a shallower part where your speed is still reasonable. This, of course, has to be a compromise and not too hard or too easy.

STEP 9. DEAL WITH THE PRESSURE

It is a good idea to run lower tyre pressures on wet days and steep roads. Rolling resistance is negligible at the speeds you'll be doing up a steep climb, but the energy you're wasting if you're struggling for traction and your tyres aren't in proper contact with the road is huge. Anyone who has got out of the saddle on a steep climb on a wet, mucky day will know the feeling of losing traction and momentum, so do what you can to avoid it.

STEP 10. BREAK IT DOWN

It is a good idea to break your climb down into smaller segments. This is especially true of long climbs, but can also be useful on shorter, sharper ascents, where the worst sections of gradient will actually make up only a small part of the climb.

When you recce the hill you will be racing on, pay attention to how the gradient varies between the bottom and the top and plan your attack. It can pay to give it your all on the steepest sections of the climb, where you know others will struggle, and then have a micro-recovery on a flatter section where you can maintain a higher pace even as your level of effort eases slightly.

On longer climbs it can be good to break it down into bite-size chunks just for the psychological boost of ticking them off as you go. Make sure you leave enough to change up near the top and sprint for the line!

It's not easy to wring every ounce of energy out of yourself when your body is screaming at you to ease off.

171

LEARN FROM THE EXPERTS

Learning from different branches of the sport can make you a better rider. Here's how...

At the highest levels of cycle sport, victory tends to go to the specialist. Grand Tour contenders are a different breed from Classics riders, who differ from pure sprinters, who contrast with climbers. If you want to win at a high level you find what you're good at and you stick with it.

But there are exceptions to this rule. Riders like Peter Sagan, who can sprint, climb a bit and last the distance in the Spring Classics, show there's still a place for the true all-round talent. And for regular amateur riders there's a lot to be gained by taking a break from our favoured branch of cycling and trying something different.

Whether you prefer sportive riding, sprinting for points in your local road race, or testing yourself in a local time trial, learning from different disciplines will help build a better biker.

BUILD A BETTER... TIME TRIAL RIDER

Anyone who has seen the likes of Bradley Wiggins or Tony Martin at full pelt will be in awe of their sheer speed and ability to hold a streamlined body position for mile after mile. Want to do the same? "It's a matter of looking at your power-to-weight ratio and reducing drag," says Matt Bottrill, who rides for Giant and is the 2015 British national 50-mile time trial champion.

Matt recommends time in the wind tunnel as the best way to cut drag, but a cut-price alternative is to examine your riding position in front of a mirror. "Look at reducing your frontal area and narrowing your shoulder width," says Matt.

Training to wind up a big gear for a prolonged period is hard work. "If you have a good base of fitness you need to start building in sweet-spot training blocks of 20 minutes to start with, until you can do up to one hour." Matt describes sweet-spot training as 85–90% of the power output you could sustain for a 20-mile time trial. "Then introduce threshold efforts of 20 minutes, and to really build the top-end, micro-burst intervals of 30 seconds to one minute (flat out) every five minutes over a block of one hour."

PROFILE
BRADLEY WIGGINS

UCI WORLD HOUR RECORD 2015
TOUR OF BRITAIN WINNER 2013
ROAD WORLD CHAMPS GOLD MEN'S TIME TRIAL 2014,
                      SILVER MEN'S TIME TRIAL 2013, 2011
TOUR DE FRANCE WINNER 2012, 3RD 2009
OLYMPICS GOLD MEN'S TIME TRIAL 2012,
          GOLD INDIVIDUAL PURSUIT & TEAM PURSUIT 2008
PARIS-NICE WINNER 2012, 3RD 2011
TOUR DE ROMANDIE WINNER 2012
CRITERIUM DU DAUPHINE WINNER 2012, 2011
VUELTA A ESPANA 3RD 2011
NATIONAL CHAMPS WINNER MEN'S TIME TRIAL 2010, 2009

BUILD A BETTER... CLIMBER

Chris Froome and Nairo Quintana may have legs filled with helium, but for ordinary mortals riding uphill is one of the most challenging aspects of cycling. "Climbing is about learning to be in a state of discomfort for a long time," says Tom Southam, former pro racer turned PR man for the Rapha Condor JLT team.

"On long climbs your mental approach can make a huge difference. You have to accept that it's going to hurt for 50 minutes or an hour. The more you can practise these kind of efforts in training the more used to it you get," says Tom. "So if you're a rider who tends to cycle a lot but at a steady pace you should include some shorter but harder rides."

There are mental games you can use to take your mind off the discomfort. "In Tim Krabbé's *The Rider*, there are some wonderful excerpts about a guy who does maths problems based on the gears he's got." For those of us less adept at mental arithmetic, Tom suggests breaking a long climb down into smaller chunks to make an epic mountain ascent seem more manageable.

Don't use where you live as an excuse. You might be miles from the nearest mountain, but you can still train to be a better climber. "You push yourself on the flat instead," says Tom. "Put in 20-minute efforts at threshold to improve your climbing." (Threshold is usually defined as the hardest effort you can sustain for one hour.)

It pays to slim down to develop a better power-to-weight ratio, but riders shouldn't get obsessed with how much they weigh. "I would never recommend doing anything other than eating a healthy, balanced diet," says Tom. "You will lose weight as a by-product of becoming fitter and riding more."

PROFILE
CHRIS FROOME

TOUR DE FRANCE WINNER 2015, 2013, 2ND 2012
CRITERIUM DU DAUPHINE WINNER 2013, 4TH 2012
TOUR DE ROMANDIE WINNER 2013
CRITERIUM INTERNATIONAL WINNER 2013
TOUR OF OMAN WINNER 2013
OLYMPICS BRONZE INDIVIDUAL TIME TRIAL 2012

BUILD A BETTER... SPRINTER

Maybe you've got tree-trunk thighs and weave from side to side when climbing a speed bump. If so, congratulations, you're a natural sprinter in the tradition of Mario Cipollini, Mark Cavendish and Marcel Kittel.

Even those of us who weren't born with a great finishing kick can learn to get one with the right training. Do a 20-minute warm-up – nothing specific, just riding steady. Then do six 10-second sprints 8–10 minutes apart. The sprint needs to be started at around 8mph in a relatively small gear such as 39x15 or 39x16 (34x18 or 34x19 on a compact). Then you sprint as hard as you can without changing gear as the speed increases. Once you've completed six sprints, warm down and finish.

This session doesn't just build power, it trains your muscles to fire in the right order and at the right time to maximize every available watt. It benefits every aspect of your riding as the body improves its timing to activate each muscle group in the pedal stroke.

A good sprinter doesn't just possess physical strength. The best will ride a canny race to arrive at the finish fresh, staying in the bunch while others chase down breaks. Starting a sprint for the line after having already made lots of unnecessary sprints will reduce your maximum power. You need to stay out of the wind and be as smooth as possible coming to the last few miles.

Successful sprinters also understand how other riders are likely to behave. Create a mental file on all the riders you compete against, so you know over many races what you can expect from them and how they respond to a number of race situations. Anyone who rides regularly with the same friends or club-mates can do the same, learning which wheels are best to follow.

PROFILE
MARK CAVENDISH

TRACK WORLD CHAMPS WINNER MADISON 2005 & 2008
ROAD WORLD CHAMPS WINNER 2011
TOUR DE FRANCE GREEN JERSEY 2011,
26 STAGE WINS
GIRO D'ITALIA RED JERSEY 2013,
15 STAGE WINS
VUELTA A ESPANA GREEN JERSEY 2010,
THREE STAGE WINS
NATIONAL CHAMPS WINNER MEN'S ROAD RACE 2013
MILAN-SAN REMO WINNER 2009

BUILD A BETTER... CYCLOSPORTIVE RIDER

The best sportive riders may not enjoy the fame of the top sprinters or fastest riders against the clock, but they are very capable athletes.

Mike Cotty's exploits have made him arguably Britain's best-known sportive rider. Last year, he rode across the Alps from Evian-les-Bains to Nice in less than 34 hours, with over 16,000 metres of climbing.

Obviously not every sportive rider is on Mike's level. "There's a vast differential in terms of ability, and it's easy to get carried away," he says. "It's better to stick to a planned pace – don't burn all your matches in the first 20 minutes."

If you want to ride to the best of your ability without blowing up, listen to your breathing. It should be deep but if you can't speak to riders around you without running out of breath you're giving it too much welly. Mike recommends a heart rate monitor as "the next step in judging your effort", if you know how to use it (see tinyurl.com/oxz6w2a for help if you don't).

What other skills does a sportive rider need? "Confident and efficient pack riding," says Mike. "Don't sit on the front of a group and tow everyone along. Take your turn, then hide from the wind and save your energy." Club runs and evening chaingangs can help you develop this skill, as well as the events you take part in.

Descending is another skill that sportive riders need. Safety has to come before speed, and that means good technique and looking out for those around you. "Moderate your speed before the bend – try not to brake through the corner, you should roll through," says Mike. "Identify a safe line and stick to it. Cutting across other riders shows no respect."

As for physical qualities, a sportive rider needs endurance, and lots of it. "You need the distance in your legs." Mike recommends gradually building base miles (ridden at a steady and manageable pace) through the winter and spring to develop your body's ability to handle long distances on the bike, with one easy week in every four to allow the body time to adapt.

BUILD A BETTER... CYCLO-CROSS RIDER

The best cyclo-cross riders, like Sven Nys, Marianne Vos or Helen Wyman, combine explosive pace with exceptional bike handling. The races are short (generally 30–60 minutes) so the pace is high, with lots of short, sharp efforts taking riders further into the red.

Here's one of the sessions that Kona rider Helen Wyman, twice European cyclo-cross champion, recommends to develop the fitness specific to this fast and punchy style of racing.

"Having warmed up, start with a full-on sprint for 10 seconds, settle back to a tempo slightly higher than endurance riding. At three minutes sprint for 20 seconds, settle back to the same tempo. At six minutes sprint for 30 seconds, then back to tempo. At nine minutes sprint for 20 seconds, then tempo pace, at 12 minutes a 10-second sprint then ride at the tempo pace until you reach 15 minutes."

The benefits of riding 'cross aren't just physical. Like mountain biking, cyclo-cross develops confident bike handling, which will make you a better rider on the road. "Sliding around in the corners gives you an understanding of how a bike feels when it begins to slip, and you'll know how to correct it," says Helen. "After racing 'cross you'll be able to balance better and corner better."

The cantilever brakes on 'cross bikes are generally much weaker than the callipers fitted to road bikes. Helen believes riding with weak brakes teaches you to use them more smoothly, which helps in a bunch back on the road. "You learn to taper your braking," says Helen. "You don't always need to slam them on."

PROFILE
HELEN WYMAN

NATIONAL CX CHAMPS WINNER 2014, 2012, 2011, 2010, 2009, 2008, 2007, 2006, 3RD 2005
WORLD CX CHAMPS 3RD 2014
EURO CX CHAMPS WINNER 2013, 2012, 3RD 2010, 2009

CYCLE TOURING

A bike is the ultimate way to enjoy the freedom of the open road. Here's all you need to know to enjoy a trouble-free touring trip

Any time on two wheels is time well spent, but if a short ride is good and a long ride is better, wouldn't the best thing be to go riding for several days, or weeks even? So isn't it about time you tried cycle touring? Touring combines the simple pleasure of riding a bike with the relaxation of being on holiday. It's not hard to get started, but our expert advice will help smooth any bumps in the road...

IT'S NOT ABOUT THE BIKE
You don't need a tourer to go touring – but it helps. Depending on the kind of tour you have in mind, just about any safe and serviceable machine can be pressed into service, but a bike designed to do the job will do it better.

A road bike is better suited to short, 'credit card' tours where the plastic takes the strain rather than your panniers. It is possible to do other kinds of touring but you'll have to accept certain privations because you won't be able to carry so much. You need to be very experienced and ready to rough it a bit.

If 'roughing it' and 'holiday' aren't words you ever put together, the load-carrying ability of a proper tourer will pay off. With a bit more air between road and rim and a more upright riding position, a touring bike will be more comfortable than a racer. But don't go thinking a tourer is only good for touring.

Narrow rubber can always be fitted and bars lowered, and with a rack and mudguards usually fitted as standard, a tourer makes a great commuter or general-purpose bike.

FROM RACEHORSE TO PACKHORSE
A touring bike might be a better option, but if you already own a road bike and don't want to buy another bike, a few modifications can make it more touring-friendly. You will probably need lower gears, depending on load carried, the terrain and your fitness. And, for comfort, use the biggest tyres you can fit with safe clearances. It could also be worth raising the bar by flipping the stem or fitting a shorter riser stem.

A few tweaks can adapt a road bike to carry loads. There are ways and means to fit a rack to bikes that don't have fittings. If your bike has mudguard eyelets on the dropouts, the bottom of the carrier legs bolt on here and take most of the load. Fit the carrier legs next to the frame and the mudguards on the outside. If you have no mudguard eyes, you can get a fitting that is held by the skewer, and use P-clips for the top fittings to the seatstays.

TRAVEL LIGHT
The lighter you travel, the less need you have for a rack. For just a night or two away, you could use an old-fashioned saddlebag, but only if there's enough space between the saddle and rear tyre.

Bar bags won't carry much but are ideal for travel documents, valuables and your camera, where they'll be easy to access.

START SMALL, THINK BIG
Maybe you like the idea of cycling all the way to the Med but lack experience. Don't be put off. Keep the goal of an epic tour in mind, but start small and learn the ropes on short trips before taking on a long-distance adventure.

Andrew Sykes, author of *Good Vibrations: Crossing Europe on a Bike Called Reggie*, rode the Pennine Cycleway as a taster the year before setting off on his six-week ride to southern Italy.

"I don't think I questioned my physical ability," he says, "but I was concerned that I wouldn't enjoy it. I was worried about the isolation of being on my own."

A shorter ride on home soil silenced any doubts he had.

" It's a good idea to do a short practice tour before setting off on an epic. "

BE FLEXIBLE

Rush out of the door with no route in mind and hastily packed panniers and you could hit trouble within miles, but planning every last mile could rob the trip of its sense of adventure.

"I knew the towns I wanted to cycle through and had a rough route," says Sykes, "but a small change would have thrown out a detailed itinerary. Instead I would sit down every morning with a coffee and a map and plan the day's route."

LOOK AFTER YOURSELF

Don't overdo the mileage and do look after your health. If you can ride 100 miles in a day without luggage, cut this to 70 on a tour, or 50 if you're carrying camping equipment.

Taking care of your body means keeping clean. "I took sterilizing gel on my trip," says Vin Cox, who set what was then the record for riding around the world in 2010. "Antiseptic wipes are useful, and chamois cream acts as a barrier to protect your skin."

PACK LIGHT, PACK RIGHT

Cox is a big advocate of the 'less is more' approach to cycle touring. "The lightest kit is the stuff you don't take with you," he says, and reckons he could have pared down the luggage he carried on his global bike ride even further. "I shouldn't have bothered with a stove – I only used it a couple of times. It's very rare to be in a part of the world where you can't find food."

If you're not racing to break a world record, though, a few creature comforts could be worth the slight weight penalty, reckons Sykes. "I took a very thin lightweight camping mat

" If you want to go further afield or carry more, you'll need a beefy bike."

on my ride and it was completely ineffective. I struggled to get a good night's sleep. I'd have been better off taking a heavier, more comfortable mat and dieting before I left!"

DRESS SENSE

On any tour it's important to make smart choices about the clothing you take with you. It pays to have a clothing system, especially on a lightweight tour where you'll pretty much be wearing cycle clothing all the time. Take many thin layers so that if you wear every stitch of clothing you'll be warm enough if it gets cold. Rather than having separate cold and warm weather clothing, you take layers off as it gets hotter.

At night you'll want to get clothes clean. Wash your baselayers when you shower. Spread the clothes on a towel, roll it lengthways and twist it. The clothes should be almost dry, and will be ready to wear in the morning.

It may not be possible to get clothes clean every night, in which case it pays to wear good-quality kit. A merino wool vest is better than one made of manmade fibre as it can be used more days on the trot without getting smelly.

GET TOOLED UP

You don't necessarily need a lot more tools than you would take on any day ride. On his round-the-world ride Cox

relied heavily on a multi-tool. "I had used the same tool to build the bike, changing any nuts or screws that the tool wouldn't fit. That way I knew I could adjust or replace most components using the one tool."

Along with a decent multi-tool, a couple of spare tubes, tyre levers and a puncture repair kit should see you through most mechanical mishaps. On longer tours you may want a little more. "I took gaffer tape, spare shoe plates, WD40 and some zip ties – they're great if a bolt has fallen out," says Cox.

THINKING ON YOUR FEET

Every once in a while something is certain to go wrong, but overcoming a mishap can be very rewarding, and a bit of ingenuity can go a long way – quite literally sometimes, as Cox reveals.

He had to use a bit of lateral thinking on his record-breaking round-the-world ride. "I was trying to get every last bit of use out of one tyre while cycling though America. I realized that it had been worn right down to the canvas, but I couldn't find a bike shop."

After cleaning the tyre, Cox decided to glue puncture repair patches all over it to create a tread. "The tyre lasted for another 300 miles before it could be properly replaced," he says.

READY FOR ADVENTURE

If you want to go further afield or carry more then you'll need a beefy bike to cope with the extra kit. For heavily laden adventure touring, even a tourer can benefit from some upgrades.

A custom-built rear wheel is advisable to handle really heavy-duty loads, although upgrading the front wheel is less important. Spokes break far more rarely in a front wheel.

If heading to really far-flung places, the received wisdom is to use a steel frame for easier repairs, and 26in wheels, which should be stronger than 700c wheels and simpler to find spares for in far-off places. Round-the-world cyclist Mark Beaumont rode an aluminium bike, though, and Cox completed his circuit of the globe on 700c wheels, so there's more than one way to get to the most remote places on two wheels.

EMBRACE THE UNEXPECTED

You'll enjoy touring more if you take each experience as it comes. The places you think will be highlights of your trip may not turn out as expected, but a welcome surprise could be just around the corner.

Sykes had been looking forward to climbing the Gotthard Pass in the Alps. "When I got to the top it was a bit of a tourist trap," he recalls.

Better was to follow near the end of his journey when he stumbled across a beautiful setting in the far south of Italy. "I arrived at a place called the Laghi di Monticchio, a lake in the crater of an old volcano. It was just beautiful. I'd be surprised if there were more than a dozen people at the campsite.

"That evening I sat down and watched the sun set on the other side of the lake. I didn't know what I was looking for when I set off from Berkshire, but that felt as if I'd found it."

GET SET FOR A SPORTIVE

Whether you're new to cycling or you're rekindling your interest, if you've never cycled a sportive before then you're in for a treat. As long as you're prepared...

Imagine a perfect world: politicians wouldn't be incorrigible fibbers, cold callers would be strapped down and pelted with rotten eggs, and you could get really fit with only a few minutes of exercise time taken out of your busy schedule. Ah, we can all dream... Though in fact one of these has already come true.

Scientists and coaches say that training for shorter amounts of time – but at a higher intensity – could get you as fit, if not fitter, than training for more time at a lower intensity. The broad idea is called high-intensity interval training (HIIT) and the original concept comes from 1990s Japan. Dr Izumi Tabata was monitoring the national speed skating team and noticed short bursts of intensive exercise seemed to be as effective, if not more so, than hours of moderate training for the Japanese athletes. He set out to prove his hypothesis.

He arranged for one group of moderately trained students to perform an hour of steady cardiovascular exercise on a stationary bike five times a week. Another group did a 10-minute warm-up on the bike, followed by four minutes of Tabata intervals (ie, at a higher intensity), four times a week – plus one 30-minute session of steady exercise with two minutes of intervals.

The results were profound. After just six weeks, the group following Tabata's plan – exercising for just 88 minutes a week – had increased their anaerobic capacity

by 28 per cent and their VO2 max (the key indicator of maximal aerobic power and cardiovascular health) by 15 per cent. An increase in heart size was also recorded. The control group, who trained for five hours every week, also improved their VO2 max, but only by 10 per cent – and their training had no effect on anaerobic capacity.

ALL-OUT EFFORT

From this research Tabata settled on his simple but demanding training protocol – 20 seconds of all-out effort, 10 seconds of rest, repeat eight times. It's not the sort of training you can do while thumbing through the latest JK Rowling novel or chatting up someone on the neighbouring treadmill. But the routine is multi-discipline, so can be done on a static bike or rowing machine, or via explosive bodyweight exercises, sprints or similar.

"All-out effort at 170 per cent of your VO2 max is the criterion of the protocol," says Tabata. "If you feel okay afterwards you've not done it properly. The first three repetitions will feel easy but the last two will feel impossibly hard."

Plus it keeps working even after you've showered. Soon-to-be-published research shows that the Tabata protocol burns an extra 150 calories in the 12 hours after exercise, even at rest, due to the effect of excess post-exercise oxygen consumption. So as well as getting you fitter, it's also getting you slimmer.

By definition, Tabata or HIIT workouts – the only real difference between the two being that HIIT tends to have longer intervals of recovery – take much less time than traditional training methods and come with a lower risk of injury as you're not stressing your body for as long. As well as for the time-poor, this also makes these methods ideal for athletes cautious about remaining injury-free.

THE POWER OF HIIT

Dr John Babraj, exercise physiologist at Abertay University and co-author of *The High Intensity Workout*, has also conducted research into the fitness benefits of HIIT, based on six-second bike sprints. He says improvements are down to the body's ability to use lactate.

"People think the chemical causes them pain and slows them down, but lactate is actually a useful fuel that the body makes during exercise to enable it to perform at a higher level for longer. The problem for athletes is they're unable to use up all the lactate, as by the time their blood is saturated with the chemical, races are often over. But this doesn't happen in shorter sprints."

HIIT is a great idea for people whose training has plateaued. "HIIT is really effective for somebody who is already training," says Dr Babraj. "When we start to get fit, we see changes quickly as our body adapts to the training stimulus, but then we start to stagnate – for a runner it becomes harder each year to produce personal

bests despite putting the training in. This is because we've stopped pushing our bodies and instead train within our comfort zone for that sport.

"HIIT is different because every session requires maximum effort. This means you're using the fuel supply in the skeletal muscle each time you exercise and this forces the muscle to adapt to each session. This can result in increased ATP resynthesis by a number of different mechanisms such as improved ability to utilize lactate as a fuel and improved fat utilization as a fuel source. It produces changes in cardiovascular function as well."

For a team sport such as football you'd be likely see improvements in sprint pace and endurance capacity (ie, you recover quicker from bursts of activity). "In terms of running you're able to maintain a faster pace for a longer period of time," says Dr Babraj, who does HIIT workouts to improve his running. "It's allowed me to produce a PB of 90 minutes for a half marathon this year while only running 10–20 miles per week. Previously I ran between 60–80 miles per week. HIIT also reduces injury risk from overtraining."

HIIT IT RIGHT

Dr Babraj recommends using HIIT to complement other training methods rather than only training in short bursts. "I would typically do three HIIT sessions per week and three run sessions. If you don't have time for this, I would recommend HIIT above other training regimes due to the magnitude of adaptation that you get in terms of muscular

and endurance adaptation. It can also be used by long-distance runners to train for the mental aspects of the sport due to psychological adaptations that occur around your perception of fatigue. Also, doing a run after a HIIT session will give your legs the same sensation as the later stages of a long-distance race."

Aren't sudden bursts of high intensity likely to be a bit of a shock to the system? "In all the HIIT studies I've done there have never been any injuries sustained by the participants. We're using HIIT protocols with people over the age of 70 without any adverse effect. If you're doing it on your own the key is to give yourself enough recovery between bouts and to not eat or drink anything for at least two hours beforehand, because it can put a strain on the gut and lead to you being sick."

THE HARDER THE BETTER

HIIT doesn't have any easy options. "There's no point in doing HIIT running on the flat as you won't have a large enough intensity – it needs to be on a hill, with the steeper the hill the more intense the exercise. I would generally recommend a five per cent gradient or above for HIIT running."

Research has also shown that HIIT has big benefits for the general health of non-sporty types. Dr Babraj joined a team of exercise biologists at Edinburgh's Heriot-Watt University and their results showed similar results to Tabata – but in preventing diabetes and related conditions such as heart disease. Their research showed that four short bursts of flat-out exercise, two or three times a week, appear to be more effective than half an hour spent jogging six times a week.

DELAY AGEING

Similarly Jamie Timmons, a professor at Birmingham University, claims HIIT workouts can combat the signs of ageing. He found that by doing just three minutes of HIIT a week for four weeks, most people can expect to see significant changes in at least four health areas.

First, insulin sensitivity – insulin removes sugar from the blood, it controls fat and when it becomes ineffective you become diabetic. The second improvement is aerobic fitness, a measure of how good your heart and lungs are at getting oxygen into your body – and a predictor of future health. Third, HIIT uses far more of your muscle tissue than classic aerobic exercise does. You're using not just leg muscles but the upper body too, so 80 per cent of the body's muscle cells are activated, compared to 20–40 per cent for just walking or moderate-intensity jogging or cycling.

Lastly, HIIT exercise breaks down the body's stores of glucose, deposited in your muscles as glycogen. Break up these stores and you create room for more glucose to be sucked out of the blood and stored – all the things that benefit both the athlete and the everyday person. So, with high-intensity interval training, it looks like less really can be more.

SET YOUR GOAL

First off, you need to choose your event. Be realistic. If you took up cycling only a couple of months ago, don't enter a monster slog through the French Alps. Challenging, yes. Sensible, no. Then think about exactly what you want to achieve on your ride. Are you completing, competing or conquering? Again, be reasonable. Set an impossible aim and you'll soon lose motivation. Once you have your goal sorted, write it down and put it in your wallet, next to your computer, on the dashboard or fridge door... anywhere that you'll see it often enough to help keep you focused.

GET YOUR LONG RIDES IN

We all miss occasional planned rides, but even if you can't do high-mileage outings all the time, don't miss your long rides at the heart of your training – they're vital. Bad weather? Go out anyway; you could get bad weather on event day. Bike's broken? Fix it, or get your bike shop to sort it – and learn how you could have solved the problem out on the road. Long rides are when your body gets used to handling the demands you'll face on the big day; they help you learn to draw on your fuel reserves more efficiently, and they get your head prepared for long, demanding efforts.

DEVELOP TECHNIQUE

Get used to incorporating technique work into your general rides as well as devoting regular sessions to improving your skills. Find a long, winding hill and time yourself down it over several runs, looking to get quicker by laying off the brakes, leaning into the corners and learning when to put the power back on. Be careful though – do this with a riding mate and only on quiet roads where you can easily see any approaching traffic. And don't think that you can make up for poor climbing just by flying downhill.

Sheltering from the wind in a group saves you masses of power output from your legs and will improve your sportive finishing time, but it doesn't necessarily come easily and there are tactics to learn, so practise in regular group rides or during local club runs. The more comfortable you are riding in close formation, the more time you can save.

MUSCLE POWER

Lactic acid is produced when your body breaks down carbohydrate for fuel, resulting in lactate in your blood that affects your muscles' performance. Are you paying attention at the back? All you really need to know is that the point at which lactate starts to accumulate faster than you can disperse it is your lactate threshold (LT), and raising this will help you ride a faster sportive. Working on your power is important too, both for increasing the amount of force you can put into every pedal stroke and also for increasing your endurance.

As you'll see from the training programmes, we recommend regular high-intensity rides devoted to LT and strength work. Get these sessions in and you'll be rewarded on the big day.

HAVE A REST

You don't get fitter when you're riding, you get fitter when you recover afterwards, which is why you need to have at least one day without exercise every week, or more if you over-stretch yourself, plus an easy week each month.

DRINK ENOUGH

You might have read that you should drink 400–900ml of fluid an hour while riding – but that's a myth. Fluid replacement varies according to your personal sweat levels. Work out precisely what you need at varying intensities and in different weather conditions by following this process over several rides:

- Weigh yourself while undressed, before putting on your cycle kit. As an example, suppose your weight is 75kg.
- On your return, note the amount that you drank and ate during your ride. We'll say it was 1,500ml, which weighs 1.5kg, and three gels of 0.06kg each, so you've taken a total of 1.68kg on board.
- Before showering, eating or drinking, dry yourself and weigh yourself again. We'll say it's now 73.2kg.
- Subtract the second weight from the first to get your bodyweight change: 75 - 73.2 = 1.8kg.
- Add the weight of the food to this to get your total loss: 1.8 + 1.68 = 3.48kg.
- Estimate any bathroom stops because this will obviously mean losses are higher.
- Divide total losses by the hours spent riding: 3.48 ÷ 3hrs = 1.16kg lost per hour.

You won't get to the end of your training ride or event at the same weight as you started, but you should eat and drink enough to be within 1–2kg. Never be more than 2–3 per cent down in mass unless it's a ride where you really can't get adequate fuel down.

BECOME FUEL EFFICIENT

You need to drink when you ride to replace the water you sweat and breathe out, but for longer training rides and during the event itself you'll need to use drinks to help provide fuel. Suffering a 'bonk' – when your body can't get the energy it needs – is bad news when you've got two or three climbs left to ride.

For both training and the big ride, try a drink that's 5–7 per cent carbohydrate. This is an isotonic level, meaning that the drink contains the same concentration of dissolved particles as your body fluids, so will be absorbed fast. Some people prefer a hypotonic drink – one with a carb level of less than 5 per cent. The only way to find out what's right for you is by experimenting in training. Also, choose a drink that contains electrolytes, particularly sodium. This speeds up the delivery of fluid to your body, so it's especially important on longer rides. Finally, it's key to go for a drink that you really enjoy the taste of – that way you're far more likely to drink enough.

Drink plenty before you go out on your bike so that you start off fully hydrated, and continue drinking afterwards – a little and often – to aid recovery. If you've trained for over an hour, make it a carb drink. Don't wait until you feel really thirsty – that's a bad gauge of need.

You should consume at least 1g of carbohydrate per kilogram of bodyweight for every hour that you're riding. This can be in the form of carb-electrolyte drinks, gels, bars, solid food, or a mix of these. But your needs could be different from the norm so it's important to experiment in training. That way you'll be able to tell exactly what you can tolerate and what you need with you on the day. If riding an event, find out as early as possible what food and drink will be available and at what points along the route, and see if it suits you. If you can't stomach the energy drink on offer, for example, take your own sachets. If you get sick of sweet stuff, check there'll be something savoury for you to grab, or carry it with you.

AVOID INJURY

When you step up the amount of riding you do you'll be adding stresses and strains on your body. You might be tempted to ignore niggles in order to stick with the programme. Don't! Riding through the pain is a great way to make minor problems major. If you get injured, take it seriously. Take some time off the bike or do some cross-training, and if it's a biomechanical problem have your riding position looked at by an expert. If necessary, visit a health care professional. Whatever you do, don't ignore a potential injury.

PACE YOURSELF

Pacing is crucial in training and on the big day, but it's hard to get right. The main trick is to climb at an intensity that won't blow your legs. This comes with experience but if you've trained by heart rate or power then you should have a good idea of what you can sustain. If you don't know how hard you should be working, don't go above 85 per cent of your max HR on even the steepest hills or you'll dip too far into your glycogen stores. Remember, you have limited glycogen and can never eat enough to make up for going too hard too soon.

TRAINING PLAN WEEKS 1-3

	Monday	Tuesday	Wednesday	Thursday	Friday	Saturday	Sunday
Week 1	Check your bike and kit over, making sure everything is ready for you to begin riding tomorrow.	1hr ride. In the morning ideally, no breakfast before (exercising fasted is a means of encouraging the use of more stored fat as fuel), at moderate Zone 1 effort, indoors or on moderate terrain.	1hr ride. Evening ride over moderate terrain, ideally with a few mates or a club so you can practise riding in a group.	Two short sessions if possible – 30-40mins am and pm. Do the morning ride fasted, and the evening ride with an 8sec fast effort every 5mins.		Endurance. 30-40% of event distance on a moderate to rolling course. Stay in Zone 1 more than 75% of ride time.	Saturday ride if it was missed. Otherwise, a 1hr ride concentrating on a higher than normal cadence.
Week 2	Recovery day. Ideally, get a massage or at least perform self-massage of your leg muscles, especially your quads.	1hr ride. In the morning ideally, fasted, at moderate Zone 1 effort, indoors or on moderate terrain.	1hr 30 ride. Evening ride, mainly low Zone 2, but include the longest hills you can find for a total of 30mins controlled hard climbing work.	Choice day working on your area of weakness. You could do extra morning fasted work up to 2hrs.	Rest	Endurance. 40-50% of event distance on a moderate to rolling course. Stay in Zone 1 more than 75% of ride time.	Saturday ride if it was missed. Otherwise, 1hr ride in a bigger than normal gear (cadence of 50-60rpm), pushing effort on inclines for the middle 20mins.
Week 3	Rest	1hr ride. In the morning ideally, fasted, at top of Zone 1 effort, indoors or on moderate terrain.	1hr evening ride with hilly terrain, working out a Zone 2 pace to stay smooth with controlled breathing.	Choice day working on your area of weakness. You could do some extra morning fasted work up to 1hr 30.	Rest	Endurance. 50-60% of event distance on a moderate to rolling course. Stay in Zone 1 more than 75% of ride time.	Saturday ride if it was missed or 1hr in a bigger than normal gear (50-60rpm), pushing on inclines for middle 20mins.

TRAINING PLAN WEEKS 4-6

	Monday	Tuesday	Wednesday	Thursday	Friday	Saturday	Sunday
Week 4	Rest. Get bike mechanics sorted, kit organized, rides planned and nutrition bought/organized.	45mins ride. In the morning ideally, fasted, at moderate Zone 1 effort, indoors or on moderate terrain.	1hr ride working on an area of weakness: could be climbing, descending, cornering or group riding.	Rest	Rest	Endurance. No more than 25% of event distance on a moderate to rolling course. Stay in Zone 1 more than 90% of ride time.	Sat ride if it was missed. Otherwise, 1hr of light spinning with 8sec efforts every 6mins.
Week 5	1hr 30 light spin on rollers/turbo or flat terrain (low Zone 1), legs feeling no pressure.	2hr ride. In the morning ideally, fasted, at moderate Zone 1 effort, indoors or on moderate terrain outdoors.	1hr 30 ride. Evening ride, intervals of 5-8mins (equal work and recovery) in mid Zone 2, or chaingang; aim for 30-45mins of hard work here.	As Tuesday. You can have two shorter sessions on this day as an option - 1hr morning and evening.	Recovery day. Optional 1hr light spin, low Zone 1, on rollers or flat terrain, legs feeling no pressure.	Endurance. 60% of event distance on a hilly course. Stay in Zone 1 on flats and low to mid Zone 2 on hills. Include 2x20min climbs if possible.	Saturday ride if it was missed. Otherwise, 1hr 30 ride in big gear, pushing on inclines for the middle 40min section.
Week 6	1hr morning or evening ride; Zone 1, either indoors or on moderate terrain.	1hr 30 ride. In the morning ideally, fasted at moderate Zone 1 effort, indoors or on moderate terrain.	1hr 30 ride. Evening ride, low Zone 2 on the longest climbs you can find for a total of 30mins hard climbing work.	Choice day working on an area of weakness; you could do some extra morning fasted work up to 2hrs.	Recovery day. Optional 1hr light spin, low Zone 1, on rollers or flat terrain, legs feeling no pressure.	Endurance. 70% of event distance on a hilly course. Stay in Zone 1 on flats and low to mid Zone 2 on hills.	Saturday ride if missed. Otherwise, 2hrs with speed practice on descents and 5-6 1min Zone 3 efforts.

TRAINING PLAN WEEKS 7-9

	Monday	Tuesday	Wednesday	Thursday	Friday	Saturday	Sunday
Week 7	Recovery day. Optional 1hr light spin, low Zone 1, on rollers/turbo or flat terrain, with legs feeling no pressure.	Light day. It's your choice of training but bear in mind what's coming up in tomorrow's session.	2hr evening ride, intervals of 10mins (equal work and recovery) in mid Zone 2, or chaingang; aim for 50-70mins of hard work.	Choice day working on an area of weakness; you could do some extra morning fasted work up to 2hrs.	Rest	Endurance. 60-75% of event distance on the hilliest course you can find. Stay in upper Zone 1 on flats and include 40-60mins of Zone 2 work on hills.	Saturday ride if it was missed. Otherwise, 2hr ride with speed practice on the descents for the middle 40mins.
Week 8	Rest	1hr ride in the morning ideally, fasted, moderate Zone 1 effort, indoors or on moderate terrain.	1hr ride in the morning ideally, fasted at moderate Zone 1 effort, indoors or on moderate terrain.	Rest	Rest	Endurance. 40% of event distance on flat terrain, staying in low to mid Zone 1.	Saturday ride if it was missed. Otherwise, 1hr light spin with 8sec efforts every 6mins.
Week 9	Rest	Bonus 45-60min morning ride. Ride fasted and keep in moderate Zone 1, either indoors or on moderate terrain.	1hr evening ride with a few mates or a cycle club. Aim for moderate terrain and work on your group riding skills.	Two sessions, 30-40mins morning and evening. Morning ride fasted, evening ride with an 8sec fast effort every 5mins.	Rest	Endurance. 50% of event distance on a hilly course. Stay in Zone 1 on flats and low to mid Zone 2 on the hills.	Saturday ride if it was missed. Otherwise, 1:20hr ride in a big gear pushing on the inclines for middle 40min section.

TRAINING PLAN WEEKS 10-12

	Monday	Tuesday	Wednesday	Thursday	Friday	Saturday	Sunday
Week 10	Recovery day. Ideally, get a massage or perform a self-massage. A 30min light spin is optional on rollers or flat terrain.	1hr ride optional. In the morning, fasted, at moderate Zone 1 effort, indoors or on moderate terrain.	1hr 30 ride low Zone 2, on the longest climbs you can find for a total of 30mins of controlled, hard climbing work.	Choice day working on an area you know is weakest; you could do some extra morning fasted work up to 2hrs.	Rest	Endurance. 40% event distance on the hilliest terrain you can find. Stay in upper Zone 1 on flats and Zone 2 on hills.	Saturday ride if you missed it. Otherwise, a 1:30hr ride with descending at speed practice and 5-6 1min efforts in Zone 3 with a 2-3min spin recovery in between.
Week 11	Rest	Two short sessions if possible, 30-40mins am and pm. Do the morning ride fasted and the evening ride with an 8sec fast effort every 5mins.	1hr ride on hilly terrain, climbing at Zone 2 pace, staying smooth and relaxed throughout.	Rest	Rest	Endurance. 30-40% event distance on a moderate to rolling course. Stay in Zone 1 for at least 75% of the time.	Saturday ride if you missed it. Otherwise, do a 1:20hr ride, practising descending at speed for 30mins.
Week 12	Rest	1hr ride with some top of Zone 1 3-5min climbs on moderate terrain. Aim for 30mins of hard work.	1hr ride working on an area of weakness - perhaps climbing, descending or feeding while in the saddle.	1hr light spin with 8sec efforts every 6mins to test your legs' responses. No more; it's time to store glycogen.	Rest	Some riders like a light spin on the day before an event to keep their legs loose, others don't - it's your choice.	GOAL EVENT

GLOSSARY

aero bars: extension of the handlebars allowing the rider to set an aerobic position. Often found on time trial bicycles.

aerobic exercise: brisk exercise that promotes the circulation of oxygen through the blood and is associated with an increased rate of breathing.

aerodynamic: a design or shape that reduces wind resistance.

aero tuck: an aerodynamic riding position requiring the hands to be brought near the stem and the torso bent as low as possible.

allen key: a hexagonal L-shaped tool that is used to turn a screw with a hexagonal hole in the top.

anaerobic: exercise above the intensity at which the body's need for oxygen can be met. This intensity can be sustained only briefly.

antioxidant: nutrients and proteins in your body that assist in chemical reactions. They are believed to play a role in preventing the development of many chronic diseases.

attack: an aggressive, high-speed ride away from other riders.

audax: a ride where a group cycles together at a steady pace of about 22 kph.

bar: a unit of measure for tyre inflation and air pressure in some suspensions.

bead: the edge along each tyre's inner circumference that fits into the rim.

beats per minute (BPM): a measure of heart rate.

blood glucose: a sugar that is the only fuel that can be used by the brain.

blow out: a puncture that occurs while the bike is in motion.

blow up: to lose the ability to maintain pace due to overexertion.

bottom bracket: the part of the bike that connects the *crankset* to the bicycle frame and allows the *crankset* (pedals, crank arms and chain rings) to rotate freely.

break, breakaway: a rider or group of riders that has escaped the pack.

bunch: the main cluster of riders in a race. Also called the group, pack or *peloton*.

cadence: the number of times during one minute that a pedal stroke is completed.

calliper: the assembly in bike brakes that forces the brake pads against the wheel rim.

carbohydrates: sugars and starches, found in foods such as vegetables, grains, rice, breads, and cereals, which are broken down by the body into glucose, the body's principal energy source.

cardiovascular exercise: any exercise that exerts the heart, lungs and associated blood vessels.

cassette: the set of gear cogs on the rear hub. Also called a freewheel, cluster or block.

chaingang: a fast training ride with riders riding in close proximity – in either a single pace line or double pace line.

chainring: a sprocket on the *crankset*. There may be one, two or three.

chainstay: the thin frame tube that extends from the *rear dropout* to the *bottom bracket*, where the bike's crankset is located. There is a chainstay on each side of the rear wheel.

circuit training: a weight training technique in which you move rapidly from exercise to exercise without rest.

cleat: a metal or plastic fitting on the sole of a cycling shoe that engages the mechanism of a *clipless pedal*.

clipless pedals: pedals requiring a special cycling shoe with a cleat fitted to the sole, which locks into a mechanism in the pedal.

cog: a sprocket on the rear wheel's cassette or freewheel.

core strength: the power of the muscles of the torso, extending from the shoulders to the pelvis. It is the body's centre of power.

crank: one of the two arms of a *crankset*; each arm connecting a pedal to the *bottom bracket*.

crankset: the pedals, crank arms and chainrings that convert a cyclist's pedalling into forward motion.

criterium (crit): a mass-start race covering numerous laps of a course that ranges from one to five kilometres in length.

crosstraining: training in different sports in order to improve general fitness and performance.

cyclo-cross: an autumn and winter event contested off-road over courses that include obstacles, steps and steep hills that force riders to dismount and run with their bikes.

degreaser: chemical product (often bio-degradeable) that dissolves water-insoluble substances such as greases and oils.

derailleur: device for shifting gears that lifts the chain from one sprocket to another.

disc brakes: brakes that slow the bike by acting on a disc mounted on the hub of the wheel, most commonly used on mountain bikes, hybrid bikes and some touring bikes.

drafting: riding closely behind another rider to take advantage of the windbreak (*slipstream*) which reduces the effort required to ride at the same speed.

drivetrain: the components directly involved with making the rear wheel turn - the chain, *crankset* and *cassette*.

drops: the lower part of a road bike's down-turned handlebar which offers the rider an alternative and more aerodynamic position.

echelon: a staggered riding formation in which the riders angle off behind each other to get maximum draft in a crosswind.

electrolytes: substances such as sodium, potassium, and chloride that are necessary for muscle contraction and maintenance of body fluid levels.

fat: the most concentrated source of food energy, supplying nine calories per gram. Stored fat provides about half the energy required for low-intensity exercise.

feed zone: a designated area on a race course where riders can be handed food and drinks.

frame: the central structural component of the bicycle to which the rest of the components are attached.

front mech: the mechanism that causes the chain to shift between different-sized chainrings on the bicycle's crank.

full tuck: an extremely crouched position used for maximum speed on descents.

glutes: the gluteal muscles of the buttocks. A key set of muscles for cyclists.

glycaemic index (GI): how fast and by how much a food raises blood glucose levels.

glycogen: a fuel – the primary energy source for high-intensity cycling – derived as glucose (sugar) from carbohydrate and stored in the muscles and liver.

glycogen window: the period within an hour after exercise when depleted muscles are most receptive to restoring their glycogen content.

gran fondo: a long-distance road cycling event in which a large number of participants ride a marked route.

grimpeur: a rider who excels at steep climbs, particularly mountains.

groupset: all the parts that make up the gearing and braking system on the bike.

hamstrings: the muscle on the back of the thigh, not well developed by cycling.

headset: the parts at the top and bottom of the frame's headtube, into which the handlebar stem and fork are fitted.

headtube: the short tube through which the steerer of the fork passes.

heart rate (HR): the number of *beats per minute (BPM)* – during exercise the heart pumps faster to get more blood, and therefore more oxygen, to working muscles thereby increasing the heart rate.

High-Intensity Interval Training (HIIT): any workout that alternates between intense bursts of activity and fixed periods of less intense activity or even complete rest.

hip-flexor: muscles, attached to the hip joint that allow the knee to pull up.

hoods: the upper portion of road bike brake levers, often with a rubber cover, that provides an additional hand hold.

hybrid: a bike that combines features of road and mountain bikes.

index gears: system in which a single click of the *shifters* changes the gear.

jockey wheels: small semi-toothed wheels that help feed the chain through the transmission.

jump: a quick, hard acceleration.

King of the Mountains (KOM): the accolade or award given to the best climber in a road race.

knee flexion: the movement of the knee towards the chest.

lactate threshold (LT): the point where the production of lactic acid due to exercise is greater than the body's ability to eliminate it. This is marked by muscle fatigue, pain and shallow, rapid breathing. Also called anaerobic threshold (AT).

lactic acid: a body chemical which helps supply energy to muscles. The more carbs the body uses, the more lactic acid accumulates in the muscles and blood. Also called lactate.

line: the path a rider takes through a corner. Usually the straightest path through the turn, resulting in the smallest amount of speed loss.

mass start: events such as *road races*, cross-country races and *criteriums* in which all contestants leave the starting line at the same time.

mobilizers: fast twitch fibre muscles that produce power but lack endurance. They assist rapid movement and produce high force.

oxygen debt: the amount of oxygen that must be consumed to pay back the deficit incurred by anaerobic work.

panniers: large bike bags used by touring cyclists or commuters. Panniers attach to racks that place them low on each side of the rear wheel, and sometimes the front wheel.

peak: a relatively short period during which maximum performance is achieved.

peloton: the main group of riders in a race or large event.

personal best (PB): the record time achieved by each individual in a particular event.

pilates: a system of exercises designed to improve physical strength, flexibility, and posture.

pinch puncture: an inner-tube puncture marked by two small holes caused by the tube being squeezed against the rim.

plyometrics: exercise involving repeated rapid stretching and contracting of muscles (such as jumping and rebounding) to increase muscle power.

presta: the narrow European-style valve found on some inner tubes. A small metal cap on its end must be unscrewed before air can enter or exit.

protein: nutrient required for tissue growth and repair. Protein is not a significant energy source unless not enough calories and carbohydrate are consumed.

quadriceps (quads): the large muscle in front of the thigh, the strength of which helps determine a cyclist's ability to pedal with power.

randonnee: a long-distance event in which riders must navigate a prescribed course while passing through intermediate checkpoints within certain time limits.

randonneur: a rider who participates in *randonnees*.

reach: the combined length of a bike's top tube and stem, which determines the rider's distance to the handlebar.

rear dropout: the slots into which the rear wheel axles fit.

repetition: each individual exercise in an interval workout.

road race: a mass-start race on road that goes from point to point or covers one or more circuits.

saddle sores: skin problems in the crotch that develop from chafing caused by pedalling action.

schrader: an inner tube valve identical to those found on car tyres. A tiny plunger in the centre must be depressed for air to enter or exit.

set: a specific number of repetitions in interval or weight training.

shifters: mechanism for changing the bike gears. Usually positioned on or near the handlebar for easy reach.

slipstream: the pocket of calmed air behind a moving rider. Also called the *draft*.

spin: to pedal at high cadence.

stabilizers: slow twitch fibre muscles used for endurance and postural control.

stage race: a multi-day event often consisting of various types of races. The winner is the rider with the lowest elapsed time for all races (stages).

Strava: a website and mobile app used to track cyclists' performances through GPS recording.

Stem: the component on a bike that connects the handlebar to the steerer tube.

time trial (TT): a race against the clock in which cyclists ride individually, starting at set intervals.

tops: the part of a drop handlebar between the stem and the brake levers.

top tube: part of frame connecting the top of the headtube to the top of the seat-tube. Also called the crossbar.

Torx: a screw with a head having a socket shaped like a six-pointed star and a screwdriver with a tip that fits it.

turbo trainer: training equipment in which the bike's back wheel is placed on a roller to make it possible to ride while remaining stationary.

Union Cycliste Internationale (UCI): the world governing body of bicycle racing, headquartered in Geneva, Switzerland.

V-Brakes: a Shimano trademark for a direct-pull cantilever brake. Their comparatively greater power means they are usually used on mountain bikes.

VO2 max: the maximum amount of oxygen your body can use during exercise. A way to measure your level of fitness.

watt: a measurement of power produced. It measures the force being applied to the pedals.

INDEX

PICTURE CREDITS

The publishers would like to thank the following sources for
their kind permission to reproduce the pictures in this book.

Steve Behr: 90, 162
Joseph Branston: 16
Russell Burton: 3, 8, 10-11, 20, 52, 55, 62, 67, 68, 69, 78, 86, 89, 117, 138, 139, 149
Anthony Calvert: 48–49
iStockphoto: 94–95, 96–97, 99, 101, 172
Frédéric Pactat: 186
Seb Rogers: 42, 73, 168, 169, 170, 171
Shutterstock: 12R, 15, 60-61, 75, 98, 132B, 133T, 143, 144, 151, 152-153, 155, 156, 157, 158, 159, 160, 161, 174, 175, 177
Paul Smith: 121, 122, 123, 138, 141
Robert Smith: 6-7, 18, 30–33, 50-51, 57, 58, 70, 76, 77, 81, 82, 86, 93, 114, 116, 117, 118, 119, 124, 130, 134, 136, 141, 146, 150, 154, 165
Alex Tyler: 183-185
Geoff Waugh: 132

All other photographs © Immediate Media/*Cycling Plus*

Every effort has been made to acknowledge correctly and contact the source and/or
copyright holder of each picture and Carlton Books Limited apologizes for any unintentional
errors or omissions, which will be corrected in future editions of this book.